A Field Guide to the

British Countryside

Alfred Leutscher
Edited by Nigel Sitwell

A Charles Herridge book
published by

**NEW
ENGLISH
LIBRARY**

© Copyright 1981 by Charles Herridge Ltd

First published in Great Britain by New English Library Ltd, Barnard's Inn, Holborn, London EC1N 2JR in 1981.

Produced by Charles Herridge Ltd Tower House, Abbotsham, Devon
Designed by Bruce Aiken
Typeset by Toptown Printers Ltd, Barnstaple, Devon
Printed in Italy by New Interlitho s.p.a., Milan

ISBN 0 450 04818 7 (cased edition)
ISBN 0 450 05055 6 (limp edition)

Acknowledgments

Illustrations by
Graham Allen
Trevor Boyer
Jim Channell
John Francis
Tim Hayward
Stuart Lafford
Alan Male
Colin Newman
Eric Rowe
Rod Sutterby

by courtesy of Linden Artists Ltd, London

Photographs
Institute of Geological Sciences,
RIDA Photo Library (p.305),
Ardea Photographics,
RIDA Photo Library (p.307),
R.K. Pilsbury (p.309).

CONTENTS

INTRODUCTION

The purpose of this guide is to help the non-specialist to identify the wildlife he or she encounters, and thus to enjoy the countryside more. There are a number of more specialised books on individual groups, such as birds, mammals, butterflies, wild flowers, and so on, but this guide covers more or less the whole range. It also includes rock formation and climate.

An innovation, not usually found in books of this kind, are the sections dealing with farm animals and crops. Non-specialists, especially those who live in town and cities, will find these as unfamiliar, but just as interesting, as the wild animals and plants.

The 'struggle for existence', as Charles Darwin termed it, has produced a world of specialists, with most animals and plants equipped and adapted for life in their own particular habitats. For example, a squirrel is built for climbing. It is born, grows up, and lives among trees. Its nibbling teeth are admirably suited for the food a tree provides, such as nuts and acorns, bark and buds. It is a woodland animal.

A frog, on the other hand, is built for swimming. It can hibernate under-water, where it also spawns and where its young (tadpoles) grow up. It is a pond animal.

The earthworm is built for burrowing. It feeds on soil and lays its eggs there. It is a soil animal.

Bearing in mind these essential needs of wildlife, the naturalist can usually anticipate what kinds of animals and plants will occur wherever he or she goes.

But wildlife is not necessarily remote and limited to wild places, although it is true that some animals and plants have retreated from man's presence and sought refuge in remote areas. Many species can be found on our very doorsteps. This is where nature, the great opportunist, exploits the many man-made habitats which we have unintentionally created for her use.

Wherever men have settled and built homes and amenities, nature moves in as well. The garden or park is the equivalent of a woodland, the reservoir a lake, the sewage works a mudflat, and the building a cliff. Some of the creatures which live with us (called commensals) are enjoyed and made welcome — creatures like butterfly, blue tit, and ladybird. Others, like rats, dandelions, and furniture beetles, are another matter.

So a temporary rain puddle in a city street can provide as much fascination for the naturalist as a mountain crag. Whether we make adventurous journeys of discovery, or look with curiosity at the more familiar habitats of home and garden, our pleasure will be enhanced by a closer understanding of the wildlife around us.

Much has had to be omitted because of the wide coverage of this guide. But by concentrating on the most common, conspicuous, and characteristic species, it should enable the reader to recognise the type of animal or plant which he or she encounters, and decide to which group or family it belongs.

COUNTRYSIDE LAW AND
THE COUNTRY CODE

All visitors to the countryside should know what rights of access they have, and what they may or may not do. All land is owned by somebody, whether a private owner, local government, or the Crown. The following points should be borne in mind when out in the countryside: most of them amount to no more than courtesy and common sense.

Countryside Law

Footpaths. Paths where the public have a right to walk are shown on the Ordnance Survey maps as red dotted lines. Bridlepaths for walking, or riding a horse or a bicycle, are marked with red dashes. Where a path is obstructed, or has been ploughed over due to lack of use, the right still exists, but to avoid damage to crops it is better to walk round the edge of the field. Footpaths should be signposted.

Parking. Cars should not be parked so as to obstruct passage, especially in narrow lanes. Parking on private land requires permission. On council property or common land a notice will usually indicate where parking, if any, is permitted.

Trespass. Usually there is no prosecution, but a landowner can sue for damage, and is allowed to eject the trespasser.

Firearms. These require a certificate for a shotgun, and a special licence for shooting game in season. Game animals and birds have their separate close seasons. So do fishes. The public have no right to shoot anywhere, except with the land-owner's permission.

The Seashore. The public have a right to fish or sail along the seashore, in estuaries, and in tidal rivers. The foreshore between low and high tide marks belongs to the Crown Estate Commissioners, and here walking and bathing are usually allowed. The beach above the high tide mark may be private, so to reach the shore it may be necessary to use a footpath or right of way.

Common-land. This is unfenced land owned by some authority, and where local commoners by tradition may exert their rights to graze their cattle, ponies or sheep (right of common), liberate pigs to feed on acorns and beech-mast (pannage), gather fire-wood or bracken (estovers), lift peat (turbary), and fish (piscary). Public access is usually allowed on such places. In towns such rights have usually lapsed, and a common owned by the local authority is maintained for public use.

Camping and caravanning. If done on private land without permission this is a trespass. Lists of authorised camp sites may be obtained from the Camping Club of Great Britain and Ireland, and the Caravan Club, both based in London.

Animals. Dogs (or other pets) should be kept under control. The owner may be liable to damages if farm animals are worried or injured, and the farmer is entitled to shoot the dog concerned.

General. Airfields and land used by the Ministry of Defence have restricted access for the public, as do playing fields, golf-links, and parts of Forestry Commission plantations. Consult the notices or owners.

The Country Code

To avoid unnecessary conflict with country-folk such as farmers and land-owners a visitor should follow the advice given in this code.

Risk of fire. Do not throw away a lighted match or cigarette, or knock out a pipe. A fire started by one careless act may cause enormous damage, and harm wildlife. Do not discard glass bottles, which may catch the sunlight, and so start a fire, or trap small animals.

Footpaths. Keep to authorised foot-paths, especially on farmland. Crops, even grass, can be damaged when walked on. Keep to single file on narrow paths.

Gates, hedges, and walls. Avoid damaging these, and shut all gates, lest animals may stray and come to harm.

Litter. This is not only unsightly but may cause harm to animals. Take it home. Do not pollute ponds or streams with litter as these may be used by farm animals.

Country roads. If driving always be prepared for oncoming farm tractors, sheep, cattle, ponies or deer. When walking keep to the right. Avoid parking in narrow lanes.

Wildlife. Try not to do anything that will disturb wild animals. Many birds and other creatures are now protected by law. It is illegal to collect birds' eggs, so leave birds' nests well alone. It is better to observe or photograph butterflies and other insects than to collect them. Do not pick wild flowers, as some species are rare and protected, and besides, this practice destroys other people's pleasure. It is illegal to uproot **any** wild flower without the landowner's permission. Avoid carving your name on trees and rocks.

BIRDS

Nearly half — about 200 out of 470 — of the birds which can be seen in Britain are permanent, year-round residents. Others, called migrants, include summer visitors like the swallow and the cuckoo, which fly north from warmer countries to breed here. Winter visitors, such as geese and waders, fly south from the arctic where they have bred, in order to escape the northern winter weather. Yet other visitors, the passage migrants such as the arctic tern, use Britain as a staging post on longer journeys north or south.

Spring and autumn are the best times to watch birds, as the greatest number of species are in evidence. Confusion in recognising a bird may stem from its brief appearance, rapid movement, or the medley of different calls, especially in spring. However, with only a minimum of knowledge, it is possible to recognise a number of birds by regular watching, and noting the following points:

Size. The most obvious character. Compare it with the size of one of these familiar birds, listed in ascending order: blue tit, house sparrow, blackbird, pigeon, duck, swan. (Measurements given in the text are adult average, from tip of beak to end of tail).

Shape. Is the body plump (robin), slim (warbler), long-necked (goose), streamlined (grebe)?

Wings. Are they long and pointed (swift), short and rounded (owl)?

Tail. Can be long (magpie), short (partridge), forked (swallow), rounded (cuckoo), square-ended (starling).

Legs. Can be short (swallow), long (wader), webbed (gull).

Beak. Can be short and pointed (warbler), short and stubby (finch), hooked (bird of prey), dagger-shaped (heron), flat (duck).

Colour. Most birds are rather drab, in browns, greys, and yellows, also black — but some are conspicuously coloured or marked (kingfisher, magpie, green woodpecker).

Flight. Straight and fast (duck), undulating (woodpecker), hovering (kestrel), soaring (skylark), with long glides (gull).

Posture. Holds its tail cocked (wren), bobs it up and down (wagtail), sits with tail down (flycatcher), sits bolt upright (owl).

On the ground. Hops (house sparrow), shuffles (hedge sparrow), walks (crow).

On water. Sits high in water (moorhen), low down (diver), dives under (grebe), upends (mallard), taxis along surface (swan).

Nest. Bird is seen flying from bush (songthrush), a tree (woodpecker), cliff (herring gull), ground (pheasant).

Song. This is learned and is specific, but remember that some birds are good mimics. Listen to the 'dawn chorus'.

Calls. Alarm calls, food calls, etc., are inborn and can be heard all year round. Some knowledge of a bird's normal surroundings is helpful, as are recordings. Better still, join an expert on a bird-watching outing.

Birds have one distinctive feature in common, a covering of feathers. These were originally used as a means of conserving heat. Latest research suggests that the earliest known bird, the famous *Archaeopteryx,* was a ground- and tree-dweller, not a flyer, derived from ancestors in common with dinosaurs. Birds survived and achieved flight by modifying their fore-limbs into wings (see illustration). Their feathers are cleverly designed to overcome gravity, by providing lift, and to give manoeuvrability. They can easily be repaired if damaged, an important consideration when flight is a means of escape.

A bird's anatomy is fairly stereotyped. Unlike land animals such as mammals, which come in many forms — burrowers, hoppers, runners, climbers, and even flyers (bats) — most birds have limited their shape and size for flying. Their bodies combine lightness and strength. Bones are hollow, and extensions of

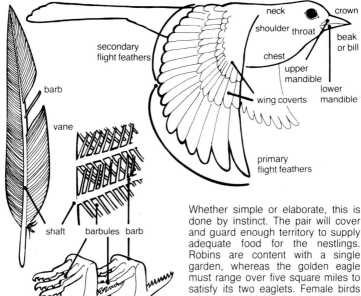

secondary flight feathers

barb

vane

shaft   barbules   barb

neck   crown
shoulder   throat
    beak or bill
chest
upper mandible
    lower mandible
wing coverts

primary flight feathers

the lungs fill internal body spaces. Their high metabolic rate is shown in body temperature and other functions, much higher and faster than ours. A house sparrow breathes 50 times a minute, and as much as 200 under stress. Its heart-beat averages 400 per minute.

Birds have excellent sight, especially birds of prey; good hearing (especially owls); but indifferent taste and smell.

Bird-watching is particularly worthwhile during the breeding season, when much interesting behaviour can be seen. Bird song — much romanticised by poets — is a serious matter enabling a bird to recognise its own kind, call a mate and warn off rivals from its territory, especially during spring. The male's brighter colours serve to attract a mate during courtship, or as a warning threat to other males (for example, the red breast of the robin, which is strongly territorial).

After courtship, which can involve many kinds of display, a nest is built.

Whether simple or elaborate, this is done by instinct. The pair will cover and guard enough territory to supply adequate food for the nestlings. Robins are content with a single garden, whereas the golden eagle must range over five square miles to satisfy its two eaglets. Female birds tend to be dull-coloured and well camouflaged, a necessary precaution when brooding, especially among ground-nesters.

Bird-watching can start at home. With a gradual loss of countryside, such as hedgerows, woods and wetlands, many birds have adapted to more artificial habitats provided by man, and to more urban areas. Woodland birds take to parks and gardens where there are bushes and trees. Water birds turn up on ponds, lakes and reservoirs. Rock-nesters use buildings. Many can be encouraged by setting up bird-tables and nest-boxes, also by planting suitable berry bushes which provide both food and nest-sites.

Since 1954 the Protection of Birds Act has safeguarded most birds, their nests and eggs, including birds of prey which were once heavily persecuted. Where certain species cause damage, such as wood pigeons, carrion crows and bullfinches, there may be exceptions. Waterfowl and game birds may be shot but have their respective close seasons, when they are protected.

Tits

Small, plump, acrobatic birds. Some familiar in gardens and attracted to nest-boxes and bird-tables. Useful insect-feeders, gathering in flocks during winter. Produce large families. Song and call-notes somewhat wheezy. Sexes similar.

1 Great Tit length 5½in, 14cm

Larger than blue tit, has glossy blue-black head and neck, yellow underparts and distinctive black band down centre of breast. Seen in gardens and will use nest-box. Has learned trick of pulling up food on string while holding on to branch with foot. Song and calls much varied, but commonly a two-toned 'tee-chew'. Occasionally mimics. Useful to gardeners.

2 Bearded Tit length 6½in, 16½cm

Not a true tit. Beard is actually a black 'moustache' on sides of white cheeks of males, missing in females. Body a tawny-brown, pinkish-grey below. Black under long tail. Habitat is reed-beds, mainly in East Anglia. Much reduced due to drainage and hard winters, also egg-collectors, now given sanctuary on reserves such as at Minsmere, Suffolk.

3 Blue Tit length 4½in, 11½cm

A universal favourite, common in gardens. The only tit with blue on crown, wings and tail. Cheeks white with black stripes across eye and around neck, yellow underneath. Small white spot on nape. Originally a woodland bird, is attracted to garden nest-boxes and is useful to the gardener as it feeds on caterpillars. Also well known for opening milk bottles to steal cream. In winter, flocks roam the woods, feeding on seeds. Song a trilling but wheezy 'tsee-tsee-tsee'.

4 Goldcrest length 3½in, 9cm

Minute bird, smallest in Britain, similar to tit but in separate family. Plump olive-green body, white below a bright yellow crown bordered in black, and orange stripe through centre. Two pale bars on wings. Call a rather shrill 'zee-zee-zee' and song of thin repeated double notes ending in a twitter — 'seeda-seeda-sissapee'. Habitat mainly in conifer woods. Builds suspended nest under tip of branch. Related to firecrest, distinguished by black stripe through eye and white above. Winters in southern England.

5 Crested Tit length 4½in, 11½cm

Distinguishing feature is the prominent crest of black feathers with white tips and white cheeks. A tit of conifer woods, at one time driven into Highlands due to extensive tree-felling in Scotland. Has since increased into forestry plantations, but still only nests in Highlands, in tree stumps. Call limited to a soft 'tsi-tsi-tsi' and a soft churring sound.

6 Long-Tailed Tit length 5½in, 14cm tail 3in, 7½cm

Small size. Colour pink and black above, white below and a long graduated tail. White stripe on crown. Restless and acrobatic inhabitant of hedgerows and thickets, slipping from branch to branch to reach its elaborate domed nest. Not often in gardens. In winter roosts in groups huddled together. A variety of calls such as 'tsirrup' and 'tsi-tsi-tsi'.

Warblers

Small birds with slender beaks. A large and diverse family, all insect-feeders. Rather dull greenish or brown plumage above, white below, and not always easy to recognise even by experts. Knowing the song and habitat helps in identification. The sexes are alike. All are summer visitors from Africa, apart from the resident Dartford warbler which is confined to gorse-covered heaths in southern England. Nests are built in or near the ground in low vegetation. They are divided into three groups: leaf warblers which occupy the tree canopy; scrub warblers which are found more in the undergrowth; and marsh warblers which are found among reeds and by the waterside.

1 Blackcap length 5½in, 14cm

Male has a glossy black crown down to eye level, which is reddish-brown in the female. Upperside greyish-brown, pale below. Song is a rich warble becoming louder towards the finish. Inhabits woodland glades and thick hedges nesting in bramble, evergreen, etc. Nest is attached by 'handles'.

2 Willow Warbler length 4¼in, 11cm

Commonest summer visitor. Slightly paler than the chiff-chaff and with a distinctive song, a melodious cadence which descends the scale and quietly fades away. Less arboreal than the chiff-chaff, it keeps more to low vegetation but its nest is similar. It is also a leaf warbler, but arrives a little later.

3 Reed Warbler length 5in, 13cm

Brown above, pale below, and a pale eye ring. Rather shy bird and lurks in reed beds, mainly in southern England. Has a characteristic suspended nest built around reed stems. Its warbling song contains repeated phrases such as 'churruc-churric'. Is parasitised by the cuckoo. In the same habitat, it can be confused with the sedge warbler, which has streaked upper parts and a bold, creamy eye-stripe, and nests in low vegetation. The sedge warbler's song is more musical and liquid than the reed warbler's, which is a succession of trills and chattering but rather grating.

4 Chiff-Chaff length 4½in, 11½cm

A leaf warbler which inhabits woodland and searches for insects among tree leaves. Closely resembles the willow warbler but has blackish legs and a distinctive song after which it is named — 'chiff-chaff-chiff-chiff-chaff'. Rather arboreal and builds a domed nest in undergrowth of bramble and evergreen. An early arrival in mid-March. May enter gardens.

5 Whitethroat length 5½in, 14cm

Male has pale grey cap, pure white throat, rusty brown upperside, pale pink breast and white outer tail feathers. The female is duller. A rather restless scrub warbler, moving in and out of bushes, bramble, gorse, etc., in fairly open country. Song is a vigorous, rather short warble, often while sitting in full view on top of a bush. Visits gardens.

Sparrows and Buntings

Perching birds with short stubby beaks. Beaks thicker at base. Mainly seed-eaters. Related to finches.

1 House Sparrow length 5¾in, 14½cm

Restricted mainly to built-up areas, towns, villages and farmland, this familiar and gregarious bird is said to have been introduced by Neolithic farmers. Male has a dark grey crown, chestnut nape, whitish throat and a black 'bib'. Female and juvenile are dull brown, lacking bib. Song consists of noisy chirping and grating noises, especially when excited. Movements local, and flocks gather to roost in noisy groups. During courtship several males surround and pursue a female. An untidy nest built on buildings, in corn-ricks and among ivy.

2 Corn Bunting length 7in, 18cm

Larger and more heavily built than the house sparrow. Plumage sandy brown, streaked above and below, and with dark 'bib'. Sexes similar. When perched on a post or telegraph wire sings a distinctive rapid jingle, like shaking a bunch of keys. Habitat is open farmland or downland. An untidy nest built on the ground in coarse vegetation. Male said to be polygamous, in charge of several females over which it keeps watch from a song-perch. Distinguished from lark by stubby beak.

3 Snow Bunting length 6½in, 16½cm

Mainly a northern species, moving to Britain for winter, along coast where it feeds on grass-seeds. Appears brownish on ground but almost pure white during flight as white patches on wing and tail are exposed. An airborne flock resembles drifting snow flakes. Male hovers during courtship and sings its lark-like song. Breeds rarely in Britain, then only in the Highlands. Nests in rock crevices.

4 Wren length 3¾in, 9½cm

A small, plumb, streaky-brown bird with short upturned tail. Very active, keeping to undergrowth, and foraging in litter in mouse-like fashion. Song strident with many trills, heard almost all year round. Common in gardens and hedgerows, building a globular nest in a convenient hole.

5 Dunnock or Hedge Sparrow length 5¾in, 14½cm

Not related to true sparrows. A rather drab bird with streaky-brown and black plumage, slate-grey below, and a slender pointed beak. Sexes similar. Rather solitary and feeds mainly on the ground, moving with shuffling gait in search of insects and seeds. Song a pleasing jingle heard most of the year. Call a shrill 'tseep'. Builds a cup-shaped nest of moss, grass, hair and wool in a bush.

6 Tree Sparrow length 5½in, 14cm

Smaller than house sparrow with chocolate-brown crown and black spot on white cheeks. Sexes alike. A more rural bird than the house sparrow, living in loose colonies in parks, orchards and woods, nesting in holes in trees, nest-boxes and haystacks. Chirrups like house sparrow but more high-pitched, with a persistent 'tek-tek' call.

Finches

Small, stubby-beaked, short-winged songbirds. Seed eaters. Distinctive wing patterns. Song helps in recognition. Cup-shaped nest built in bush or tree.

1 Hawfinch length 7in, 18cm

Britain's largest finch. It has a large and powerful beak capable of cracking open cherry stones. Main colour is a rich brown with a black throat, white shoulder patches and short, white-edged tail. A shy bird of woods, orchards and large gardens, feeding mainly on berries and soft fruit, including the stones. May attack peas. The occasional song is very subdued.

2 Goldfinch length 4¾in, 12cm

The most colourful finch, the 'seven-coloured linnet', once in great demand as a cage bird before this practice became illegal. Its colours are a contrasting black and yellow on wings, with a scarlet, white and black head. Sexes similar. Usually seen in flocks (or 'charms'), feeding on thistle heads as it moves through gardens, wasteland, roadsides and airfields. Song a soft canary-like, liquid twitter. Nests in trees.

3 Chaffinch length 6in, 15cm

One of the commonest British birds, distinguished by the double white wing-bars and white outer tail feathers visible in flight. Male has a pinkish breast, chestnut back and greyish crown. Female is pale olive-brown. The cheerful song varies in 'dialect' according to district, but usually ends in a flourish — 'chewoo'. Call a loud 'pink-pink'. A gregarious bird, mixing with other finches during winter. Flocks of males form bachelor parties. Occurs mainly in hedgerows, woods and gardens.

4 Greenfinch length 5¾in, 14½cm

Male is olive-green with a yellow-green rump and yellow on wings and tail. The female is much duller with less yellow. The song is an attractive canary-like twittering, interspersed with a long, nasal 'tswee-e-e'. It inhabits gardens, orchards and copses and nests in bushes and small trees. It is much attracted by human habitation and is a common visitor to the bird-table.

5 Brambling length 5¾in, 14½cm

A winter visitor arriving from across the North Sea in large numbers from breeding range in the Baltic. Feeds in beechwoods on mast (fruit). Male has a conspicuous white rump and orange shoulder patches. In spring, head and back turn black. Female resembles chaffinch but with white rump. Song not normally heard but can be identified by grating call-note — 'ts-week'. May breed occasionally in Britain.

Finches contd

1 Crossbill length 6½in, 16½cm

A bird of conifer forests, mainly in Scotland and the East Anglian forestry plantations. Population fluctuates with invasions from the Continent. Male brick-red with dark wings and tail, female more olive-green. The curious crossed beak is used for twisting open cones for the seeds. A gregarious, rather tame bird. Song a mixture of warbles and trills not unlike the greenfinch. Call a loud 'chip-chip'. Breeds in Scotland as early as January.

2 Bullfinch length 5¾in, 14½cm

Readily recognised. Male is a striking bright rose-red below, blue-grey above, with black cap and chin, white rump and dark beak. Female similar but more pinkish brown below, buff-grey above. Shy and secretive, seen usually in pairs, and keeping to cover in bushes, gardens, hedgerows and orchards. Song a series of subdued warbling and creaking notes. Can be harmful to fruit growers because it strips buds from bushes and trees, and thus unpopular in places like the orchards of Kent.

3 Linnet length 5¼in, 13½cm

Once the popular cage-bird of London cockneys during Victorian and Edwardian times, and caught extensively by bird-catchers, as were other finches, especially goldfinch. Were blinded to encourage song. Now protected. (Wild canary has been domesticated and crossed with other finches to produce familiar cage breeds.) Male has a red forehead and breast as distinct from redpoll. Female a streaky grey brown. Song a varied musical twitter, often in chorus, also a call-note — 'tsooeet'. Inhabits scrub-covered open country on commons, heaths and downland. A gregarious bird and may occur in large flocks. Nests in bushes close to the ground.

4 Redpoll length 5in, 13cm

Distinguished from linnet by its red forehead, pinkish breast and black chin in both sexes. Prefers alder and willow thickets, feeding on seeds, in mountains as well as lowland. Sociable, mixing with other finches in winter flocks. Song a series of long trills. Flight call a rapid 'chuch-uch-uch'.

5 Yellowhammer length 6½in, 16½cm

A finch of open farmland, commons and along country roads. Usually seen perched on a post or telegraph wire singing its rapid song ending in a long drawn-out note — 'a-little-bit-of-bread-and-no-cheese'. Male is lemon-yellow on head and underside, with chestnut rump. Female less yellow. White outer tail feathers show up in flight. Nest is built well hidden and low down in hedge bank.

Swallow, Martins and Swift

Slim and streamlined birds, graceful in flight, with long pointed wings, small feet and short beaks with wide gape. Insects caught during flight. All are migrants from Africa. Sexes similar.

1 Swallow length 7½in, 19cm

Best recognised by the long tail streamers, shorter in juveniles. Dark, glossy-blue uppersides, chestnut-red throat and forehead, white underside. Swooping flight, usually in parties in vicinity of breeding sites. Arrives in April, often returns to same nest, in open cultivated country where nest sites available. Attracted to ponds and meadows where hunts for insects. Builds cup-shaped nest of mud and straw lined with feathers on ledge or rafter in barn, cowshed, stable, chimney, even porch or garage. Song a soft, pleasing twittering. Numbers have decreased due to increased hygiene on farms and consequent decline in number of insects.

2 House Martin length 5in, 13cm

Smaller than swallow and readily recognised by pure white rump and shorter, forked tail lacking streamers; similar habits but more sociable. Flight more fluttering and at higher altitude. Nests colonially. Cup-shaped nest with entrance at top, made of mud pellets mixed with saliva and attached under eaves of houses and barns. May also build on cliffs. Excited parties gather prior to departure for Africa.

3 Sand Martin length 4¾in, 12cm

Smallest British member of swallow family. Arriving in March, they first gather over water to hunt gnats, then visit their previous nesting site, where tunnels are dug on face of cliffs, sand and chalk pits, or railway cuttings. Tunnels up to three feet long are dug and lined at end with grass and feathers. Movements of colony are sudden: one moment birds are everywhere as they swing into nest holes, then they disappear as quickly. Known in Spain as mountain butterflies. Colour brown above, white below, with brown band across breast. Gather in large parties in reed-beds prior to departure for Africa.

4 Swift length 6½in, 16½cm

Although similar in build, is not related to swallows. Larger size, sooty black-brown plumage and long, sickle-shaped wings. Helpless on the ground because its legs are small and weak. Constantly in flight by day, sleeping on air currents by night. Arrives late from Africa and departs early — late April to mid-August. A common sight is a party of screaming birds swooping and diving at speeds of up to 60 mph. A nest of straw cemented with saliva built under eaves of tall buildings, such as high-rise blocks, also cliffs. Parents fly for miles in search of food, usually over water.

Thrushes

Medium-sized songbirds with alert upstanding posture, a slender pointed beak and square-ended tail. Eyes fairly large. Juveniles spotted. Familiar as garden birds. Build cup-shaped nests in bushes or trees. This section also includes chats, closely related to thrushes but smaller. The wheatear, robin, stonechat and nightingale are chats.

1 Mistle Thrush length 10½in, 27cm

Larger than song thrush with greyish-brown back and bolder spots. Named after its liking for mistletoe berries. Also called stormcock after its habit of singing from tree during winter gales. Song of repeated phrases, rather like blackbird's but more monotonous. Inhabits woods, large gardens and orchards, and nests in fork in tree. Flocks roam countryside in winter, in company with fieldfares searching for berries.

2 Song Thrush length 9in, 23cm

Well-known and welcome garden bird. Distinguished from fieldfare and mistle thrush by brown upper parts and paler breast with smaller spots. Sexes alike. Song loud and musical, phrases repeated two or three times with short pauses between. Alarm call a loud 'tchuck tchuck'. Feeds on open ground searching for earthworms and snails, the latter being taken to a stone — the thrush's 'anvil' — to be broken up. Cup-shaped nest of grass and leaves lined with mud contains light blue eggs with black spots.

3 Blackbird length 10in, 25½cm

The jet-black male with its orange beak is unmistakeable, but sooty-brown hen with mottled breast could be mistaken for song thrush. Albino males sometimes occur, but these should not be confused with the ring ousel. Male's flute-like song lacks repetition of song thrush and has long pauses between. Dominates the dawn chorus and considered by some to be more melodious than the nightingale. Alarm call a persistent 'pink-pink', also a scolding chatter when warning of cat, fox or owl. Cup-shaped nest is lined with mud with extra layer of grass on top. One of our commonest birds, in woods, parks and gardens, even penetrating inside large cities.

4 Redwing length 8¼in, 21cm

Winter visitor from Scandinavia, slightly smaller than song thrush, distinguished by prominent eye-stripe, reddish patches on flanks and streaky, rather than spotted, breast. Song not normally heard, but call a high-pitched 'see-ip', heard as migrating flocks fly overhead at night. Roams countryside, often with fieldfare, on farmland, playing fields and occasionally in gardens. Breeds in Scotland, usually in birch woods.

5 Fieldfare length 10in, 25½cm

Another winter visitor from Scandinavia. Distinguished by pale grey head and rump, chestnut back and black tail. In flight, grey rump and white under wing show up. Roams the hedgerows in search of berries. A harsh chattering call of 'chack-chack'. Now breeds in small numbers in Britain.

Thrushes contd

1 Wheatear length 5¾in, 14½cm

A smallish thrush-like migrant from Africa, arriving early in March on its way north and west to more hilly country and moorland and also dunes, pausing at intervals on journey there and back. A restless bird, flying from perch to perch with much bobbing and fanning of tail. Once trapped to be eaten as a delicacy. Both sexes have white rump and tail, the latter with T-shaped black centre. Blue-grey back, pinkish breast, and black 'mask' on face, with white stripe over eye. Song a short, lark-like warble, call note a harsh 'chuck-chuck'. Nests in holes in walls and rabbit warrens.

2 Robin length 5½in, 14cm

Chosen as Britain's national bird in 1961, this friendly garden and woodland species is renowned for tameness and confiding behaviour, ever ready to pick up a worm from the gardener's fork. Is far shyer on the Continent, where it keeps more to deep woodland. Strongly defensive of its territory, the male puffs out its orange-red breast at any intruding rival, sometimes even fighting. The sweet, plaintive warble is heard most of the year. Female of similar appearance builds a nest of grass, leaves and moss in a hollow, tree-hole, tin-can, nest-box, and even a ledge inside a shed or garage. Young at first speckled brown. Call-note a persistent 'tic-tic'.

3 Stonechat length 5in, 13cm

A plump resident which inhabits heathland and commons, nesting low down in gorse and bracken. Male has a conspicuous black head and throat with white on neck, dark upper parts and red-brown below. A squeaky song is delivered from a perch or during a dancing flight. Female has more brownish upper parts but no white on rump. Recently distribution has become more localised due to loss of nest sites and severe winters. May be confused with whinchat, a summer visitor which has dark cheeks, clear eye-stripe and white on tail.

4 Nightingale length 6½in, 16½cm

Like a small and slender song thrush in build. Colour of uniform warm brown, paler below, with chestnut tail. Sexes similar. A celebrated songbird which arrives from North Africa in April to establish its territory in southern England before the females appear. It chooses glades and bushy places, where it keeps out of sight. Nest is built low down in dense undergrowth. Its melodious song is heard as much by day as by night, and more often than the bird is seen. Flight and posture, with bobbing tail, is similar to robin.

5 Ring Ouzel length 9½in, 24cm

Very similar to blackbird, this summer migrant is a uniform dull black with a broad white crescent across chest and dull grey patch on wing. Female more brownish with duller half-collar. In Britain makes for hilly country and high moorland in west and north, usually near a stream where it nests.

Tree Climbers

Sharp-beaked birds adapted for climbing trees and clinging to bark, nesting in tree-holes or behind bark. Woodpeckers brightly coloured in both sexes, with sharp, wood-boring beaks for drilling in trees. Long tongues for probing after food. Strong feet with two toes pointing forward and two pointing back to give firm grip on bark. Stiff tail helps as support. Strong undulating flight. Makes drumming sound on resonant dead branch. The three native species share the woodland at different levels. Nuthatch and tree-creeper also efficient climbers. Recognised by size, colour and calls.

1 Nuthatch length 5½in, 14cm

An active tree climber moving in jerks in all directions, including downwards. Compact build with blue-grey upper parts and crown, chestnut below, and black stripe through eye. Sharp beak used for opening nuts, etc., which it has wedged in bark. A variety of calls, frequently using a schoolboy whistle 'chwit-chwit'. Nests in tree-hole, occasional nest-box, plastering entrance to correct size with mud. Found in woods, parks and gardens in England and Wales.

2 Tree Creeper length 5in, 13cm

Small, brown, shy and silent mouse-like bird with thin curved beak used for probing tree trunks for insects. Song a high-pitched 'tee-tee-titit-tooee' and prolonged tit-like call 'tsee'. Climbs trees in spiral, flies to base of next tree and repeats; never moves downwards like nuthatch. Nests behind loose bark, in ivy, occasional nest-box. Seen in woods, parks and gardens.

3 Lesser Spotted Woodpecker length 5¾in, 14½cm

Has closely barred black and white upper parts. Male has crimson crown, whitish in female. Rather shy, keeping to upper branches in search of insects. Call a repeated high 'pee-pee'. Drumming softer but more prolonged than great spotted woodpecker. Seen mostly in Wales and southern England. Not easy to see unlesss first heard.

4 Great Spotted Woodpecker length 9in, 23cm

Also called pied woodpecker because of black and white plumage. A large white patch on short wings, crimson under tail. Male has black crown with crimson nape, missing from female. In juvenile entire crown is crimson. Keeps much to trees among middle branches, seldom on ground. Both sexes drum loudly. Found in deciduous woods, parks and sometimes pine woods. Enters large gardens. A nut-feeder, it wedges food in crevice in bark and splits it open with its beak. Also bores for beetle grubs. Call a sharp 'tchick'. The most widespread species.

5 Green Woodpecker length 12½in, 32cm

Largest woodpecker in Britain. Green above, pale grey-green below, crimson crown, yellow rump. Male has black 'moustache' with red centre, all black in female. Juvenile paler and more spotted. Also called 'yaffle' after loud laughing cry. Seldom drums. Often seen searching for ants, a favourite food, on lawns and in fields with mole-hills. Has increased due to spread of forestry and consequent increase in wood ants. May attack bee-hives.

Larks, Pipits and Wagtails

Average-sized, mostly streaky brown birds which sing in the air and nest mainly on the ground. Larks resemble pipits but are less slender. Pipits similarly marked but with white outer tail feathers. Wagtails have long bobbing tails. Mainly terrestrial and with musical voices, especially larks. Gregarious during winter.

1 Grey Wagtail length 7in, 18cm

The most colourful wagtail. Despite its name is bright yellow below, contrasting with blue-grey back and very long black tail. A white eye-stripe above and below eye in male, also a black throat. Usually found in hilly country by rivers and streams, nesting in holes in banks and walls, and under bridges. Similar call to pied wagtail. Can be mistaken for yellow wagtail, a summer visitor which has a yellow eye-stripe and lacks black throat.

2 Skylark length 7in, 18cm

Widely known and popular with poets. This is Shelley's 'blythe spirit' and Wordsworth's 'ethereal minstrel'. Its sustained outpouring, lasting up to five minutes, fills the air as its ascends almost out of sight, then circles down to earth. A bird of open country. It nests on moors, downs, marshes, dunes and fields. Streaky brown plumage has conspicuous white on outer feathers of long tail. Small head crest. Flocks gather in winter.

3 Pied Wagtail length 7in, 18cm

A common resident bird of gardens, farms and towns. Runs with bobbing tail. Black back, crown and throat; dark wings white below. Nests in hole in walls, buildings or rocks. A specialist in catching winged insects, formerly abundant on farms and in fields with livestock, but modern hygiene has deprived it of many feeding areas. An interesting roosting habit, as with starling, is its assembly at night in thousands on trees or buildings, notably in Dublin's O'Connell Street. Flight undulating. Call a high-pitched 'tschizzik'; song a simple twittering.

4 Tree Pipit length 6in, 15cm

Bird of heaths, open woodland, commons and country roads where a tree or telegraph pole can serve as a song post. Inconspicuous plumage, but song-flight unmistakable. Climbing steeply, it sings musically with long trills, then descends in a glide back to the same tree perch, ending in a slow 'chew-chew-chew', like a run-down gramophone. Nests on ground. (Closely similar meadow pipit is more terrestrial and seen in more open country such as moors, rough pasture and dunes. Song-flight continues down to ground. Is often host to the cuckoo.)

5 Woodlark length 6in, 15cm

Similar size to skylark with shorter tail and conspicuous eye-stripe. Inhabits grassland with shrubs on edge of woods, hillsides and sandy heaths. Less common than formerly, now found mainly in East Anglia and south coast of England. Song less powerful or sustained than skylark's but more melodious as it spirals upwards, then circles down to drop silently for the last 100 feet to earth.

Plovers

Plump wading birds with large eyes, mainly terrestrial. Usually inhabit open country or seashore. Call note helps to identify.

1 Golden Plover length 11in, 28cm

A bird of hilly moorland, mainly in west and north. Winter flocks on farmland and estuaries. Assembles in breeding areas where males skirmish and chase females. Pairs disperse to breed, and will attack intruders, even lying on ground with thrashing wings as if injured. Winter plumage dark brown spotted with gold, paler below; black face and underside during summer. Sexes similar. Call note a liquid 'tlui-i' and song a rippling trill.

2 Ringed Plover length 7½in, 19cm

A bird of the seashore, clearly marked in grey-brown above, white below, with a white collar and black band across breast. Legs orange. Active on ground and flight rapid. Typical nest site is sandy beach or shingle. Fewer sites now due to spread of beach huts and caravans and disturbance by visitors. Nesting female and young well camouflaged. Performs 'broken-wing' trick to distract attention from young. Now protected on some nature reserves.

3 Lapwing length 12in, 30½cm

Also called peewit after its call — 'kee-wi' — and green plover because of colouring. A greenish-black back with black throat and crown and longish head crest. Broad, rounded wings. A slow flapping wing beat exposes pure white underside during a twisting and erratic flight, with wings making a lapping sound. Friend of the farmer, now protected. Gregarious — sometimes in huge flocks, especially in winter. Inhabits farmland, marshes and moors. Eggs were once a gourmet's delicacy.

4 Dotterel length 8½in, 21½cm

A bird of bare, stony heights, severely decimated due to former demand as a delicacy, also egg collecting. Now restricted to some eighty pairs confined to the Scottish Cairngorms. Smaller male has a white band on brown breast, black crown, broad white eye-stripe, and black belly. Song a rapid trill. Nests among grass tussocks. Male incubates eggs and tends young. When disturbed will stay close as it runs around in a crouch, even flopping about with open wings. Call a repeated, piping 'siti-ri-siti-ri'.

5 Turnstone length 9in, 23cm

A robust plover of coastal areas, so-called after its habit of turning over stones, driftwood, seaweed and shells with its probing beak for concealed insects and small shellfish. Common winter visitor to Britain. Mottled 'tortoiseshell' pattern of back gives good concealment, and first sight is when it flies, revealing black and white underparts and wings. Most birds return to Arctic to breed. Noisy bird keeping up a rapid cry of 'kit-a-kit'.

Pigeons and Doves

Plump birds of rapid flight with small heads and crooning song. The larger pigeons have square tails; smaller, more slender doves have tapering tails. Mainly grain feeders. Families hatched in pairs.

1 Collared Dove length 11in, 28cm

A new arrival to Britain which spread across Europe from Middle East to reach Lincolnshire coast in 1952. Is now found in small colonies all over the country, even in towns and villages, where food such as grain is available. Prefers to nest in conifers. Resembles the turtle dove and identified by black half-collar behind neck. Main colour grey brown. Tail in flight shows much white. Call a deep 'coo-*coo*-coo', also a nasal flight call — 'hwee'. Has been linked with the Biblical dove.

2 Town or Domestic Pigeon length 13in, 33cm

Feral birds descended from ancestral stock of wild birds bred in dove-cotes, a practice begun by Romans. Originally bred as food, then selected by fanciers who produced such breeds as the pouter, fantail, tumbler and homing pigeon. Escapees returned to cliffs or into towns and villages to roost and nest on buildings and in railway stations, which are not unlike cliffs and caves. Town birds vary greatly from typical ancestral stock and can be white, tan, reddish and black. Male courts with bowing and circling. Two fledglings raised on pigeon's 'milk'. Does not normally perch in trees.

3 Wood Pigeon or Ring Dove length 16in, 40½cm

A large species recognised by broad white band across wing and small white patch on side of neck. Normally seen near trees and may gather in large flocks. Usually very shy in rural areas but very tame in town parks and squares. A familiar song of five syllables with accent on the second — 'coo-*coo*-oo-coo-coo'. Courtship of male is an up and down flapping flight. A flimsy raft of twigs built as nest on a branch. Can be destructive to farm crops.

4 Rock Dove length 13in, 33cm

Inhabitants of remote, rocky sea-cliffs in Britain and confined mainly to Scottish and west Irish coasts. Blue-grey plumage reflects green and purple sheen around neck. Distinguished by pale rump and two broad black bars across wings. Nests in crevices in rocks and caves. On other coasts, similar-looking birds probably domestic stock gone wild. Cooing similar to town pigeon, with accent on second syllable — 'co-roo-roo'.

5 Turtle Dove length 11in, 28cm

A slender summer visitor. fawn-coloured with rounded, white-bordered tail. Nests in open country in bushes and low trees. Song soft and purring.

Crows

Large perching birds with powerful beaks, and nostrils covered with bristles. Mostly dark coloured with harsh calls. Given to scavenging and raiding other birds' nests. Much persecuted by farmers to protect crops and game and have tended to move into built-up areas for safety. A tendency to steal bright objects. The most intelligent of birds.

1 Carrion Crow length 18½in, 47cm

All black, best recognised by size and black feathered beak. A tendency to remain solitary or in pairs, although do occur in roosts and family groups. Notorious thief of eggs and fledglings. An enemy of the farmer and gamekeeper. Now a common sight in towns where it builds a bulky nest in trees in parks and squares. A hoarse cry of 'kraa' repeated twice or three times (see rook). Very much a scavenger, hanging around rubbish tips and lay-bys, and exploring seashore.

2 Hooded Crow length 18½in, 47cm

Distinguished from carrion crow and rook by grey back and underside. Will interbreed with carrion crow (of which it is a sub-species) where ranges overlap. This so-called 'hoodie' or 'corbie' is resident in northern Scotland, Ireland and Isle of Man. Lives on moorland and shot by keepers to protect grouse, its favourite prey.

3 Raven length 25in, 63½cm

Largest of the family. A large dark beak, wedge-shaped tail, loose neck feathers, and makes a deep, croaking 'kaa' or 'kronk'. Acrobatic in flight, even flies upside down. Once a scavenger in the streets of London, now only guards the Tower. In the wild is now confined to hilly country in west and north, nesting in trees and on cliffs. Preys on seabirds and searches for carrion in sheep and deer country.

4 Rook length 18in, 45½cm

Distinguished from carrion crow by bare, whitish face and beak (but juvenile has feathered face). Feathers loose and baggy around thighs. A variety of calls less harsh than crow, such as 'kaw' and 'kaa'. Very sociable, usually in groups. Nests in colonies, or rookeries, returning to repair nests early in year. Aggressive behaviour in defence of territory has given rise to idea of 'rook parliaments', sitting in judgement on those accused for stealing nest material from another bird. Male feeds incubating female with much bowing. Useful to farmer as eats wireworms and leatherjackets. Gleans food from stubble.

Crows contd

1 Jackdaw length 13in, 33cm

Smaller than carrion crow with grey on back of neck. Call a distinctive short 'tchak'. Very sociable, with definite 'pecking-order' within colony. Nests on buildings well above ground, and is at home anywhere from towns to remote cliffs. Commonly attached to ruins and old houses with nest sites. Feeds regularly with rooks. Will pluck hair and wool from backs of horses and sheep for nest material. A notorious thief but makes an interesting pet. Much studied to interpret their social behaviour. A young bird treats its human owner as 'boss' and when mature may even make courtship overtures or attempt to offer food.

2 Starling length 18½in, 21½cm

A familiar bird in towns, gardens and on farms and is much attached to man. Belongs to a separate family of stocky birds with short tails and long pointed beaks. Colour is black and speckled white, with glossy purple, green and blue sheen. Very gregarious, usually in flocks, and with habit of roosting on buildings or trees in towns and cities, as in London's Trafalgar Square, moving out by day to forage in gardens and fields. Can be seen moving rapidly along flight paths into town at dusk. Large numbers of winter visitors from Continent augment residents. Moves with waddling gait, feeding around bird-table or in fields among cattle in search of leatherjackets. Fond of apples. Nests in holes in buildings, nest-boxes and trees. Song a mixture of twitters and whistles, also a harsh 'tcheer'. An excellent mimic. Seen here in winter plumage.

3 Magpie length 18in, 45½cm

Unmistakable, contrasting black and white plumage, long tail and loud rapid call — 'chak-chak-chak'. Inhabits farmland and open country with hedges and trees. Builds a domed nest. Usually missing from game preserves due to control by keepers, and is now penetrating towns, mainly in suburbs. Is well inside Dublin city but not in London. Like jackdaw, is an egg-stealer and attracted to bright objects. Much associated with superstitious beliefs.

4 Jay length 13½in, 34½cm

A handsome crow, easily recognised by its harsh penetrating cry — 'kraak' — sounding like tearing linen, when alerted by a fox, owl, cat or human, yet very secretive and silent during breeding. Annoying to naturalists and called 'policeman of the woods'. Very much a woodland bird and common in town parks and gardens. Preys on eggs and nestlings and will gather and bury acorns in squirrel fashion. A pinkish-brown body with white rump and black tail and conspicuous blue and black barred feathers on wings.

5 Chough length 15½in, 39½cm

Resembles a carrion crow but with curved red beak and red legs. Lives on cliffs in Wales, Scotland, Ireland and the Isle of Man, in small colonies now much reduced. Nests on cliffs or in caves. Name (originally pronounced 'chow' but now 'chuff') is taken from its long, high-pitched call — 'kyaw'.

Game Birds

Mainly ground birds shot for sport and protected by game laws which provide a close season and the need for a licence to shoot them. Consist of pheasants, partridges and grouse. Beaters drive birds which fly towards guns, and kills are recovered by dogs.

1 Ptarmigan length 14in, 35½cm

A grouse of high, stony, barren mountain-tops. In summer male is brown, hen grey, both with white wings and black tail. Red wattle over eye. In winter both turn pure white, but retain black tail. Voice a harsh croak. Crowing song during courtship with fanning of tail and drooping wings. Keeps mainly above tree-line, feeding on green shoots and berries. Nests in a scrape among rocks.

2 Red Grouse length 15in, 38cm

The only bird unique to Britain (but introduced into Belgium). Stout body and short wings. Male has dark rufous plumage, darker on wings and tail, red wattle over eye and white feathered legs and toes. Female brown and more barred. Inhabits moorland and peat areas in north and west, feeding on young heather and berries, especially on grouse moors in Scotland. Call a crowing 'kowk-ok-ok'. Males challenge rivals by leaping in air with outspread wings and extended neck with cries of 'go-back, go-back'. Flies with whirring wings. Can endure severe weather. Shooting commences on August 12th.

3 Pheasant length 30-35in, 76-89cm

Introduced possibly by Romans but definitely established by Norman times. The so-called Old English Pheasant has its origins in central Asia and China. A later introduction from eastern Asia has white neck ring. Both occur today in about equal numbers. Males' gay colouring quite variable due to cross-breeding. Runs for cover rather than flies. Strong, short flight with noisy take-off. Prefers open woods with undergrowth. Nests in hollow on ground under cover of low vegetation. Crowing male has strident double note 'korr-kok'. Thousands reared and released in time for first shoot on October 1st.

4 Partridge length 12in, 30½cm

Chubby, chicken-like game bird with rufous upperside, grey neck and underside, pale chestnut head. Male has conspicuous brown patch on lower breast. A crouching walk, squats or runs swiftly when alarmed. Whirring flight with alternate glides. Habitat mainly on farmland, nesting in hedge bottoms. (Red-legged or French partridge more common in eastern England, preferring drier surroundings. Has red beak and legs, white throat bordered in black and grey, heavily barred sides. Habitats generally similar.) Many eggs destroyed by predators.

5 Black Grouse length 21in, 53½cm

Male or blackcock has glossy blue-black plumage with lyre-shaped tail, white underneath. Female or greyhen (actually more brownish) heavily barred with black. Birds assemble at courting ground, the lek. Males polygamous, display and engage in mock fighting, with a sustained chorus of bubbling notes. Feed on birch buds and conifer shoots, live in vicinity of trees by moorland and marshy places. Mainly confined to Scotland and Wales but increasing with spread of conifers.

Waders

Long-legged birds with long slender beaks. Wader is a general term for a large group of birds adapted for paddling in shallow water and probing for food in mud and sand. Habitat is seashore, moorland, mudflat and marshy places. Plumage is well camouflaged pattern of browns and greys in most cases, especially in females, which nest on the ground.

1 Common Sandpiper length 7¾in, 20cm

Named after its shrill, piping 'twee-wee-wee', this wader inhabits much of Northern Hemisphere. It arrives in summer to nest alongside clear streams, trout brooks and mountain lochs in the west and north. Colour is dark olive-brown above, more so than other waders, with white on sides and below. Low flight of shallow wing-beats, and glides with deeply curved wings revealing white wing-bar. Constant bobbing of head and tail when on ground. Like other ground-nesters, it will play the 'broken-wing' trick to lure away intruders.

2 Redshank length 11in, 28cm

A greyish-brown, resident wader; paler below with long orange legs. White back and rump, and white border to wings revealed in flight. Usual call is a ringing 'tleu-lu-lu', also a musical, repeated yodelling cry — 'tu-udle-tu-udle'. Habitat is on marshes, moorland, sewage farms, wintering on mud-flats and estuaries. (Somewhat similar but paler greenshank has greenish legs, a winter visitor to Scotland.)

3 Avocet length 17in, 43cm

Was absent from Britain from 1825 due to drainage and shooting for feathers; after Second World War birds returned, probably from Holland, to start nesting on Minsmere bird reserve and Havergate Island off Suffolk coast, both established by the RSPB. Both colonies have increased, especially on Havergate. Easily recognised by bold black and white plumage and upturned beak, used in sideways sweeps to sift small seafood from water. Nests close to shallow water on mud-flats and sand-banks. Voice a fluty 'kloo-it', also a yelping alarm cry.

4 Oystercatcher length 17in, 43cm

One of the easiest waders to recognise. Also called the 'sea-pie', it has a conspicuous black and white plumage with orange beak. Common on the beach at low tide, searching for shellfish which it can split open with its sideways-flattened beak. Flocks rest on sand-bars and islets between tides. Normally nests along shore and on cliff-tops and is spreading into moorland and farmland.

5 Curlew length 21-23in, 53½-58½cm

Britain's largest wader, seen mainly on moorland during breeding season, moving to coast for the winter. Not to be confused with smaller whimbrel, both having downcurved beaks. Whimbrel confined to Scottish moors and has striped crown. Curlew's unmistakable call is a pure ringing 'coor-li', after which it is named, and a liquid song delivered slowly and ending in a trill.

Ducks, Coot and Moorhen

Ducks are aquatic birds with webbed feet and flat beaks with serrated borders used for straining water plants. So-called surface ducks feed by up-ending or dabbling, springing vertically from surface when taking off. Diving ducks patter along surface for take-off, and dive for food. Drakes (males) more brightly coloured, both sexes usually with bright-coloured wing patch, called the speculum. Plumage of duckling and of drake in late summer (the 'eclipse'), resembles that of female. Coot and moorhen are dark-coloured marsh dwellers.

1 Moorhen length 13in, 33cm

Smaller than coot, black with red frontal shield and beak, white streaks on flanks. Conspicuous white under tail which shows in flashes as it swims buoyantly and jerkily. Flight weak. Common on ponds, marshes, sewage farms and in town parks. Territorial, and males will fight. Nests in thick cover close to water. Call a loud croak — 'kurruk'.

2 Coot length 15in, 38cm

A plump, black water-bird which inhabits marshland, open waters and reservoirs; commonly seen in town parks. Larger than moorhen, it has a white frontal shield and beak. Flight clumsy, landing with a splash. Swims with bobbing head and dives frequently. Patters along surface when taking off. Rather quarrelsome and territorial, lowering head and raising wings in attack. Toes separately fringed with webs. Sexes alike. Call a loud 'tewk'.

3 Mallard length 23in, 58½cm

Familiar and widespread surface duck, very tame in villages and towns. Drake has iridescent green head, white collar, brown breast, and tail with curled feathers. Duck a mottled brown. Both have purple speculum. Flight rapid, moving down to coast at night and for winter. Duck quacks loudly, drake has quiet whistle. Nests on ground, occasionally in hollow tree or on flat roof-top.

4 Pochard length 18in, 45½cm

Diving duck, common in town parks, sometimes in large flocks on reservoirs and lakes. Drake a uniform chestnut on head and neck, black breast and pale below. Tends to stay on water, where it sleeps. A quiet bird with drake making an occasional wheezing call, duck a more growling note. Most birds fly to eastern Europe to breed.

5 Tufted Duck length 17in, 43cm

Diving duck common on ponds and park lakes, in company with mallard. Drake black and white with drooping crest, duck browner with smaller crest and small white patch at base of beak. Call of drake a soft whistle.

6 Shelduck length 24in, 61cm

A coastal duck, somewhat goose-like in build and flight, clearly marked in dark green, black and white with chestnut band around foreparts. Beak red. Sexes alike but drake has knob on beak. Largest British duck. Usually nests in rabbit burrow in sand dune. A mass movement to northern Europe takes place after breeding, in order to moult.

Divers

Streamlined fish-hunting birds with pointed beaks, nesting on or by freshwater lakes, etc. In Britain they include true divers, grebes and kingfishers. Divers are large birds of open water, rather shy and quick to submerge. Swim low in water, sometimes with only head and neck showing. Clumsy and awkward on land. Nest close to waterside. Smaller grebes more aquatic, building nests on water. Swim with neck erect. Toes separately webbed. Kingfisher dives for fish from overhanging perch, nests in hole. Easily recognised by bright colours.

1 Great Northern Diver length 27-32in, 68½-81½cm

Largest diver, size of small goose. A chequered black and white body, black head and neck, white collar. In winter dark grey-brown, white cheeks, throat and underside. Takes off from water clumsily and lands with a splash. Powerful swimmer and diver, catching a variety of food with powerful beak. In Britain winters mainly on coast of Scotland. Occasional non-breeding birds present in summer.

2 Red-Throated Diver length 21-24in, 53½-61cm

Smaller than the great northern diver but with similar streamlined build. In summer a dark brownish-black, grey head and neck with red throat patch, white below. Black-throated diver similar size, build and habits, has black throat and striped neck. Call of both a guttural 'krouck', also high wailing cries. Both inhabit Scottish lochs to breed, wintering along coast. May be seen farther south in severe winters.

3 Great Crested Grebe length 19in, 48cm

Largest British grebe. Identified by black ear tufts and chestnut frill around slender white neck. Streamlined body appears tailless and is held low in water. Greyish brown above and pure white below. Frill missing in winter. Low flight shows white on wings. Sexes alike. Once nearly exterminated due to demand for feathers for women's hats. Has now greatly increased with protection and more suitable habitats (disused gravel pits, reservoirs) even inside towns. Birds now nesting on Serpentine in London. A floating nest is attached to nearby vegetation. An elaborate courtship of circling, neck rubbing and 'kissing', also offering tokens of water weed. Call a shrill 'er-wick' or barking 'karr-arr'.

4 Kingfisher length 6½in, 16½cm

Gaudiest of British birds, a brilliant blue-green above, chestnut-orange below. Seen as a streak of colour in rapid and direct flight up or down stream, or sitting on a fishing perch. Plunges into water for fish or may hover and dive. Fish taken to perch, beaten, and swallowed head first. Nest-hole, dug in bank alongside water, contains fish bones. The head and large stabbing beak look out of proportion to body. Colour is protective as flesh is foul-tasting.

5 Little Grebe or Dabchick length 10½in, 27cm

Smallest British grebe. Widespread on lakes and ponds even in town parks. Stocky, oval-shaped body, short neck and blunt tail. Dark brown above, paler below. Cheeks and throat chestnut. Flight low and fast. Call a repeated 'wit-wit'. Courtship accompanied by trilling song as birds face one another.

Geese

Related to ducks, these larger, long-necked, more bulky water-birds spend much time feeding on land. Many make long journeys north to breed, wintering (in Britain) in Scotland and Wales, and on reserves such as the Wildfowl Trust at Slimbridge, Gloucestershire. Flocks roost in estuaries and marshes, moving to feeding grounds to crop grass and other shoots, also rootcrops. Beak is triangular with broad base, used as a cutting tool. Numbers much reduced due to wildfowling and shooting by farmers, and partial loss of habitat and feeding grounds. There are two types — black and grey geese. Flight is powerful, usually in V-formation.

1 Brent Goose length 22-24in, 56-61cm

Smallest British goose, little bigger than the mallard. Has entirely black head, neck and breast, with small white spot on neck. Much reduced, largely because of disease and loss of its favourite food, the marine eel-grass (Zostera). Very much a sea-going goose, roosting on the water during high tides. Winters in estuaries, especially at Foulness, Essex, also Wash and Fens, flying from roosts to feeding grounds on arable fields. Ban on shooting has saved it from possible extinction.

2 Barnacle Goose length 23-27in, 58½-68½cm

A black goose readily recognised by black and white pattern, white face and forehead. Winters in Scotland having bred in the Arctic. Feeds mostly at night on short turf on dunes and sea meadows. Larger than similar-looking brent goose. Now protected from shooting. Is named after mediaeval belief that it originated from the goose barnacle which is washed ashore on driftwood, and somewhat resembles a goose in appearance.

3 Pinkfoot length 24-30in, 61-76cm

Grey goose with blue-grey plumage and pink feet and beak. A small dark head and neck. Large winter flocks a familiar sight in Scotland around the Firth of Forth, flying from roosts to feeding grounds.

4 Canada Goose length 36-40in, 91½-101½cm

Largest goose, introduced from North America as ornamental bird. Numbers have escaped and are seen on lakes, ponds and meres, also in town parks. Colour grey-brown with black head, long black neck and pale breast. Distinctive white patch on throat and cheek. Tends to move around. Grazes in fields and may up-end in water. Keeps to fresh water.

5 Greylag length 30-35in, 76-89cm

Grey goose, the ancestor of domestic breeds. Only greylag and Canada goose breed in Britain. A pale grey with thick orange beak. Absence of any black and larger size distinguishes it from other grey geese. Nests mainly in Scotland, beside lochs. Voice same nasal gabbling as farm goose — 'aahung-ung', sounding in distance like a bleating sheep.

Swans and Herons

Swans are large, white-coloured cousins of ducks which cannot be mistaken. Of the three native species the largest, resident, and often tame mute swan is most familiar. Bewick's and whooper swans are winter visitors. Feed with serrated beak similar to ducks. Take off from water by pattering along surface. Grey heron and bittern are long-legged fishing birds. Swans fly with neck outstretched, herons with neck tucked between shoulders.

1 Bewick's Swan length 28in, 71cm

Named after the eighteenth-century bird artist, Thomas Bewick. Smaller than mute or whooper, with smaller, more rounded yellow base to beak. Flight call more goose-like. In winter, flocks from Soviet Arctic visit the East Anglian fens, and a large flock goes to the Wildfowl Trust at Slimbridge.

2 Whooper Swan length 60in, 152½cm

The shyest and noisiest swan. Holds neck stiffly erect and has a bugle-like flight call. Beak is black, without knob, with lemon-yellow base which tapers to a point on both sides. Found in herds along coast or on lakes during winter, mainly in Scotland.

3 Mute Swan length 60in, 152½cm

A familiar swan seen almost everywhere in towns, villages, sea-shores, even remote lakes and marshes. Recognised by graceful curved neck and black knob (the 'berry') on beak, larger in male (or cob), smaller in female (or pen). Cygnet at first a fluffy brown, turning grey during first year. Said to have been originally introduced from main stronghold in the Low Countries, but may have been resident all the time in the East Anglian fens, though overlooked. An ornamental bird once eaten at banquets. Is powerful in flight, with creaking wing-beats. Hisses and snorts when annoyed and can become aggressive. Mates for life. Legendary 'swan-song' as it dies is a myth. Considered a royal bird; the crown once controlled ownership through special courts — the swainmotes. Birds were marked on beak or webs to identify ownership. Annual ceremony of 'swan-upping' still practised on the Thames every July.

4 Grey Heron length 36in, 91½cm

Usually seen standing like a grey sentinel in or beside water, waiting for a fish or frog, or during flight with slow flapping wing-beats and head tucked into shoulders, legs dangling. May range many miles to fishing grounds and will steal goldfish from ponds. Birds return each year to same heronry, in tall trees, mostly in river valleys, fens and marshes. Normal call, at rest or in flight, a deep harsh 'fraarnk'. Colony very noisy during nesting, with much croaking, chattering and clatter of beaks.

5 Bittern length 30in, 76cm

Resembles a short-necked heron, more brownish, heavily mottled and barred. Lives and nests among reeds, mainly in East Anglia. When alarmed will freeze with neck and beak stretched upwards in perfect camouflage with surrounding reeds. Produces a deep booming note. Once nearly exterminated, now protected on reserves. Keeps much to cover, moving in a hunchback manner.

Gulls

Long-winged seabirds with squarish tails. Familiar, buoyant fliers and swimmers, mostly white with grey or black above. Wings with white tips. Different species best recognised by size, wing pattern and colour of legs. Juveniles more mottled in brown. A rough nest built on cliffs or ground containing three or four pear-shaped speckled eggs. Nests in colonies. Much time spent along shore and inland during winter.

1 Great Black-Backed Gull length 29in, 73½cm

Largest British gull, black above with pale pink legs. A ferocious predator of nestlings, eating almost anything it can find or steal. Swoops at intruders to defend its own eggs. Confined mainly to coast along Atlantic seaboard. Small colonies occur on ground, on clifftops, coastal moors and islands. Does not breed inland. Call a herring-gull-like 'kyow-kyow' and a chuckling 'auk-auk-auk'. Lesser black-backed gull similar but smaller and has yellow legs.

2 Black-Headed Gull length 15in, 38cm

Most familiar gull, of average size, with chocolate-black head, crimson beak and legs and white front edge to wings. Since end of nineteenth century has penetrated inland during winter to scavenge in towns on rubbish tips and railway sidings. Fed by well-wishers. Seen on most ponds and lakes in parks and on rivers, moving out of town at dusk to roost on reservoirs and coming back to same feeding area next morning. Much studied by ringing. In spring birds fly north to breeding sites alongside lochs, lakes and marshes in northern England and Scotland, or fly across North Sea to Baltic shores. Nests in colonies on ground. *Note:* in winter black head reduced to dark smudge behind eyes.

3 Kittiwake length 16in, 40½cm

The most sea-going gull, seldom seen inland, only coming ashore to breed. Size of common gull, with black wing tips and black legs. At sea, food is picked off water surface. Breeds on tall cliffs in noisy colonies, uttering its name — 'kitti-waak'. Unlike other gulls it builds an elaborate cup-shaped nest.

4 Common Gull length 16in, 40½cm

Resembles small herring gull with same grey upper parts and black and white wing tips, but legs greenish yellow and beak yellow. Call higher but similar to herring gull. Often seen inland during winter. Colonies breed on moors and islands, or shingle beaches, mainly on Scottish islands and in Highlands on lochsides. Feeds on refuse, soil animals and carrion. Not Britain's commonest gull despite its name.

5 Herring Gull length 22in, 56cm

Large, grey-backed, with black and white wing tips and pink legs. The commonest gull and familiar to holidaymakers. Follows ships and haunts fishing ports and harbours. Has increased enormously. Large colonies nest on cliff ledges, islands and in dunes, even roofs of buildings near coast. Call a strident 'kyow' and a laughing 'gah-gah-gah'. Common inland during winter, following the plough. Eats almost anything. Chick pecks at red spot on parent's beak to encourage regurgitation of food.

Other Seabirds

Besides gulls, other seabirds that inhabit and nest along our shores include auks, fulmars, shearwaters, gannets, terns and petrels. Points to look for: auks — black and white diving birds of stocky build, short necks and whirring flight; fulmars — gull-like, fly with long glides on stiff wings; shearwaters — gull-like with thinner beaks and similar stiff flight; gannets — large sized and plunge into sea after food; terns — white with black head, slender and gull-like, forked tail and thin pointed beak, graceful in flight, hover and plunge for food; petrels — small and dark, usually skim close to waves, visiting shore after dark (patter over calm water as if walking, hence 'petrel' derived from St Peter, after Biblical account of walking on water).

1 Fulmar length 18½in, 47cm

Resembles gull but more stubby build and thick neck, more gliding flight on stiff wings close to water surface. Short, thick, yellow beak with tubed nostrils (as in albatross and other 'tube-noses'). Clumsy on land. Birds of open sea, greatly increased probably due to offal thrown from fishing boats. Breeds on cliffs or hollows in turf. Ejects foul-smelling fluid if disturbed.

2 Puffin length 12in, 30½cm

Also called sea-parrot. Readily noticed by triangular, red, blue and yellow, sideways flattened, parrot-like beak, white face, black and white body and orange legs. Appears large headed during rapid and whirring flight. Breeds on turf-covered cliff-tops and islands, using rabbit burrow, or digs own hole with beak, shovelling soil away with webbed feet. Not very vocal but makes growling sounds — 'arr-arr'. Spends winter at sea when beak loses horny sheath and appears duller.

3 Guillemot length 16½in, 42cm

Black and white auk with curved white wing-bar, similar to razorbill in build but with slender pointed beak and thinner neck. Some individuals have white line behind eyes. An efficient diver after fish. Breeds in dense colonies on cliff-faces and cliff-stacks. In February a noisy breeding season begins with much overcrowding and harsh notes of 'arra-arra'. Birds take part in display flights and 'dancing' on water. Single pear-shaped egg laid on bare rock. In August birds leave to spend rest of year at sea.

4 Razorbill length 16in, 40½cm

Differentiated from guillemot by thicker head, more squat body and laterally compressed beak crossed halfway by white line. When swimming keeps tail cocked. Breeds on sea cliffs, often close to guillemots. Voice a querulous growling. Named after shape of beak.

5 Common Tern length 14in, 35½cm

Differs from other terns in red beak with black tip and shorter wings. A summer visitor, breeding on ground in colonies on beaches, shingle, dunes and islands. Dives on intruders with shrill cries of 'kik-kik-kik'. Hovers then dives for fish, especially sand-eels. Most widely distributed breeding tern in British Isles, mostly on coast but inland nesting common in some areas.

Other Seabirds contd

1 Storm Petrel length 6in, 15cm

Smallest petrel, all black with conspicuous white rump and square black tail. Keeps well out to sea, following ships. Comes ashore only at night to enter nest burrows when breeding, mainly on islands along Atlantic coast. Makes purring and crooning noises, ending in a kind of hiccup. At sea keeps to troughs in waves.

2 Cormorant length 36in, 91½cm

Large black fishing seabird with long neck, pointed beak, white cheeks. (Smaller shag more greenish black, no white on face and small head crest.) Swims low in water with erect neck and beak pointed upwards. Dives for fish. Usually seen flying in line low over water or standing on rock with wings half open, necessary to dry feathers because of lack of waterproof oil. Inhabits coasts and estuaries, sometimes on inland waters such as reservoirs and rivers. Normally breeds colonially on rocky ledges.

3 Gannet length 36in, 91½cm

Largest seabird, goose-sized. All white with black wing-tips, pointed beak and pointed tail. Wing span six feet. Juveniles blackish brown. Wheels and glides and plunges with wings closed in a spectacular dive into sea after fish, from 100 feet or more. Call a barking 'arragh'. Very maritime over Atlantic, coming ashore to breed in dense colonies on rocky islands, as at St Kilda in Outer Hebrides and Bass Rock in Firth of Forth.

4 Manx Shearwater length 14in, 35½cm

Sooty black above, pure white below, with slender beak. Somewhat gull-like in build. Largely oceanic, gliding over water on narrow, stiffly held wings, following wave movements. Breeds locally along Atlantic coast in burrows, coming ashore at night. Will use rabbit holes. A constant eerie crooning heard after dusk. Travels long distances on migration, even reaching South America and Australia. Moves clumsily on land.

5 Arctic Skua length 18in, 45½cm

Hawk-like seabird. Two variants, one blackish brown with white below and on cheeks and neck, the other uniformly dark. In flight shows flash of white on wings and extended feathers beyond curved tail. A summer visitor and Britain's rarest seabird. Breeds on moorland in north and west Scotland, mainly Orkney and Shetland. Voice a wailing 'ya-aaow'. Skua known as pirate of the sea, will harass other seabirds (gulls, terns) in hawk-like manner until they disgorge food. Will rob nests and defend its own extremely aggressively.

6 Arctic Tern length 15in, 38cm

Most numerous tern in British Isles, but more northerly distribution than common tern and colonies almost entirely on or near coast. Beak wholly red in summer and wholly black in winter. Travels to Antarctic for winter, a journey of some 10,000 miles.

Owls

Mostly nocturnal birds of prey with large head, flattened face and circle of feathers around forward-placed large eyes giving good binocular vision. Hooked beak, sharp claws and short tail. Excellent hearing. Soft feathers give noiseless flight. Hooting call. Sexes alike. After a meal regurgitates food pellets containing bones, skulls, hair and beetle remains. Three to four round white eggs in clutch. Generally useful and protected by law.

1 Tawny Owl length 15in, 38cm

The most familiar owl. A woodland species, often found in towns; roosts in trees, nests in tree-holes. Feathers mottled and streaked in browns, eyes black. Hunts small mammals, occasionally birds. Call a familiar tremulous 'hoo-hoo-hoo-oo-oo'. Also a more shrill 'ker-wick', but never at the same time. Can be spotted roosting by excited 'mobbing' by small birds. Has been known to attack humans close to nest-site. Young sometimes fall from nest and are rescued and raised as pets.

2 Long-Eared Owl length 14in, 35½cm

Medium sized. Inhabits conifer woods and recognised by long ear-tufts (not visible during flight). Very nocturnal and normally seen only when roosting. Slimly built and will stretch up its body when alarmed, and may also threaten with snapping of beak, hissing and outspread wings. Call a soft, sighing 'oo-oo-oo'. Prey mainly mammals and birds. Uses old nest of squirrel or crow.

3 Barn Owl length 13½in, 34½cm

Pale coloured and long legged with white face. Golden buff above, unstreaked white below. Also called white or screech owl, it has a ghostly appearance in flight at dusk. Call a long wild screech, also hisses and snorts. Usually associated with man, on farmland and around villages where suitable roosts and nest-sites occur, as in barns, church towers and lofts. Eggs laid on heap of food pellets.

4 Short-Eared Owl length 15in, 38cm

Bird of open country, on marshes, moors, downs and dunes, nesting on ground among heather or marram grass. A pale tawny colour with streaked underside and barred wings. Short ear-tufts. Flight low as it patrols ground, even in daytime. Voles a favourite food and birds will move into areas suffering from vole 'plagues'.

5 Little Owl length 8½in, 21½cm

The smallest owl, about the size of a starling. Introduced at end of last century and has spread rapidly. Often abroad by day and usually seen sitting on a post or telegraph wire in open country, bobbing its body. Has a flattened face and yellow-ringed eyes giving a fierce expression. Feeds mainly on insects and small mammals. Nests in tree-holes and burrows. Call is a plaintive, cat-like 'kiew'.

Birds of Prey

Birds with hooked beaks and sharp talons for hunting prey during daylight. Much persecuted in past and have suffered from effects of pesticides and habitat changes, some almost to the point of extinction. Now protected and slowly recovering. Best recognised in flight by silhouette shape. Eagles are large with broad wings and squarish tails. Falcons have large heads, broad 'shoulders', pointed wings and long narrow tails. Harriers have smallish heads, long slim bodies, angled wings and long tails. Buzzards have heavy bodies, broad wings and short wide tails. Hawks have short rounded wings and long tails. Females in some species are larger than males.

1 **Golden Eagle** length 30-35in, 76-89cm

Recognised by large size, majestic soaring and gliding. Seen mainly in mountains and remote sea-cliffs in Highlands and, rarely, in Lake District. Territory covers up to 20 square miles in which it hunts grouse, ptarmigan, hares and occasional sick lambs. Will also scavenge. Pairs for life. Nest or eyrie built on inaccessible rock ledge and used yearly. Usually only one of the two fledglings survives. Young bird has white on wings and base of tail. Call an occasional yelping 'kya'. So-called 'king of birds', but title undeserved as it is rather cowardly.

2 **Osprey** length 20-23in, 51-58½cm

Summer visitor, once extinct in UK but returned in 1950s to breed at Loch Garten on Speyside and elsewhere in Scotland. Also called fish-hawk, it will swoop to catch fish. Resembles small eagle, dark upperside, snow-white below and whitish head. Wings long, narrow and angled. Protected by RSPB and a tourist attraction at Loch Garten. Eyrie built in tree.

3 **Goshawk** length 19-24in, 48-61cm

A large hawk once persecuted and rare, but now recovering. Inhabits wooded country, pursuing small birds in a low dashing attack typical of hawks. A short chattering cry — 'jig-jig-jig'.

4 **Marsh Harrier** length 19-22in, 48-56cm

Distinguished from other harriers by larger size, broader wings and no white on rump. Low hunting flight typical of harriers, quartering ground with occasional wing-beats and long glides. Male chestnut-brown with pale grey tail and grey on wings, female more uniform brown. Call a high-pitched 'kwee-a'. Inhabits fens and marshes as summer visitor, especially in East Anglia (e.g. at Minsmere, Suffolk). Nests on ground among reeds.

5 **Buzzard** length 20-22in, 51-56cm

Usually seen in flight, soaring in circles, almost out of sight, uttering a plaintive cat-like 'pee-oo'. Mainly in Scotland, Wales and West Country, but range extending. Pounces on prey, mainly rabbits. Numbers much reduced because of loss of food due to myxomatosis. Nests on rock ledges and in trees. (Not to be confused with kite, once a street scavenger in towns, now rare and confined to Wales. Kite has deeply forked tail and white under wings. Also soars. Call similar.)

Birds of Prey contd

1 Peregrine length 15-19in, 38-48cm

Prized by falconers for their ancient sport, the falcon is renowned for its speed and its skill in capturing prey in air. Will 'stoop' (dive down with closed wings) at speeds of up to 160 mph, striking victim hard, even breaking off head. Much reduced due to shooting to protect homing pigeons during Second World War, also later from pesticides. Is slowly recovering. Male, or tiercel, is a third smaller than female, and has a slatey-grey back, whitish below narrowly barred with black. Female darker. Young bird dark brown. Has wide range in wild open country, from moor to mountain. Nests on cliffs, mountain ledges, occasionally on towers and church spires.

2 Merlin length 10½-13in, 26½-33cm

Small falcon. Male little larger than blackbird. Blue-grey back, slate-blue tail and heavily striped reddish-brown below. Larger female similar with dark brown above. Lives and hunts in open country, pursuing with dexterity the twists and turns of small birds. Although much persecuted is holding its own in Wales and on moors in northern England and Scotland.

3 Kestrel length 13½in, 34½cm

A falcon with typical pointed wings and long slim tail. Male has spotted chestnut back, grey head, rump and tail. Female more rusty-brown with barred upperside. Is very adaptable to different surroundings, such as farmland, downs, moors. Usually seen hovering in air as it scans ground for prey such as voles and mice. A common sight along roads, perched on a post. Nests in trees, on sea-cliffs, also in towns on buildings. Call a shrill repeated 'kee-kee-kee'. The commonest day-flying bird of prey.

4 Hobby length 12-14in, 30½-35½cm

Resembles a small peregrine but has more streaky underside and reddish feathers around thighs. Dashing, agile flight. Preys on small birds and insects, and can even catch a swallow or a bat. A summer visitor to southern England, on downs, commons, open woodland. Breeds in trees in old nests.

5 Cuckoo length 13in, 33cm

Familiar summer visitor, described here because of possible confusion with sparrowhawk. Has similar build, flight and long tail, as well as colouring. Note difference in beak and grey on upper breast. Once thought to turn into a hawk during winter. 'Cu-coo' call of male unmistakable; female gives more bubbling call. Well-known habit of laying a single egg in other birds' nests, each female concentrating on a particular host species.

6 Sparrowhawk length 11-15in, 28-38cm

Average size and distinguished from other small birds of prey by short, rounded wings and long tail. Male slate-grey above, reddish-brown below with crossbars. Larger female similar but has grey underside. Hunts small birds and game birds along hedgerows and in woods. Cry a loud, rapid 'kek-kek-kek'. Has suffered much from pesticides and persecution. Given legal protection in 1966 and is now recovering.

MAMMALS

Warm-blooded vertebrates which grow hair and suckle their young. Today's most advanced animals. British mammals consist of insectivores, bats, the rabbit and hares, rodents, carnivores and deer. Seals and some whales occur in coastal waters. Altogether about 60 species.

Insectivores

Small, restless and often quarrelsome, with pointed snouts, small brains, short legs and five clawed digits on each foot. Sharp pointed teeth. Feed on a variety of soil animals such as earthworms, beetles and grubs.

1 **Hedgehog** body 10in, 25½cm

Plump body on short legs. Upperside covered with sharp, dark brown prickles, a form of modified hair which is soft when animals are young. Underside and head covered with earthy-brown, coarse hair. Inhabits dry areas, avoiding dense woodland, marshes and moorland. Common on farmland, in open woods, along hedgerows and in gardens. Mainly active at dusk, moving and feeding noisily. Squeals loudly when hurt or attacked. Eats soil animals, eggs, frogs, even snakes. Curls up when alarmed, prickles raised. Hibernates in nest of leaves, in ditches, undergrowth, etc.

2 **Common Shrew** body 3in, 7½cm tail 1½in, 4cm

Small, somewhat mouse-like build, with heavily whiskered and pointed snout and small ears. Short fur, rusty brown above, grading to white below. Tips of teeth red, small eyes. Restless and active, nose constantly twitching as it hunts invertebrates, especially beetles and earthworms. Apparently fearless. Hunted by owls but otherwise left alone when killed due to musty smell. Widespread in leaf litter and undergrowth of hedges, woods and plantations. Voice a shrill squeak. Nests on surface, under a log, stone or root.

3 **Water Shrew** body 3½in, 9cm tail 2½in, 6½cm

Largest of three British shrews. A dark, slatey black above, white below. Row of stiff hairs under tail and along hind legs aids swimming. Very much confined to waterside, usually of slow-running streams. Hunts small water animals, including small frogs and fish. Nests in tunnel in bankside.

4 **Pygmy Shrew** body 2½in, 6½cm tail 1½in, 4cm

Smallest British mammal. Similar to common shrew in build and habits, but paler and relatively longer tail. Widespread from sea-level to mountains. Only shrew in Ireland. Habitat as for common shrew.

5 **Mole** body 6in, 15cm

Barrel-shaped body with large spade-like forelimbs built for digging. Short tail held erect. Plush, velvety black fur lies in any direction. Eyes buried by fur and may even be covered with skin. No outer ears. Mainly subterranean but may venture above now and then. Wide range of habitats in workable soil, especially on farmland. Presence indicated by mole-runs and casts; mole-hill or 'fortress' may be turf-covered and contain nesting chamber. Feeds on soil animals, mainly earthworms. Solitary and quarrelsome. Swims well.

Bats

Only mammals capable of true flight. Wings consist of membranes stretched between greatly elongated fingers and connecting along sides of body with hind leg and most of tail. Hook-like thumbs and hind toes used for crawling and gripping on to resting place. All hunt insects and hibernate. Single young may be carried in flight by mother. Much decreased, possibly due to effects of pesticides. Hang from roof with wings folded around body. Two different types in Britain: typical bats have plain nose and an organ inside ear (the tragus), probably used in echo-location or sonar; horseshoe bats have faces with leaf-shaped appendages — a flat horseshoe-shaped fold in front, a saddle-shaped 'sella' in the middle and an erect 'lancet' above — and no tragus.

1 Noctule body 3in, 7½cm wingspan 16in, 40½cm

Largest British bat. Robust build, has long slender wings, short rounded ears, broadly spaced, and greyish fur. A lowland bat flying boldly at tree-top height, over woods, parks and gardens. Dives steeply. Sleeps in hollow trees, sheds, rarely in caves, in summer and winter.

2 Long-Eared Bat body 2in, 5cm wingspan 10in, 25½cm

Readily recognised in flight by long ears carried forwards, which are folded at rest. Fur reddish. Widespread, inhabiting woodland, avenues, orchards, often close to buildings. Emerges late and flies throughout night. In summer sleeps in spaces behind shutters, in lofts and cellars. Hibernates in cellars, caves and mines, hanging from roof. Rather unsocial.

3 Greater Horseshoe Bat body 2½in, 6½cm
wingspan 14in, 35½cm

A species of mountain-country bat confined to south-west England and Wales. Has become rare and is now legally protected. Grey-brown fur (male more reddish), pale grey below. Ears large, wings short and broad. Flight heavy and labouring, with much gliding. Gregarious, sleeping in colonies in roofs and cellars, hibernating in caves, quarries and mine shafts, hanging from roof. Lesser horseshoe bat is more common, extending into Midlands, Yorkshire and East Anglia, and has lower, more erratic flight.

4 Daubenton's Bat body 2in, 5cm wingspan 9½in, 24cm

A small bat, usually seen flying over water in daytime, hunting insects. Flies low and fast in circles, often touching water surface or hovering. Widespread (but not in mountains), usually seen in woods and orchards not far from water. Fur reddish brown, ears short. Sleeps in hollow trees, buildings and cracks in walls. Hibernates in caves and mine shafts. Can swim.

5 Pipistrelle body 2in, 5cm wingspan 8in, 20½cm

Commonest and smallest species. Widespread along woodland borders, glades, orchards and parks, often inside towns and villages. Fur rusty brown. In summer sleeps in buildings, hollow trees, behind bark and ivy, emerging soon after dusk. Flight rather fast and erratic, fairly high along regular beat, hunting gnats. Hibernates in buildings, entrances to caves, hollow trees. Seen early in spring, sometimes during mild weather in winter.

Rabbit, Hares, and Squirrels

Rabbits and hares, once classified with rodents, are now placed in a separate group. Special features are the extra pair of upper incisors, elongated hind limbs for hopping and, in British species, a short tail and long ears. Squirrels are true rodents adapted for climbing. (Other rodents appear on following pages.)

1 Rabbit body 16in, 40½cm

Original home in Iberian peninsula. Introduced by Normans in thirteenth century for its fur and meat and strictly protected in areas called warrens. Has spread throughout country on farms, downs, heaths, dunes and woodland borders, becoming a serious pest to farming and forestry. Greatly reduced by myxomatosis virus, first detected in Kent in 1953, but now more or less recovered. Colony usually centred on warren, recognised by many openings and heaps of droppings. Eats first of its droppings, a process called reingestion. Like sheep, keeps turf short. A prolific breeder, young born blind in separate burrow. Screams when caught or wounded. Colour a mixture of yellow, brown and grey hairs.

2 Brown Hare body 24in, 61cm

Larger than rabbit — more leggy, longer ears with black tips. Attains speeds of up to 40 mph. Lives above ground in open country such as fields, downs and dunes. Since myxomatosis it has penetrated more into woodland, in absence of rabbit. Sits in hollow or 'form'. Young (leverets) are born above ground with eyes open and furred, and are visited by doe. Bucks compete in spectacular boxing matches, hence 'mad March hare'. Screams in distress.

3 Mountain Hare body 20in, 51cm

Smaller than brown hare, with shorter ears. Summer coat similar but no black on tail. Also called blue hare. Turns white in north, retaining black ear tips. Occurs mainly in mountains of Scotland, northern England, Wales and Lake District. Sits in form between rocks. Feeds on mountain plants such as heather and sedges.

4 Red Squirrel body 8in, 20½cm tail 7in, 18cm

Reddish brown coat in summer, tail bleached almost white, darker in winter. Has ear tufts. Suffered much from disease in past and has retreated to strongholds in conifer woods and plantations in Highlands, Lake District, West Country and East Anglia. The only squirrel in Isle of Wight. Eats a variety of food, mainly cones for seed. Food remains can be found on tree stumps. Nest a 'drey' of bare twigs lined with grass and moss in a conifer. Rather shy.

5 Grey Squirrel body 10in, 25½cm tail 8in, 20½cm

A native of eastern Canada and USA, introduced since 1876. Has ousted the smaller red squirrel in many areas. Mainly greyish but with some reddish patches in summer coat. Inhabits deciduous woods, less numerous amongst conifers, also found in parks and gardens. A problem for foresters where too numerous. Nest a drey of twigs with leaves attached, in a tree fork or hollow tree. Voice a harsh chatter. Does not interbreed with red squirrel. Food much varied — buds, bark, bulbs, fungi, eggs. Buries acorns. Rather bold.

Rodents

One of the largest and most successful groups of mammals, far outnumbering other kinds in Britain. Consists of mice, rats, voles, dormice and squirrels. Front teeth curved and chisel-shaped for gnawing. Canines (dog-teeth) missing. Mainly vegetarian. Prolific breeders.

Mice and Rats

Large ears, pointed snouts and long tails in contrast to voles.

1 House Mouse body 3in, 7½cm tail 2½in, 6½cm

A universal pest living under cover in buildings, food stores, farms, corn and hay stacks, even in refrigerated stores and mines. Spreads into hedgerows in summer. Orignal home central Asian steppes but now world-wide. Colour mouse-grey above, paler below. Omniverous and causes much damage to food.

2 Wood Mouse body 3½in, 9cm tail 3in, 7½cm

Old name long-tailed field mouse. A little larger than house mouse, with larger ears, bigger looking head. Colour more reddish brown, grey to white below. Widespread, inhabiting open woodland and hedgerows, plantations and rural gardens. An active leaper and climber, feeding on seeds, buds, berries and nuts. Digs tunnel for nest with food store nearby. Larger yellow-necked mouse has yellow collar round neck and chest and occurs in scattered colonies mainly in parts of southern England.

3 Harvest Mouse body 2¼in, 5½cm tail 2in, 5cm

Smallest British rodent. Colour reddish brown, white below. An active climber using prehensile tail for support. Mainly active by day. Occurs mainly in southern and eastern England. Once common in corn fields but driven out by modern harvester and stubble burning. has taken to reed-beds, tall grass, hedgerows and woods bordering cultivation. Builds a compact rounded nest attached to reed stalks and grass stems. Winters in corn ricks, barns and stables. Has become very localised, even rare, and given protection.

4 Black Rat body 7in, 18cm tail 8in, 20½cm

Smaller than brown rat, ears larger and more translucent, tail relatively longer, more pointed snout. Three colour forms — all black; grey-brown with white below; and grey-brown with grey below. Keeps largely under cover in buildings. Nocturnal and an excellent climber. Original home was in trees in Indian region. Brought bubonic plague to Britain during twelfth century. Rare today due to control and confined to ports.

5 Brown Rat body 9½in, 24cm tail 9in, 23cm

Larger than black rat, normally greyish brown, occasionally black. Introduced in early eighteenth century and now widespread, having replaced shyer black rat. Occupies anywhere undisturbed where food is available — in winter in buildings, cellars, store rooms and sewers. In summer moves out to farms, canal banks, rubbish tips. Digs burrows and swims well. Can do severe damage and spread disease.

Rodents contd

Voles, Dormouse and Coypu

Voles are small rodents with blunt snouts, small ears and short tails. The dormouse belongs to a separate family and has a bushy tail. The coypu is a very large South American rodent.

1 Field Vole body 4in, 10cm tail 1in, 2½cm

Also called short-tailed vole. Plump body a little larger than wood mouse. Colour a dark mixture of black and brown, grey on flanks, grey-white below. Widespread in rough pasture, young plantations, woodland glades and moorland. Runs fast, keeps under cover, seldom climbs. Commonest mammal in Britain. Occasional vole 'plagues' cause damage to sheep country. Feeds mainly on grass, roots and bark. Makes runways above ground through grass. Nests on surface under shelter of log or grass tussock.

2 Water Vole body 8in, 20½cm tail 4in, 10cm

Largest British vole, about rat-sized. Recognised by vole features of plump body, small ears and short tail. Brownish-black fur, sometimes entirely black in parts of Scotland and eastern England. Usually found close to water along borders of slow-running streams, also canals and marshy places. Nests in tunnel in bank side, with entrance below water. Feeds on waterside plants, bark and water snails, using a feeding platform near tunnel — a flat patch where plants have been bitten down. Usually heard diving into water, or seen sitting upright and motionless, often for minutes.

3 Bank Vole body 4½in, 11½cm tail 2in, 5cm

A little larger than field vole and more.hump-backed. Colour rusty red above, brown on flanks, greyish white below. A lowland vole inhabiting mixed woodland, hedgerows and ground vegetation. Active in daytime, climbs well. Nest connected to a system of superficial burrows. Feeds on seeds, bark, buds and berries.

4 Coypu body 24in, 61cm tail 18in, 45½cm

Large rat-like rodent. South American origin, introduced in 1930s for use in fur farming. Escapes established themselves in fen country and the Broads of East Anglia. Intensive control campaign in operation because of damage to root crops and dykes. Fur a rich silky dark chocolate, long rat-like tail, webbed hind feet and large orange incisors. Normally docile but bite severe. Inhabits reed-beds, river banks and marshes. Does not hibernate and suffers in severe winters. Food mainly water plants and root-crops. Precocious young swim soon after birth and can feed in water from teats along sides of mother's body. Voice a loud moaning sound, also screams. Active at dawn and dusk, sometimes in the day. Moves with a crouching gait but can also hop.

5 Common Dormouse body 3in, 7½cm tail 2½in, 6½cm

Mouse-like rodent with plump body, rich chestnut coat and furry tail. Nocturnal, inhabits hedgerows and bushy thickets. An active climber, builds a round nest above the ground. Feeds on nuts, berries and bark. Goes into deep hibernation under cover, usually between roots. Becoming rare.

Carnivores

Flesh-eating mammals with large dog-teeth (canines) and senses well developed for pursuit of prey. Have been persecuted for fur or sport and to protect game and stock. Some now rare, surviving only in remote places.

1 Fox body 24in, 61cm tail 16in, 40½cm

Only surviving British member of the wild dog family, holding its own in spite of hunting and trapping, sometimes penetrating villages and even towns. Mainly nocturnal but often active by day in undisturbed places. Has pricked ears and white-tipped bushy tail, a reddish-brown coat, darker on shoulders, white below. A larger, more greyish hill fox present in Scotland may be of Scandinavian origin. Preys on small mammals and birds — rabbits, game and poultry; will attack lambs and fawns. Has strong scent glands, leaving 'foxy' smell. Makes den in enlarged rabbit burrow, badger sett or among rocks in mountains. Call of a dog a repeated triple yap; vixen screams.

2 Badger body 24-30in, 61-76cm

Largest member of weasel family. A powerfully built ground dweller on short legs with strong claws for digging (French *bécheur* — digger). Coarse coat of stiff grey and black hairs. Belly and legs black. Conspicuous black stripe over each eye and ear contrasts with white face. Family life in a home or sett, an extensive network of tunnels with numerous entrances heaped with piles of earth, some fresh and in current use. Usually found in woodland or among rocks in hills. A clean animal, it digs its own latrines. Omnivorous feeder on plants, roots, beetles, wasp grubs, small mammals and especially earthworms. Nocturnal, rarely destructive and now enjoys legal protection, especially from badger-baiting.

3 Wildcat body 30in, 76cm tail 6in, 15cm

Confined mainly to Highlands, though slowly spreading. Not to be confused with feral tabby cat (domestic tabby gone wild), with which it sometimes interbreeds. Wildcat has larger, more leggy build, larger feet and rounded, more robust head. Colour greyish with yellow tinge, marked with well-defined black bars, especially on more bushy blunt-ended tail. Occurs in mountain woodland, rocky heights and high moorland. Prey is game birds, rabbits, hares and small mammals. Screams and caterwauls loudly. Rather solitary.

4 Otter body 26-33in, 66-84cm tail 12in, 30½cm

Streamlined animal built for swimming, with broad flattened head and whiskered muzzle, small ears, webbed feet and thick tapering tail. Short, thick, brown fur, darker when wet. Shy and nocturnal, wandering far, but tends to inhabit river courses, lakes and reservoirs. Leaves trail of air bubbles when swimming underwater. Day-time resting places among reeds or heather. Breeding quarters or holt in river bank, hollow tree or drainpipe. Today widely scattered and much reduced in numbers due partly to hunting but also to water pollution and lack of food. Hunts fish, especially eels, also crustaceans, water birds and other animal food. Main stronghold in clean rivers in Scotland, Wales, West Country and East Anglia. Also semi-marine off Scottish coast and islands. Rather solitary. Call a thin high-pitched whistle. Does not cause serious damage except in fish hatcheries.

Carnivores contd

1 Stoat body 10in, 25½cm tail 4½in, 11½cm

Weasel-like in build but larger. Reddish brown above, yellowish white throat and underside. Permanent black tip to tail. Turns white in winter in northern mountains (then called ermine). Mostly nocturnal but may appear in daylight. Widespread in lowland and mountains, in woods and on farmland. Favourite prey is rabbit, which it tracks by scent, entering burrows. Moves with bounding gait, back arched. Kill made by bite behind neck. Also takes other small mammals. Sometimes hunts in family packs. A good climber. Cry a shrill repeated 'kee-kee' with much chattering and spitting. Reduced by trapping.

2 Weasel body 8in, 20½cm tail 3in, 7½cm

Smallest British member of its family. Colour and build much like stoat, but shorter tail without black tip. Does not turn white in winter in Britain. Widespread, mostly on farmland, along lanes and hedgerows, also moorland, often close to human habitation. Rather inquisitive, will stand up and look around. Hunts smaller prey such as mice and voles, therefore useful to man although treated as vermin. Numbers reduced by trapping. Runs with body close to the ground. Call a high-pitched screaming bark, also hisses.

3 American Mink body 18in, 45½cm tail 6in, 15cm

An escape from fur farms, first seen breeding in wild in 1956 along River Teign, Devon, but now widely established along rivers. About size of ferret. Fur a rich, glossy, deep brown, darker below. Similar to European mink (now confined to south-west France) which has white on upper lips and chin. Nocturnal and solitary, keeping close to water. Excellent swimmer, hunts small mammals, also birds and fish. Can become a serious threat to farm stock, also to nesting wildfowl because of its ability to reach islands.

4 Pine Marten body 18in, 45½cm tail 12in, 30½cm

Britain's rarest mammal, once hunted for its fur, now confined to remote areas of Highlands, Lake District, Wales and Ireland. Keeps mainly to conifer woods up to tree line, also on rocky open ground in some areas. A mountain-dweller and expert tree climber. Large hairy feet for gripping branches. Fur a rich chestnut brown, darker below and on legs, with creamy white 'bib' on throat. Shy and nocturnal. Hunts small mammals and birds and can catch a squirrel. Den among rocks or in old nest of magpie, squirrel or even large birds' nest-box. Call a repeated, huffy 'tok-tok', also growls, screams and moans. Old name sweet mart.

5 Polecat body 18in, 45½cm tail 6in, 15cm

Once widespread, now confined to central Wales. Formerly hunted with hounds. Lives in varied habitats, from dunes to mountains. A ground-living animal and a poor climber, but swims well. Coat blackish brown, darker below with white mask on face. Similar in size and build to ferret, a domesticated form of polecat which can hybridise with wild form to produce polecat-ferret. Hunts small game, rabbits, snakes, eels, frogs, occasional poultry. Old name foumart (foul marten) refers to its objectionable smell.

Deer

Even-toed ungulates (hoofed animals). Males grow branched antlers which are shed and regrown yearly. Red and roe deer are only true natives, others introduced. Deer, like cattle, are ruminants (cud-chewing) and mainly woodland animals.

1 Red Deer height at shoulder 42in, 107cm

Britain's largest wild mammal. Loss of woodland habitat has driven it into unnatural open areas, such as Highlands, Lake District and Exmoor. Smaller herds occur elsewhere, such as in Thetford Chase and Ashdown Forest. Summer coat dark reddish brown; longer, more grey brown in winter. Powerful build with nervous bearing. Stag has compact neck with mane. Antlers have pointed branches (tines) which increase in number with age. Rutting or mating period in autumn, when sexes come together and stags compete for hinds, roaring or 'belling' with deep-throated coughs. In Highlands there is a seasonal movement from open moorlands above tree-line in summer to sheltered valleys in winter. Feeds on grass, heather, young shoots and bark, on farmland root-crops, cereals and vegetables, doing some damage. Hunted with horse and hounds on Exmoor, stalked in Highlands.

2 Roe Deer height at shoulder 30in, 76cm

Small native deer about the size of a large dog. Once confined to Scotland and Lake District due to loss of woodland but has since spread to many parts of England. Prefers open woodland, especially young conifer plantations with plenty of cover, usually near water. Summer coat rich red-brown, thicker and more greyish in winter. White patch below tail. Male has pointed antlers with three branches on each side. Lives in small parties, usually with doe, new-born kid and yearling. Ruts in summer when buck chases doe, often in circles around a bush or tree, leaving an impression of a 'deer ring' on ground. Gestation is long due to delayed implantation of egg. Young, sometimes twins, are born the following May-June. Buck gives short harsh bark, doe a high-pitched whistle. Damages trees by 'fraying' with antlers during rut, also marks with scent. Feeds on leaves, berries, heather and, rarely, bark.

3 Fallow Deer height at shoulder 36in, 91½cm

Mediterranean species widely introduced to many lands (recorded in Britain from early Norman times) for ornament or for hunting. Typical park deer is deep fawn spotted with white, tail black above with white hind-quarters beneath. Many escapes now scattered in wild herds throughout the country, mainly in woodland. Remnants of ancient herds of dark animals, once hunted, still survive in New Forest, Epping Forest and Cannock Chase. Male has palm-shaped antlers, gives a grunting bark. Fawn heavily spotted, born in June. Nervous and moves jerkily. Can leap on stiff legs (buck-jumping). Feeds on grass, barks, buds, fungi and fruit.

Deer contd

1 Sika height at shoulder 30in, 76cm

Resembles a small red deer but with chestnut-red coat faintly spotted with white. Antlers small with up to four branches each. White tail and hind quarters. Originally from Japan, has escaped from parks into parts of England and Scotland. Prefers dense woodland with glades. Ruts in autumn, fawn born in May as with fallow deer. Male gives whistling call ending in a grunt.

2 Muntjac height at shoulder 18in, 45½cm

A small deer native to China and India, and kept at Woburn since 1900. Escapes have spread widely into Chilterns, Home Counties and Midlands. Coat reddish brown above, paler below. Male has single pointed antlers fixed to long base which extends as ridges down face, also large upper canines forming short 'tusks'. Two halves of hooves unequal, making characteristic track. Active by day, keeps to thick undergrowth in woods. Moves with hump-backed gait. Rutting from October through to March. Small fawn dark brown, spotted white on flanks, born in summer. Many die in severe winters. Male makes sharp bark when alarmed, thus also called barking deer.

3 Chinese Water Deer height at shoulder 18in, 45½cm

Introduced, swamp-loving deer, small without antlers, a short tail, and male with protruding upper canines. Ears large and white inside, body pale brown. Occurs in parts of Hampshire and the Home Counties, adapted to woodland. Shy and sensitive, head held high and large ears erect. Ruts from November to January. One to four tiny fawns born in May, many die in first winter.

4 Reindeer height at shoulder 42in, 107cm

Well-known deer of Arctic steppes associated with Christmas festivities. Long under domestication in Lapland and Siberia. A staple source of food for northern tribes. Probably became extinct in Britain in twelfth century. Successful reintroduction from Sweden into the Cairngorms nature reserve in 1952, when a small herd became established in the Highlands. Has increased on high moors, feeding on lichen called reindeer moss. Male has curved and branched antlers with flattened ends, also grown by female but smaller (no other female deer grows antlers). Colour variable, a mixture of brown, white and black. Rutting call a loud grunt. Swims well. Hooves make a clacking sound when on the move. One or two unspotted calves born in June.

Deer Hunting

Deer, in particular red deer, have been hunted since prehistoric times and appear in cave paintings. Archaeological remains show artefacts carved from antler and bone to make ornaments, hunting tools, even needles. Antlers found at Grimes Graves, Suffolk, were made into picks for excavating flint which was made into tools by Neolithic man — our earliest industry. Later, since Norman times, red deer became a 'roiall beaste of the Forrest', and was hunted by the Crown. A mature 12-pointer, called a royal, was the king's property. Smaller fallow deer were hunted by nobles and ladies. Deer control is necessary today because of damage to trees and crops.

Sea Mammals

Specialised mammals adapted for swimming and which inhabit coastal waters round Britain. Seals have densely furred, streamlined bodies with fin-shaped limbs; hind limbs used for swimming, but cannot be turned forward as in sea-lions; clumsy on land; pups born ashore. Whales are permanently aquatic, giving birth at sea; fore-limbs modified into flippers, hind-limbs missing; horizontal tail fin. Two kinds: toothed whales have rows of teeth and hunt fish and other prey; larger whalebone or baleen whales, mainly oceanic, have plates of 'baleen' used in filtering small sea crustaceans (krill) for food. Common porpoise and common dolphin occur around coast, other whales that are seen are usually stranded.

1 Common Seal length 54-72in, 137-183cm

Also called harbour seal. Greyish white to yellow fur, densely spotted, paler below. Rounded head with retroussé nose and small external ears. Inhabits mainly sandy coasts offshore, sandbanks and estuaries (e.g. the Wash and along East Anglian coast), also bays around Scotland and outer islands. Pup born white in mid-summer on flat beach, soon moults. Deserted by mother but follows her out to safe rock or sandbank to suckle. Rather silent apart from plaintive bark. Hunts fish and molluscs.

2 Grey Seal length 7-8ft, 2.1-2.7m

Also called Atlantic seal. Larger than common seal, colour variable from dark grey to brown, with paler underside and irregular dark spots. Head more flattened with depressed snout, especially in bull. Inhabits rocky coasts and islands on Atlantic side, also North Sea coast down to the Wash, and Farne Islands. Pups born on rocky shore or in caves September to October. Hunts fish and molluscs, may attack salmon. Voice a drawn-out, girlish 'hah-ee'. Pup makes child-like bawling when hungry. Said to be one of rarest seals but concentrated around Britain.

3 Common Porpoise length up to 6ft, 1.8m

Small robust whale. Blunt snout without beak. Black above, white below. Inhabits coastal waters in small schools. A slow swimmer, does not normally leap. Hunts fish, mainly herring.

4 Common Dolphin length up to 8ft, 2.4m

Rather longer than porpoise, has slender body with elongated beak and dorsal fin curved backwards. Deep chocolate brown above, white below, with stripes along flanks. Roams the warmer seas in schools, often accompanying ships; around Britain mainly south and west coasts during summer. Playful, leaps out of water. Hunts fish (mackerel and herring), also cuttlefish.

5 Pilot Whale length up to 20ft, 6.1m

Also called caa'ing whale or blackfish. Toothed whale with long slender body, bulging head and small beak. Colour black with white throat patch. Very gregarious, following leader. Sometimes whole school becomes stranded on beach. Occurs mostly around Scotland and northern England. Hunts cuttlefish.

REPTILES

Cold-blooded, scaly-skinned vertebrates which in Britain all hibernate. Six native species — three snakes and three lizards. Fond of basking.

---

1 Adder length 24in, 61cm

Also called northern viper. Rather small with stocky build; female longer. Male usually brighter — grey to greyish-brown with black zig-zag stripe along back. Female more yellowish to red-brown, with dark brown stripe. Brick-red and black specimens also occur. Inhabits dry localities in woodland, moorland, dunes and mountains throughout mainland. Young born live in mid-summer. Shy and nervous and bite seldom fatal. Hunts small mamals and lizards.

---

2 Grass Snake length up to 36in, 91½cm

Longest British snake. Slender build, usually olive-grey to brown, with yellow or orange black-bordered 'collar' behind head. Dark bars along flanks, chequered black below. Lively and active, quickly retreats from danger. Does not bite but may produce foul-smelling glandular secretion or feign death. Normally inhabits open woods, ditches and places near water. Excellent swimmer. Hunts frogs, toads, newts, fishes and occasional small mammals. Eggs laid in rotting vegetation. Harmless.

---

3 Smooth Snake length 18in, 45½cm

Slender build. Male brownish, female more grey. Dark band through eye and along neck. Series of separate markings along back. Smooth skin without ridges on scales. Inhabits dry localities in open woodland and heaths, confined to Hampshire Basin in and around New Forest. Now extremely rare and legally protected. Hunts mainly lizards. Bite harmless. Young born alive.

---

4 Viviparous Lizard length 6-7in, 15-18cm

Common and widespread. Body fairly slender, generally coloured brown above, tinged with green, and dark band along each flank. Male more orange-yellow, stippled black below; female more yellowish, unspotted. Inhabits glades, heaths, dunes, quarries and wasteland where food such as insects and spiders is available. Young born alive, black at first. Tail often ruptures and regrows as a stump.

---

5 Sand Lizard length 8-9in, 20½-23cm

Larger than viviparous lizard and more heavily built. Colour brown to grey with rows of 'eye-spots' along back and flanks. Male coloured green in summer. Habitat sand dunes and dry heaths. Female lays eggs in soil. Restricted to New Forest area, Dorset, East Anglian coast and Lancashire dunes. Rare.

---

6 Slow-Worm length up to 18in, 45½cm

Lizard with a limbless snake-like body covered in small polished scales. Usually coloured grey or reddish-brown, occasionally with scattered blue spots. Young born alive. Widespread in quiet places along woodland borders, hedgerows, cliffs and quarries, railway embankments and churchyards. Tends to burrow and retire under logs and stones. Hunts earthworms and slugs. Long tail easily fractures. Harmless.

AMPHIBIANS

Six native species — one frog, two toads, three newts. Skin naked. Gill-breathing tadpole changes by stages into lung-breathing adult. Rather secretive, avoiding exposure to sun. All hibernate.

1 Common Toad length 2½in, 6½cm (female usually larger)

Squat build, more rounded snout than frog, dry skin heavily warted with prominent parotid glands behind eyes. Colour grey, brown or reddish. Smaller males, usually more numerous during breeding, compete for females in a 'knot' of toads. Eggs laid in long strings. Males give high-pitched, repeated croak. After hibernation toads make for certain ponds along migration route at night. Eats worms and various insects, especially ants. Rather nocturnal. Protected by bitter secretion from skin.

2 Common Frog length 3in, 7½cm

Smooth moist skin, pointed snout, long legs and lively manner. Colour and markings variable. Widespread in vicinity of water. Assembles in colonies in spring to pair and lay clumps of spawn. Tadpoles browse on water plants, turning into froglets about ten weeks later. Adult catches earthworms and various insects with its tongue. Male gives dull croak.

3 Natterjack length 2½in, 6½cm

Small toad coloured olive-brown or olive-grey, with yellow stripe along back. Often active by day and runs in brief bursts on short legs. Breeding similar to common toad but more protracted. Male gives loud trilling song. In Britain inhabits sand dunes and heathland centred on pond. Can breed in brackish water. Now extremely rare and protected.

4 Crested or Warty Newt length up to 6in, 15cm

Largest newt. Skin warty, almost black with black markings, orange-yellow below with black spots. Breeding male has high serrated crest. Breeds in deepish water. Eggs laid singly, stuck to water plants in coating of jelly. Tadpoles feed on minute water animals. After breeding, adult leaves water to hide under stones, etc., emerging at night to hunt small prey. Can then be mistaken for a lizard (which is scaly). May hibernate in water.

5 Smooth Newt length up to 4in, 10cm

Commonest newt and widespread. Avoids mountains. Brown to olive-brown, covered in darker spots; below yellow to orange with darker spots. Male has wavy crest. Breeds in ponds and ditches. General habits as for crested newt.

6 Palmate Newt length up to 3in, 7½cm

Smallest newt. Can be mistaken for smooth newt. Distinctive features are low, straight crest in male, webbed hind feet and fine thread extending from truncated tail. Also more finely spotted but throat unspotted. Largely a mountain species, often in pools on acid soils. Breeding habits as for other newts.

INSECTS

Judged by their numbers and variety, the insects are surely the most successful group of animals, having occupied almost every available habitat, apart from the open sea. They are found everywhere, from deep underground to high mountains, from equator to arctic snow, within and on the soil, and within and on animals and plants, including ourselves.

Damage caused to crops, farm animals, food, dwellings and property means that a constant war is waged against insects by gardeners, foresters, farmers, veterinary and pest-control officers, as well as householders. However, some insects, like butterflies, give us pleasure. Others perform a variety of useful roles as far as man is concerned. Ladybirds attack greenfly, while bees provide honey and pollinate flowers. And, of course, insects provide food for innumerable other animals.

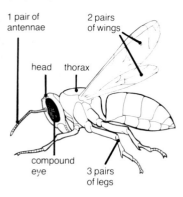

1 pair of antennae
2 pairs of wings
head
thorax
compound eye
3 pairs of legs

The insects belong to an enormous group of invertebrate animals called Arthropods ('jointed legs'). Besides insects, these include the eight-legged Arachnids (spiders and scorpions), the many-legged Myriapods (millepedes and centipedes), and the wingless, hardshelled Crustaceans (crabs, shrimps, wood-lice).

Insects may be recognised by their bodies, which are in three parts. The head has a single pair of antennae and compound eyes, with mouth-parts modified for biting, sucking, or piercing. The chest or thorax carries three pairs of legs and two pairs of wings (though some have no wings and the flies only have one pair). The main body or abdomen contains the digestive and reproductive organs, and may carry a sting or egg-laying tube.

DIFFERENT MOUTHPARTS

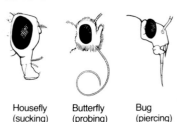

Housefly (sucking)
Butterfly (probing)
Bug (piercing)

Insects are relatively small, since they have no internal skeleton to support a large body (the biggest ones in Britain are the death's head hawkmoth and the stag beetle). Instead, they have a hard outer skeleton of dead chitin which limits size and has to be shed from time to time in the growing, larval stage. It is arranged in rings or segments, with joints in between to allow for movement. One advantage of this form of construction is that it restricts water loss.

Insects undergo a process of metamorphosis, or change in form, usually in four stages — egg, larva, pupa, adult. All the growth takes place during the larval stage. The larva — which may be called the caterpillar — can differ greatly from the adult. It feeds and grows, then changes into a resting pupa or chrysalis (for example, that of a butterfly). Great changes take place inside the pupa before the adult insect emerges.

In some groups there is no pupal stage. Dragonflies, grasshopers, and cockroaches have a larval stage (called the nymph) after which they change straight into adults. Once insects become adult they grow no more.

Like ourselves, insects breathe air. Water-living insects rise to the surface to take in a fresh supply, though some have special gills, enabling them to absorb dissolved oxygen in their larval stages (as with water beetle and dragonfly larvae). A land insect takes in air through openings called spiracles along the sides of the body. These lead to tubes (the tracheae), which convey oxygen to the blood. This is pumped by a simple heart, and can be seen in the pulsing movement of a resting bee. Blood freely bathes the internal organs and the wing veins.

The different insect groups have certain characteristics which help to identify them. Butterflies, which are mainly day-flyers, normally hold their wings closed above the body when at rest. Night-flying moths rest by day with wings folded along the body.

Beetles with hard skins, usually black or brown, are found mainly on the ground and under some form of cover. Some species attack trees and furniture.

Flies are two-winged (not four-winged), and include gnats, midges, and mosquitoes. Some hoverflies mimic the colours of wasps, while others resemble bees. The bees and the more slender wasps themselves should not be difficult to recognise.

Dragonflies are aerial acrobats, usually found not far from water where their nymphs grow up. True bugs have piercing mouth-parts used for sucking plant sap (as with aphids), and attacking other animals and ourselves. Some occur in water. Grasshopers reveal themselves by hopping out of harm's way.

LIFE HISTORIES

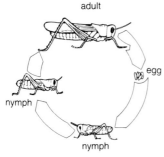

GRASSHOPPER
(incomplete metamorphosis)

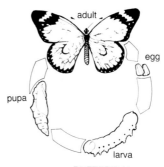

BUTTERFLY
(complete metamorphosis)

Wingless Insects

This group includes some of the most primitive creatures, such as springtails, which date back to the Devonian period over 300 million years ago, and which have never evolved wings.

1 Springtail length ¼in, 6mm

Group of small, wingless, primitive insects with a forked organ — the furcula — held at rest under body; when released this causes the insect to leap into the air. Lives in soil, leaf-litter and refuse in humid surroundings, world-wide. Some cause damage to legumes.

2 True Louse length ⅛in, 3mm

Parasitic wingless insect which feeds on birds or mammals, including man. Body flattened, with strong claws for attachment. Small eyes and short antennae. Permanently attached to host but may transfer if two hosts come together, as in nest of fledglings, litter of mammals or crowd of humans. Tendency to be host-specific; can transmit disease. Biting lice attach themselves to birds and have two claws on each leg. Sucking lice, with one claw per leg, live on mammals and humans. Eggs (nits) stick to hair. Two kinds of human louse, head louse and body louse, each keep to own area. Can transmit typhus. Another species occurs in pubic region.

3 Silverfish length ½in, 13mm

Small, wingless, with a tapering body and shiny scales. Long, thread-like antennae and three long 'tails'. Also called bristletail. Commonly found in buildings, feeding on paper, glue and spilled food in cupboards and kitchens. The similar firebrat prefers warmer places in bakeries, hot houses etc., and has longer antennae. Both are a nuisance but harmless. Some related two-tailed species live in soil or between bark in dark, moist places.

4 Flea length ⅛in, 3mm

Wingless, bloodsucking parasites found on birds and mammals. Sideways flattened body helps in movement between hair or feathers. Well known for leaping ability. Only adult lives on host. After a meal the female lays numerous eggs in communal home or nest of host, which hatch into white, worm-like larvae without legs or eyes. Larvae feed on detritus in vicinity of host, also on droppings and host's blood passed by adult. Spins a cocoon to pupate. Adult needs a stimulus to hatch, such as nearby movement, hence empty houses 'coming alive' when reoccupied. Empty birds' nests also reveal fleas when disturbed. A new host found by warmth. Human flea, now less common, probably derived from ground animal, possibly fox or badger. Diseases spread include bubonic plague from rat flea and myxomatosis from rabbit flea. Cat and dog fleas may bite humans.

5 Book Louse length ⅛in, 3mm

Not to be confused with true louse. Small and soft bodied, with or without wings. Wings held roof-wise over body. Outdoor species (mainly winged) feed on pollen, algae and fungi, and occur in birds' nests. Indoor species (usually wingless) feed on moulds, glue, neglected books and wallpaper. Food scraped off with strong biting mandibles.

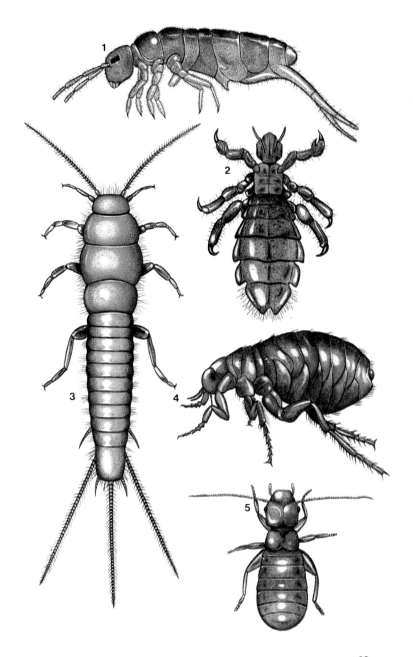

Grasshoppers and Crickets

Medium to large, with a stout body, blunt head, and saddle-shaped covering to thorax. Large hindlegs for leaping. Mainly two pairs of wings, front pair straight, hind pair broadly rounded. Normally well camouflaged but detected by song or stridulation, which is produced by rapid rubbing of series of 'pegs' (the file) over a 'scraper' along edge of wing. File is on legs of grasshoppers and on opposite wing of crickets. Antennae long or short according to group. Rather poor flyers apart from locusts.

1 House Cricket length ¾in, 19mm

One of the true crickets, differs from other species in broader, more flattened body and short front wings. Has long antennae and long ovipositor in female. Eggs laid singly in soil and crevices. Introduced from Africa and confined to warmer surroundings, in kitchens, factories and fermenting rubbish. Now less common due to improved hygiene. The original 'cricket on the hearth'. Song prolonged and more highly pitched than grasshopper, difficult to detect because sound changes in volume and appears to come from different places. Colour brownish.

2 Field Grasshopper length 1in, 25mm

Common species of grasshopper usually disturbed or heard in grass or low vegetation. Antennae rather short. Feeds on grass. Eggs laid in batches in soil covered by hardened froth for protection through winter; hatch in spring, adults appearing in June after larval or nymphal stage. Sings by moving legs up and down against wings. Related to the much larger locust which reaches Britain on rare occasions after an outbreak, spreading from Africa or Middle East.

3 Oak Bush Cricket length ⅜in, 9mm

Resembles great green bush cricket but much smaller. Commonest species, active late in day, often in neighbourhood of oak trees. Attracted to light and may fly into windows. Does not sing.

4 Great Green Bush Cricket length 2in, 50mm

Large and handsome green species. Bush crickets have long antennae and were formerly called long-horned grasshoppers. Lives among bushes in southern England near coast. Tends to walk rather than hop or fly. Female has long ovipositor, lays eggs in soil or between bark. Feeds on small insects. Sings loudly over long periods by raising wings and rubbing together.

5 Mole Cricket length 2½in, 63mm

A single British species. Large size, stout brownish body covered in hairs. Greatly developed front legs, toothed and used for digging. Most of time spent underground in dampish soil. Female lays and guards eggs in underground nest, nymphs mature in following year. Male sings by rubbing wings, producing long bursts of churring sound on warm evenings, usually from inside burrow. Feeds on plants, roots and grubs. Confined to southern England and rather localised.

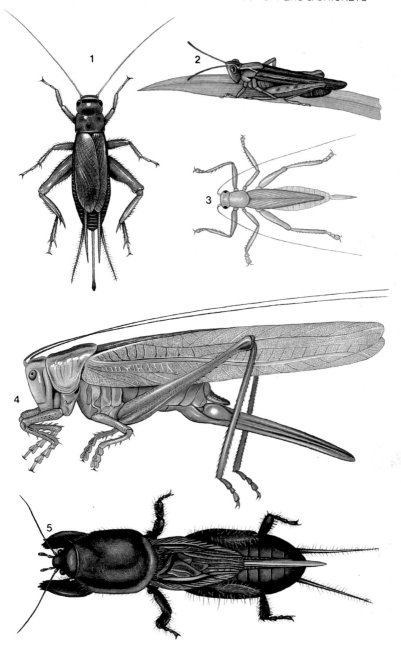

Cockroaches, Earwig and Stick Insect

Mainly tropical insects, cockroaches have flattened bodies, two pairs of wings held flat over back, head and thorax covered by a shield (pronotum), and long antennae. Related to grasshoppers but without jumping legs. Tendency to run fast and seldom fly. Usually keep hidden by day, mainly in buildings, in warm places such as kitchens, warehouses, breweries and green-houses. Omnivorous, feeding on any available food. Chief harm caused by contamination of food due to deposit of offensive and characteristic smell. When disturbed by light will scuttle for shelter under floorboards, wainscot, air vents, etc. Eggs, laid in container carried by mother, hatch into nymphs passing through several moults, as with grasshoppers. Nine British species.

1 German Cockroach length ⅜in, 9mm

A small cockroach, yellow-brown colour.

2 Common Cockroach length 1in, 25mm

Chocolate brown in colour. Often called the 'black beetle', although not a beetle.

3 American Cockroach length 1½in, 38mm

The so-called American cockroach, the largest, originates in Africa as do the German and common cockroach. All three found mainly in England and Wales.

4 Earwig length ½in, 13mm

Elongated shape, with short, leathery forewings and large hind ones. Latter folded up under forewings in elaborate manner and seldom used for flight. Strong pincers at rear of body, curved in male, straight in female, and raised when alarmed. Broad head with slender antennae. Biting jaws for feeding on plants, other insects and dead larger animals. Winter spent below ground. During summer hides by day in dark places, feeding at night. Useful scavenger but harmful to plants and flowers. Can be trapped with flower pot containing paper inverted and balanced on stake. Superstition that earwig enters ear of sleeping human is completely unfounded. Mates in autumn. Eggs laid in soil and guarded through winter by parent, who feeds young which hatch in spring. Five British species, of which the most widespread is the common earwig.

5 Stick Insect length 3in, 76mm

Readily recognised by long, slender, green or brown body resembling a twig, giving excellent camouflage. Wings small, if present at all. Mainly tropical, a few in southern Europe. Occasional escapes in Britain, probably arriving in imported plants, or for laboratory use and as pets. Males are absent — female parthenogenetic, laying fertile eggs scattered over ground. Most likely species to turn up is the laboratory stick insect, seen in greenhouses, occasionally in hedgerows in southern England.

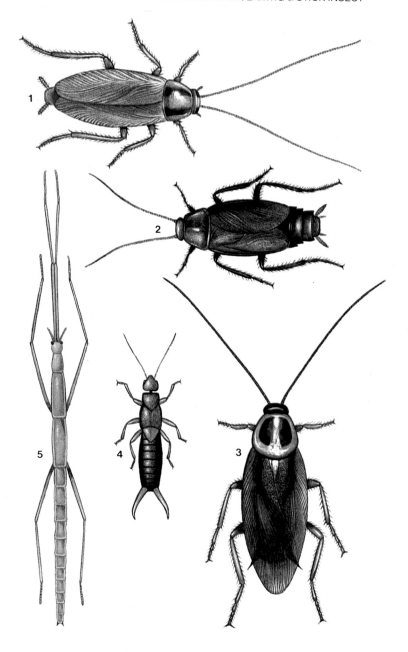

Bugs

A term loosely used for most insects. True bugs belong to the Order Hemiptera. Piercing mouth-parts for sucking plant and animal juices. Divided into two groups: the Heteroptera, in which base of front wing is leathery and tip membranous, and wings lie flat (e.g. bed-bug); the Homoptera, which have entirely uniform front wings held roof-wise (e.g. frog-hopper). Plant bugs spread viruses and weaken plants. All British species small, apart from rare cicada found in New Forest.

1 Aphid length ⅛in, 3mm

Large group of homopterous bugs, popularly known as greenfly and blackfly, or plant lice. All small with pear-shaped bodies. Enormous rate of reproduction. Overwinter as eggs, producing in spring the wingless females. These produce by virgin birth further female generations, wingless alternating with winged forms, which spread to other plants. In autumn both male and female appear, and fertilised winter eggs are laid. Some aphids restrict activities to certain plants (e.g. bean aphid, rose aphid, cabbage aphid). So-called woolly aphid secretes for protection a waxy substance seen as white patches on infected apple trees. Some aphids exude a sweet, sugary liquid from anus derived from plant sap (the honey-dew) making leaves of trees sticky, especially those of oak and lime. Aphids 'milked' by ants for honey-dew (see p.126).

2 Hawthorn Shieldbug length ½in, 13mm

Heteropterous bug with broad flattened body shaped like a shield. Flies with hindwings, covered at rest by forewings as in beetles. Common on hawthorn, feeding on berries, occasionally oak leaves. Also called stinkbug.

3 Frog-Hopper length ¼-½in, 6-13mm

Homopterous, and named after shape and ability to leap. Coloured green or brown. Common among grass and in hedgerows. Eggs laid in plant stems in autumn, hatch as larvae in spring, feeding on sap. Larva exudes sticky fluid and blows it into a frothy covering (cuckoo-spit) as protection and to prevent drying up. Adults emerge in June.

4 Scale Insect length ¼in, 13mm

Also called mealy bug. The females are motionless, holding on to host plants with mouth-parts, which secrete a hard, waxy covering which blends with bark. Males resemble small midges. A prolific breeder, the female produces many eggs. Hatched nymph moves away on legs, then settles, loses legs, and builds scaly coat. Serious pest on fruit trees, may turn up in greenhouses.

5 Lacewing length ¾in, 19mm

Belongs to separate Order Neuroptera, which includes alderfly (p.248). Soft-bodied, brown or green, has large flimsy wings with network of veins, held roof-wise over body. Long, thin antennae, large eyes. The green lacewing, a delicate green with golden eyes, is frequently attracted to light, entering houses, where it may hibernate. Useful to gardeners as larva feeds on greenfly. Lays eggs on stalks under leaves. Larva covers body with skin of victims as means of camouflage.

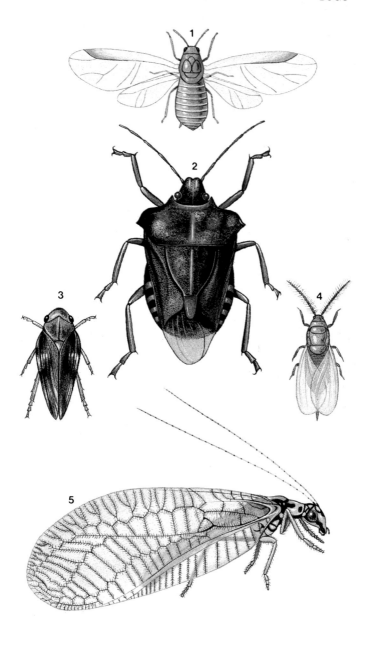

Butterflies

Both butterflies and moths are insects with veined wings covered in scales (Lepidoptera), and have well-developed antenna. Mouth-part is a long sucking tube (proboscis), extended for feeding by pumping in blood, coiled at rest. Adult feeds on nectar and other liquids. Life history has four stages — egg, larva (caterpillar), pupa (chrysalis) and adult (imago). Only caterpillar grows and has silk glands used by some species for spinning cocoon or building a 'tent' for protection. Some well camouflaged, others covered in hairs or distasteful and brightly coloured as deterrent against birds. Butterflies generally differ from moths in having a slender body, club-shaped antennae, wings coloured above and held together over head so that dull undersides act as camouflage. Fly by day. Some hibernate, others migrate. About 70 British species.

1 Large White body 1¼in, 32mm

Familiar butterfly attracted to fields and gardens where eggs are laid on wild or cultivated members of cabbage family. Numbers sometimes augmented by migrants from Continent. Destructive caterpillar (1a) remains on leaf surface, stripping the leaf down to skeleton. Pupa hangs attached to plant stem or fence by silken thread. The small white is equally destructive, and green caterpillar usually bores into heart of cabbage.

2 Orange Tip body 1in, 25mm

Member of 'white' group of butterflies, with orange-coloured tips to forewings (males only). Underside dappled green and white as camouflage when at rest. Eggs laid on plants of wild cabbage family — wild mustard, cuckoo-flower, jack-by-the-hedge, etc. Caterpillar (2a) tends to be cannibalistic. Pupa resembles a long seed-pod.

3 Brimstone body 1¼in, 32mm

Originally the 'butter-coloured fly' from which the whole group gets its name. Male butter-yellow, appears early after hibernation, a little before greenish-yellow female. Inhabits hedgerows. Eggs laid on buckthorn against which the green caterpillar is well hidden. Related to clouded yellow, a more orange, summer migrant, arriving in large numbers along southern coast of England in some years. Caterpillar (3a) feeds on clover in open grassland.

4 Meadow Brown body 1¼in, 32mm

Common member of the 'brown' group. A single 'eye-spot' on each forewing. Common on grassland. Similar to smaller hedge brown or gatekeeper which occurs along hedgerows. Both slow in flight. Green caterpillar (4a) feeds on grass.

5 Swallowtail body 1¾in, 44mm

Most handsome and rarest British butterfly, confined to Norfolk Broads. Bright black and yellow wings with blue and red markings, and 'tail' on hindwings. Eggs laid on milk parsley growing among reeds, sometimes on carrot. Caterpillar (5a) at first black and white resembling bird droppings, then turns conspicuous green with black and white markings. Can produce a Y-shaped horn from behind head if disturbed. Pupa overwinters attached to reed stem.

Butterflies contd

1 Common Blue body ¾in, 19mm

The 'blues' are small butterflies, males easily recognised by colour, although the females are usually dark brown. Underwings are spotted. Most species inhabit grassy areas mainly in southern England in chalk country. Caterpillar (1a) of common blue feeds on bird's-foot trefoil. Two broods, of which the second hibernates. A secretion from honey-gland attracts ants in some species of blues.

2 Painted Lady body 1¼in, 32mm

A migrant from North Africa arriving in May, often damaged from journey. Numbers vary yearly. Wings marked in black, orange and white. Caterpillar (2a) lives and pupates in silken tent on nettle. Adults return south for winter and cannot survive in Britain.

3 Red Admiral body 1¼in, 32mm

Handsomely coloured in black, red and white, and formerly called 'red admirable' butterfly. Widespread migrant arriving from Mediterranean in about May. Eggs laid on nettle. Caterpillar (3a) covered in spines, living solitary life in folded tent of leaves. Emerging adult feeds on garden flowers, sap from trees, and fallen fruit. Only a few survive winter.

4 Small Tortoiseshell body 1in, 25mm

Well-named after colour pattern, but well camouflaged when at rest, resembling dead leaf. Common and widespread and attracted to garden flowers, especially buddleia, the 'butterfly bush'. Caterpillars (4a) covered in short spines; usually keep together in silken tent on nettle. Large tortoiseshell more localised in East Anglia, caterpillars feeding on elm leaves. Can be confused with comma butterfly which has more ragged edge to wings and distinctive white 'comma' under hindwings. Tortoiseshells and comma hibernate among leaf litter or in hollow trees.

5 Peacock body 1½in, 38mm

Obviously named after bright coloured 'eye-spots' on wings resembling those on peacock's train. Virtually invisible when at rest due to camouflaged underwings. Flash of colour as it takes off thought to deter birds. Common and widespread in woods and gardens in autumn, feeding on flowers and rotting fruit. Eggs laid on nettle. Caterpillars (5a) black speckled with white, spin leaves together with silk to make a protective tent, live in colonies, pupating during mid-summer. Adult hibernates, sometimes in buildings.

Moths

Mainly differ from butterflies in having stouter bodies, more feathery antennae in males, wings dull coloured above for camouflage, and folded flat, scissor-wise along body. Mainly nocturnal, a few day-flyers usually brightly coloured for protection. About 2000 species, mostly of small size.

1 Oak Eggar Moth body 1½in, 38mm

Well built day-flying moth with hairy body, reddish-brown wings, an egg-shaped mark on each forewing. Male darker and smaller. Hairy caterpillar (1a) feeds on bramble, heather and fruit trees, hibernating as larva in south and as pupa in north. Adult emerges the following July. Avoided by birds. Adult has short life and does not feed. Fairly widespread.

2 Pine Shoot Moth body ³⁄₈in, 9mm

Has contrasting colours of brick-red forewings marked with transverse silvery lines, and dark grey hindwings. Appears in June and eggs laid on pine needles. Brown caterpillar (2a) bores into bud, hollowing out chamber lined with silk as protection against resin. Pupation in following years inside a stem. As a result of injury the shoot grows in a curved attitude, or may sprout many small shoots into a 'witch's broom'. A serious pest of forestry, especially in pure stands of pine.

3 Goat Moth body 1½in, 38mm

Large, speckled, brownish moth named after the strong, goat-like smell given off by caterpillar (3a). Adult lacks proboscis, cannot feed. Female attracted to exuding sap on tree where eggs are laid. Caterpillar bores into wood, mainly willow or poplar, where it lives for up to three years, causing damage. Leaves tree to pupate in soil throughout winter. Adult emerges in July.

4 Leopard Moth body 1¼in, 32mm

Large white moth speckled with grey on long narrow wings, related to goat moth. Attacks timber. Grey spotted caterpillar (4a) spends two or three years burrowing in various deciduous trees. Pupates under bark, emerging in June. Larger female has pointed end to body to facilitate egg-laying between bark. Mainly south-east England.

5 Puss Moth body 1½in, 38mm

Easily recognised by its furry whitish body, patterned with dark lines on forewings. Reddish eggs laid on willows, resembling spots of disease on leaves. Caterpillar (5a) at first black, turning green. Last pair of legs (claspers) modified into two whips which are raised and waved to deter predators. Also ejects formic acid. Greatly swollen front end has red mask and false 'eyes' giving fierce expression. By September colours darken to match bark on which it spins a hard cocoon. Moth uses a chemical to soften cocoon in order to emerge.

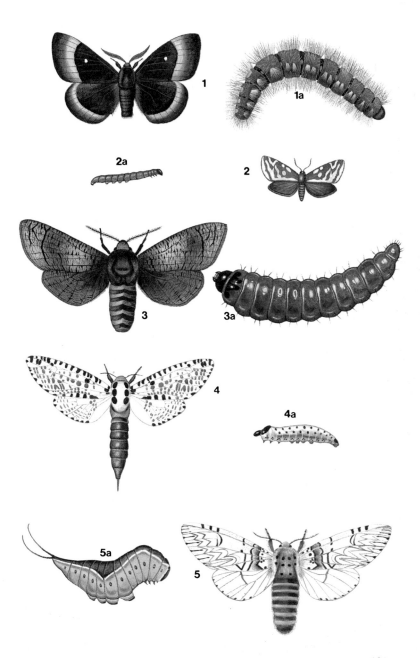

Moths contd

1 Red Underwing body 1 ¼ in, 32mm

A large, stout-bodied species with dull, grey-brown forewings, well matched to bark or wall when resting. Hindwings bright red and black, exposed when disturbed so as to confuse enemy. Flies on summer nights, mainly in south-east England, and is attracted to light. Eggs laid in bark crevices of willow or poplar, hatch in following spring. Dull grey caterpillar (1a) rests close to bark and not easy to find. Pupates in leaf-covered cocoon. Belongs to the large family of Noctuid moths, mostly stout-bodied, dull-coloured and nocturnal. Some caterpillars feed on plant roots of vegetables, severing plants and known as cutworms.

2 Hornet Clearwing body ¾ in, 19mm

A good example of mimicry in which moth resembles a hornet. Body striped in yellow and brown, transparent wings. Caterpillar (2a) burrows into wood of poplar or willow, pupates after two or three years. Chrysalis has projections on hind end and can push through exit hole made by caterpillar before pupation. Adult emerges in May leaving empty pupal case sticking out of hole. Mainly in eastern England.

3 Tiger Moth body 1 ½ in, 38mm

Powerfully built moth in conspicuous warning colours. Forewings patterned in black and white, hindwings red with black and blue markings. Very exposed at rest. Dark, hairy caterpillar (3a), called a 'woolly bear', left alone by birds except cuckoo. Hatches in August, feeding on nettles and garden plants, then hibernates. Pupates in cocoon the following May, adult emerging shortly afterwards. Adult has no proboscis and cannot feed but lives on food reserves from caterpillar stage. Widespread and common.

4 Magpie Moth body ¾ in, 19mm

Conspicuous, distasteful to birds. Wings brightly coloured with orange and black markings on white background. Caterpillar (4a) equally brightly coloured, often found in gardens and hedgerows, feeding on leaves of fruit bushes and trees. Called a 'looper' from habit of crawling by moving front end forward, then drawing up hind end to meet it.

5 Emperor Moth body 1 ½ in, 38mm

Related to large, tropical silk moths, and lives on heaths and moorland. Prominent 'eye-spots' on wings. A day flyer. Smaller male has feathered antennae and can detect female (shown here) up to a mile away. Eggs, laid on heather or bramble, hatch into green caterpillars (5a) ringed with black and red — an excellent match to the green heather leaves and red flowers. Spins a brown cocoon with an exit made of stiff hairs pointing outwards so that the moth can emerge but no enemy enter. Male arrives almost immediately after female emerges.

Moths contd

1 Cinnabar body ¾in, 19mm

A conspicuous moth resembling burnet but in separate family. Forewings brownish with red markings, hindwings reddish. A common day-flyer on grassland such as downland. Eggs laid on ragwort. Caterpillar (1a) brightly ringed in black and yellow.

2 Six-Spot Burnet body ¾in, 19mm

Conspicuous day-flying moth with bright, metallic colours. Forewings black with a blue-green sheen, marked in red, hindwings edged in black. Antennae club-shaped. Exudes a poisonous substance when attacked, giving ample protection. Caterpillar (2a) plump, yellowish with black spots and hides in grass. Spins a yellowish cocoon on grass stem. Commonest of seven species of burnets, seen in colonies, flying about sluggishly and feeding on flowers on open grassland.

3 Buff Tip body 1¼in, 32mm

Stout-bodied, forewings brownish with paler patches on wing tips. Hindwings pale yellow. A fringe of hair on hind border forms a hump over back when resting, giving appearance of a broken twig. Inhabits woodland. Hairy caterpillar (3a) feeds on elm, lime or hazel.

4 Tortrix Moth body ½in, 13mm

Small, pale-green and grey moth living in colonies on oak trees. Rather sedentary but rise in a cloud if disturbed. Caterpillars (4a) in some seasons may strip whole tree of leaves, and thus called defoliators. Will drop from tree on silken thread. Pupates inside a rolled-up leaf held together with silk, hence name of tortrix (from Latin meaning 'twister'). Also called green oak moth.

5 Winter Moth body ¾in, 19mm

A species which flies during early winter. Often seen on lighted windows, together with the larger mottled umber moth. Both have brown patterned forewings, paler hind ones. Female is wingless and spider-like. Winter moth lays eggs in crack in bark, especially fruit and oak trees. Green looper caterpillar (5a, see also magpie moth, p.102) feeds on leaves in June and may strip tree. Descends from tree on silk line to pupate in soil. Adults hatch in autumn. After mating, female ascends tree to lay eggs, which overwinter. Can be trapped by sticky bands placed around trunk.

6 Peppered Moth body 1¼in, 32mm

Normally coloured white and 'peppered' with black which gives perfect camouflage on lichen-covered trees where it rests. The looper caterpillar (6a, see also magpie moth, p.102) feeds on various tree leaves, especially birch. Stands at an angle from perch when resting, resembling a twig. A rare black (melanistic) form increased due to Industrial Revolution. Pollution killed off lichens and darkened trees and walls with soot and grime, providing ideal background against which black form could hide. Today black form less common due to pollution control. Normal white form predominant in cleaner west and north.

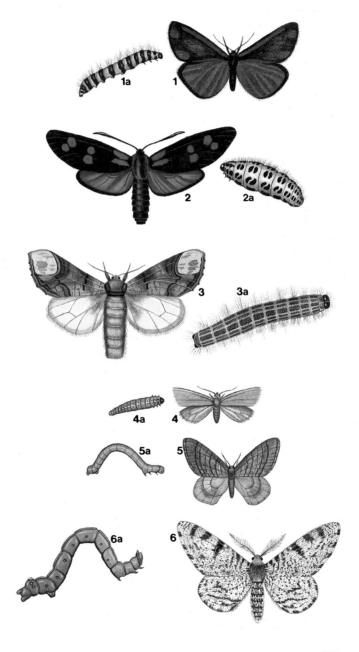

Moths contd

1 Swallowtail Moth body 1¼in, 32mm

The pale, yellow colour produces a ghostly appearance against moon or a lighted window where it may settle. Has pointed tips to hindwings. Eggs laid on ivy or privet, producing caterpillars (1a) resembling twigs. Adults seen in July. Is related to peppered moth (p.104). Common and widespread.

2 Vapourer Moth body ½in, 13mm

Also called tussock moth. Small and brownish, covered in irritating hairs. Common and widespread. Occurs on hawthorn where wingless female attracts male, which has feathered antennae. Eggs overwinter before hatching. Caterpillar (2a) black with red spots, has patches of contrasting hair which can inflame sensitive skin. Safe from birds.

Hawkmoths

Large, fast flying moths with stout bodies, narrow pointed forewings, shorter hindwings. Ability to hover in front of flowers to feed, mainly at dusk. Well camouflaged at rest. Caterpillars usually green with darker, oblique stripes, and a protruding 'tail' at hind end. Brown chrysalis buried in soil, often exposed during gardening. On emergence scales on wings soon fall off. Some species migrate. Bee hawkmoth mimics bumblebee. Largest, death's-head hawkmoth has skull-like pattern on thorax.

3 Hummingbird Hawkmoth body 1in, 25mm

A small moth of the Mediterranean, and a powerful long-range migrant which turns up in large numbers in some summers, from June onwards, mainly along coastal areas. Flies by day and hovers in front of flowers, moving rapidly from one to the next, with wings buzzing after fashion of hummingbird. Frequents parks and gardens. Colour brown and orange. Eggs laid on lady's bedstraw. Some adults known to return to Europe, many die at onset of winter.

4 Privet Hawkmoth body 1½in, 38mm

Large species common in town parks and gardens where privet grows. Named after its food plant, as are some other species such as lime, poplar, and pine hawkmoths.

5 Elephant Hawkmoth body 1¼in, 32mm

Common species with pinkish wings, lays eggs on rosebay willow-herb. May occur in built-up areas where plants grow on waste ground. Caterpillar (5a) uses spectacular deterrent when disturbed; head and trunk-like neck are retracted into thorax which swells to expose conspicuous 'eye-spots', giving snake-like appearance. The eyed hawkmoth has 'eye-spots' on hindwings, also exposed when alarmed.

Flies

Many insect names include the word fly. True flies are distinguished by having a single pair of wings (Order Diptera). Hindwings reduced to club-shaped balancing organs, called halteres. Mouth parts used for sucking liquid food, either pad-shaped as in housefly or for piercing as in mosquito. Some mimic wasps or bees in colour and shape. Larva is legless. Some aquatic (see Pond and River Life p.248). About 5000 British species made up of housefly and allies, slender mosquitoes and craneflies, and smaller gnats and midges.

1 Housefly length ⅜in, 9mm

Greyish, with four dark bands along thorax. Occurs mainly in houses and farm buildings, attracted to exposed food, decaying vegetation, carcasses and excrement. Worldwide, and a danger to health due to feeding habits. A pad-like mouth deposits saliva onto food to soften it before feeding. Germs picked up are transmitted either by the feet or by regurgitation; could result in dysentery or typhoid if from human excrement. Best avoided by personal hygiene, use of flush toilet and protection of food. White eggs laid in masses on food, which is then eaten by the resulting maggots (1a), whose skin later hardens to form pupa (1b). Life cycle completed in about 10 days during warm weather. A few adults and pupa survive the winter. The lesser housefly also occurs indoors and tends to circle around room in small groups. Has a straight-sided body. Autumn housefly enters buildings, sometimes in large numbers, in order to hibernate. During summer lives in fields, breeding on cow-pats. The stablefly breeds in farm buildings, has a pointed proboscis and bites farm animals, occasionally man.

2 Greenbottle length ½in, 13mm

Smaller size than bluebottle, a metallic green, normally stays outdoors. Lays eggs on dead animals, also on sores on bodies of sheep, etc., where larvae feed on flesh. Is also known to infect toads.

3 Blowfly length ½in, 13mm

So-called bluebottle, resembles housefly in build but much larger, and has hairy, metallic blue body. Enters house in summer (usually females) with loud buzzing. Male feeds on flowers. Eggs laid on exposed meat and dead animals. Fully grown maggot pupates in soil, hatching in two weeks. Dead flies stuck on window panes or walls and surrounded by a whitish powder have been killed by a fungus.

4 Hoverfly length ¾in, 19mm

Commonly seen in gardens and fields, usually black and yellow and mimicking wasps and bees. Is capable of hovering and darting in any direction in helicopter fashion. Swarms visit flowers in summer. Most larvae feed on aphids. So-called dronefly is shown here as a larva (4a, called rat-tailed maggot) which lives in stagnant, often foul water; it has a long telescopic breathing tube which it extends to the surface to obtain air.

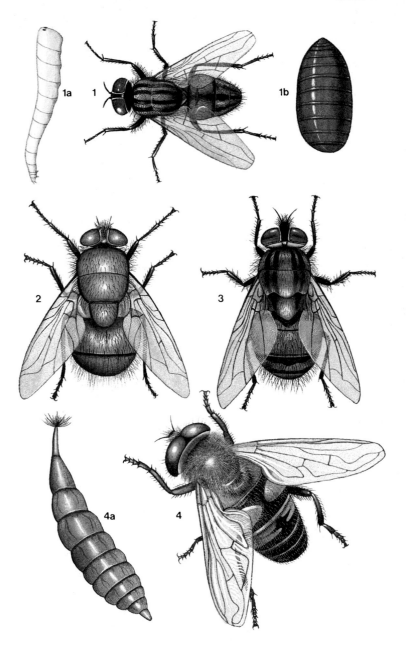

Flies contd

1 Midge length ½in, 13mm

A general term for a large number of small species of mosquito-like build. Some bite, others do not. Biting midges suck blood of other animals, including humans, and can be a nuisance in coastal areas, causing irritation, although saliva is non-poisonous. Non-biting species have no mouth-parts and live short lives, usually found in woodland or near water. Males have feathery antennae and swarm in dark clouds over trees and roof-tops. Females lay eggs in jelly coating, fixed to a support in water (e.g. sides of swimming pool). Larvae feed on decaying material. Some contain haemoglobin as in human blood, giving body a red colour, and are called 'blood-worms'. Can live in oxygen-deficient water.

2 Cranefly length ¾in, 19mm

The familiar, long-bodied 'daddy-long-legs'. Legs break off easily to help in escape from predator. Colour in most species a dull brown. Female uses an egg-tube to deposit eggs in soil. A grey and cylindrical larva — the leatherjacket — does serious harm to plants in June by feeding on roots, causing bare patches in grass in some years. Pupal stage lasts through winter, adults emerging the following summer, sometimes in swarms. Adult feeds on nectar, or uses up food reserves. Harmless.

3 Thistle Gallfly length ⅜in, 9mm

Galls are abnormal growths or swellings on plants caused by a number of agents, such as gallflies, gallwasps, mites, eel-worms and fungi. Well-known example is the oak-apples caused by gallwasp. A common gallfly is the thistle gallfly, which lays eggs in the stems of thistles, causing swellings. Resembles a housefly but with a mottled wing-pattern and tapering body. The larvae each live in a separate cell inside the gall, and feed on the tissues.

4 Fruitfly length ⅛in, 3mm

Small, yellowish fly which feeds on rotting fruit and hangs around dustbins; also seen in fruit factories. Eggs are laid in all these places. Most famous is the vinegarfly (Drosophila). Its larva's large salivary chromosomes and its rapid breeding make it ideal for the study of genetics and heredity. Also bred as food for small captive animals.

5 Ked length ⅛in, 3mm

A wingless fly with flattened body and backwards-pointing hairs which lives among hairs or feathers of various animals, using stabbing mouth-part for sucking blood. Young develop within mother and are born singly as full grown larvae. The sheep ked, entirely wingless, lives in fleece of sheep. It pupates and hatches on the host. The forest ked is winged, and common on ponies and cattle in the New Forest. Other related species live on bats.

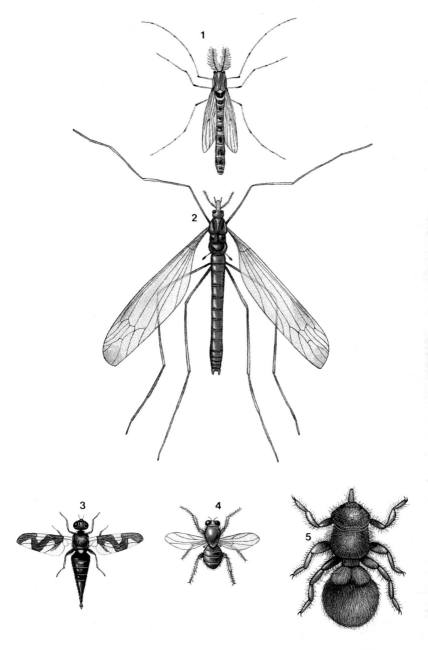

Flies contd

1 Horsefly length 1in, 25mm

Heavily built fly with large head and swollen, glistening eyes. Male feeds on nectar, female sucks blood, inflicting painful bites on horses, cattle and humans. One species, the cleg, attacks in complete silence, biting without warning. Common in damp meadows. Larva lives in damp soil, feeding on earthworms.

2 Botfly length ⅝in, 16mm

Large brownish fly with pointed abdomen and lacking proper mouth-parts. Lays eggs on front legs of horses, who lick them off and swallow them. Hatched larva attaches itself by hooks on mouth to stomach lining. Some months later larva passes out with dung and pupates in ground. Adult emerges in July. Heavy infestation affects host. Related species parasitise cattle, sheep and deer. Irritation from botfly infestation causes horses to gallop about.

3 Warblefly length ½in, 13mm

Stout, hairy fly, rather bee-like in build and colour. After mating the female lays eggs on forelimbs of cattle. Hatched larvae bore through skin, working their way towards the throat by late summer. Continue journey through winter to reach underskin of cow's back where air holes are made. Consequent inflammations are called warbles. Irritation and damage affect cow's health and holes in skin reduce value of hide. Larva drops off to pupate in soil. Adult does not feed and lives a short life. Cattle gallop around field in distress at sound of buzzing fly.

4 Dungfly length ⅜in, 9mm

Easily recognised by bright yellow, hairy appearance. Gathers in swarms around cow-pats and horses' dung in fields. Smaller female, more grey-green, lays eggs on dung. Larva feeds on this, helping in breakdown. Adult feeds on nectar and other insects.

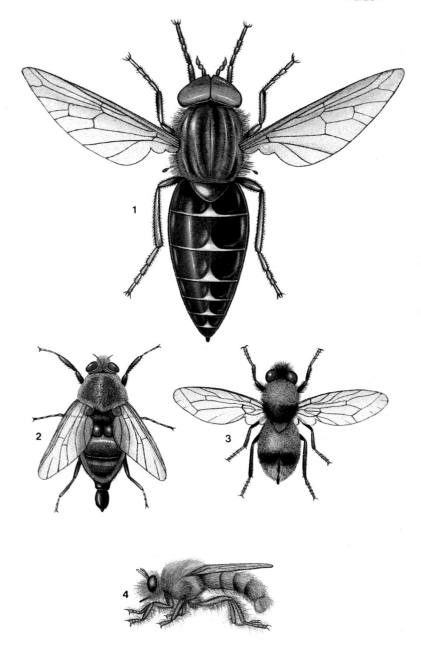

Bees

In general distinguished from wasps by plumper body, hairier legs, feathery in some for gathering pollen. The dorsal plate on thorax does not reach round to join wings, as in wasps. Food is pollen and nectar. Useful flower pollinators.

1 Bumblebee length 1⅛in, 28mm

Large, hairy bee, common in gardens, usually dark-coloured with some amount of yellow or red banding. Nest built underground. In spring queen gathers grass or moss to line nest in a hole, such as mouse-hole. Gathers pollen or nectar to make a ball of 'bee-bread' on which eggs are laid, surrounded by wax. A 'honey-pot' also made for storing honey. Queen sits on eggs to keep warm. Workers which emerge then take over to manage the hive and gather food. Later in autumn drones and young queen appear. Only queens hibernate, workers die off as with wasps.

2 Mining Bee length ½in, 13mm

Resembles honeybee, though less hairy, having a short tongue and more flattened body. Solitary bee which digs a burrow with a conical pile of earth around entrance, usually in soft soil. Often many nests built close together. Inside, cells are built and food added. Nectar and pollen rolled into ball, each containing one egg. Mother takes no further interest and offspring fend for themselves. Each female works independently.

3 Cuckoo Bee length 1in, 25mm

Parasitic bee resembling bumblebee but less hairy. Has no pollen baskets on legs. Female enters bumblebee's nest, killing off most workers and queen, then lays own eggs which are reared by the few remaining bumblebee workers until colony contains only cuckoo bees.

4 Leaf-Cutting Bee length ½in, 13mm

Also resembles honeybee but lives solitary life. The familiar sight of rose leaves with pieces neatly cut away denotes their presence. They use pieces to construct cells by rolling them into cylinders to line nest in a burrow in rotting wood, or even in a key-hole. Piece of leaf seals off store of food with an egg at far end of burrow. More eggs and food stores laid in succession along tunnel, each sealed off until complete, when bee leaves and dies.

5 Honeybee length ¾in, 19mm

Mainly a hive bee kept under domestication, but originally introduced, probably from South-East Asia. Occasional swarms settle and nest in hollow trees but usually do not last. Combs are built vertically to hold honey. Eggs laid by larger queen (5b) in hexagonal cells, built by workers (5c), in which grubs are reared. Larger cells along edge of combs produce drones (5a, males) . Large cone-shaped cells contain future queens, shortly before colony is about to swarm. Queens are determined by a special food, the 'royal jelly' fed by workers. Communication between workers through so-called 'queen substance' peculiar to each hive. The first queen to emerge kills off the others, then goes on mating flight and returns to take over from old queen. Alternatively she may take off with part of the colony to start a new nest. Bee sting is barbed and usually torn off in wound so that bee dies.

Wasps

Usually more slender in build than bees, also more brightly coloured as warning of sting. Dorsal plate reaches down to wing bases, which are folded lengthwise at rest. A short tongue, no pollen sacs. Food variable — fruit, insects and carrion. Sting has no barbs.

1 Common Wasp length ¾in, 19mm

Conspicuous bands of black and yellow, with paired wings folded at rest. Hoverflies, which mimic wasps, have a single pair (see p.108). Very social, living in colonies consisting of a large queen (1a), drones (1b), and workers (1c, infertile females). Only queen survives winter. In spring seeks out a suitable nest site, usually below ground, sometimes in hollow tree or in building. Nest has horizontal combs with cells underneath, built of paper or wood pulp, mixed with saliva. Queen builds small 'queen's nest' and rears first brood. Workers then take over with various tasks — enlarging nest, attending queen, gathering food, feeding young, etc. Useful in catching insects. A complete nest may contain 20,000 individuals. Towards autumn new queens and drones appear in special large cells. By winter whole colony has died off, apart from queens.

2 Sawfly length 1½in, 38mm

Aggressive-looking black and yellow, wasp-like but without a 'waist'. This large woodwasp or horntail has a long protruberance which is not a sting but an ovipositor which can be bored into conifer tree to lay an egg. White grub-like larva has vestigial wings, and tunnels through wood, damaging tree, taking up to three years to grow. May emerge from cut timber, even furniture. Spread by timber trade and doubtful if species is a native. Other smaller species have a saw-like egg-tube for cutting into plant stems to lay eggs.

3 Digger Wasp length 1⅛in, 28mm

One of many kinds of solitary wasp. Shown here is the sand wasp, slender and reddish in colour with body ending in a swelling. Digs a flask-shaped burrow. Catches a caterpillar which it paralyses with a sting, then carries back to nest; an egg is laid on the caterpillar, then the entrance is closed. Grub feeds on caterpillar and emerges the following spring.

4 Hornet length 1½in, 38mm

Large wasp, coloured more brown and orange (black and yellow in other species). Is somewhat rare in woodlands of southern England. Builds a paper nest in hollow trees, holes in ground, occasionally buildings. Adult feeds on nectar and fruit juices, grubs and flies. In spite of reputation is fairly docile and seldom stings.

5 Ichneumon Fly length 1¼in, 32mm ovipositor 1¼in, 32mm

Slender, wasp-like, and parasitises insects, especially caterpillars and pupae, with its eggs. One or more larvae feed on victim, then pupate in a silken cocoon. After mating, female usually hibernates. A large species shown here attacks horntail. It searches for hidden grub, then bores into tree with slender ovipositor. The two halves rotate backwards and forwards rapidly and drill down to deposit egg on woodwasp grub. Emerging larva then feeds on victim.

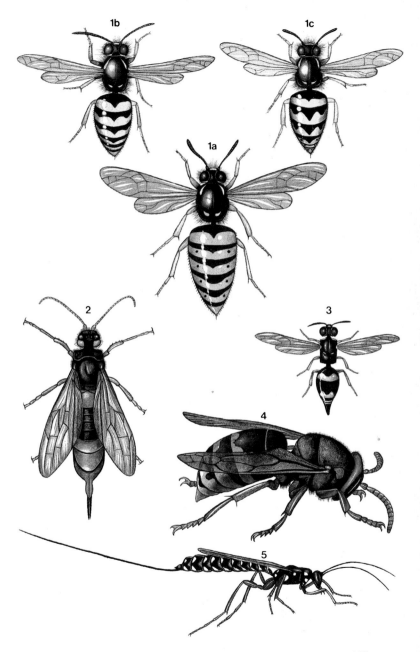

Beetles

Front pair of wings are hardened (called the elytra) and meet together to cover hindwings when not flying. Have hard outer skin, and mouth-parts for biting. About 4000 British species, some aquatic. A number are harmful to crops, trees, stored food and household property. Some are flightless.

1 Violet Ground Beetle length 1¼in, 32mm

Commonly found hiding by day under stones, logs, etc. Widespread. Has metallic sheen to wing cases which are fused together. Flightless. Moves rapidly at night, hunting caterpillars, worms, other insects. Larva also hunts.

2 Rove Beetle length up to ½in, 13mm

More than 1000 species of dark-coloured beetles resembling earwigs without pincers. Most have short elytra with large, black wings and can fly. An unusual example is the devil's coach horse. When disturbed raises hindquarters over body in order to squirt a strong-smelling vapour at enemy. Powerful jaws can give painful bite. Adults and larvae occur in rubbish dumps, in dung, under stones, etc., feeding at night on insects and decaying plant material. Some rove beetles occur in ants' nests.

3 Seven-Spot Ladybird length ¼in, 6mm

Common species of familiar beetles named after number of black spots on red elytra. Valuable to gardeners as both grub and adult feed on greenfly and other pests, although some aphids will resist by kicking. Eggs laid on plants and hatch into active grubs. Beetle emerges after short pupation. Numbers largely controlled by food supply and weather conditions. When disturbed or attacked exudes a bitter-tasting fluid; bright colour acts as warning. Usually avoided by birds. Hibernates, often in buildings.

4 Stag Beetle length 3in, 76mm

Unmistakable, especially male which has large, antler-like jaws, probably used as deterrent or ornament. Bite is weak and it does not feed. Makes courtship flights on summer evenings with droning sound. Female has smaller jaws and lays eggs in rotten tree stumps. Large, curled white grub lives and feeds for three years before pupation. The smaller lesser stag beetle has more modest jaws.

5 Green Tiger Beetle length ½in, 13mm

A fast-running, long-legged hunting beetle with powerful jaws. Green with yellow spots, occurs in drier soils on heaths and in sand-dunes. Catches other small animals. Makes short flights with distinct buzzing. Larva lies inside burrow waiting for prey.

6 Cockchafer length 1in, 25mm

Also called the maybug, flies about on summer nights with audible buzzing, often flying into windows. Brown colour, with pointed abdomen and feathery antennae. Fat, white grub lives underground for up to three years, doing much harm to roots of plants, especially grass and cereals. Sought after by birds and also called rook-worms. Adult may damage trees by eating leaves.

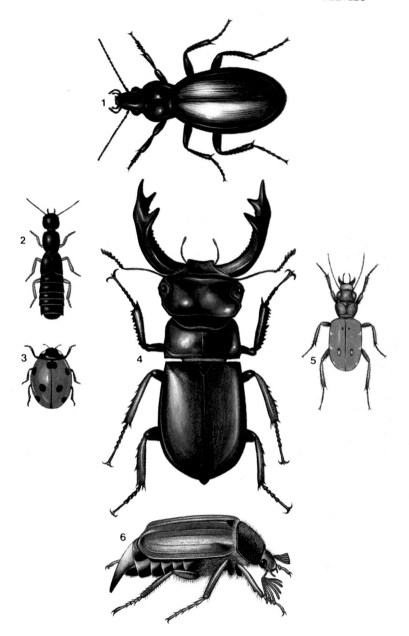

Beetles contd

1 Dermestes Beetle length ¼in, 6mm

Dull-coloured, with covering of downy hairs and clubbed antennae. Larvae are basically scavengers and can cause serious damage by eating dried animal material, e.g. larder beetle which eats stored meat and hides; related to carpet beetle which damages furs, fabrics and carpets. Museum specimens are also attacked by dermestes beetle — so it can be used for cleaning skeletons! In separate family is the flightless flour beetle which infests stored products. Larvae, called mealworms, bred as food for cagebirds, lizards, etc.

2 Furniture Beetle length ⅛in, 3mm

A notorious pest whose larva bores into dead wood if it is untreated — attacks furniture, rafters, shelves, stairs, floorboards, etc. White larva lives and feeds inside wood for up to three years. Signs of activity are appearance of fresh wood powder. In June reddish-brown adults emerge. After pairing female lays eggs in nearby crevices or in existing holes.

3 Dor Beetle length ¾in, 19mm

Also called dung beetle and related to chafers. Rounded, hard-skinned body, usually a shiny black, with strong legs for digging. Named dor after old English for drone because of loud, humming flight. Female digs tunnels under cow-pat, each provided with a pellet of dung on which egg is laid. Larvae feed on this. Droppings of other farm animals, and deer and rabbit, also exploited. Useful insects in recycling animal waste.

4 Deathwatch Beetle length ⅜in, 9mm

Prefers old timber beams in large houses, halls and old churches. Emerges in April-May. Male makes tapping sound by rapidly vibrating his head against tunnel wall; female answers. Larvae spend up to three years inside beam (see also bark beetle and longhorn beetle, p.122) Smaller powder post beetle attacks cut timber and can be a problem in timber yards.

5 Click Beetle length ¾in, 19mm

Dull brown, oval-shaped beetle with hard skeleton,named after unusual habit of somersaulting when fallen on back. Body arches so that peg-like projection engages a notch under body; when released gives an audible click, and beetle is thrown up to a foot in the air, landing right way up. Some species produce soil-dwelling larvae, called wireworms, which do considerable damage to young crops. Antennae of adult toothed or feathered.

6 Sexton Beetle length ¾in, 19mm

Usually dull-coloured, but specimen shown also marked in orange. Carrion-feeder with a good sense of smell, enabling it to detect a dead animal. Male releases scent to attract a mate. Together, they then proceed to undermine a corpse and bury it. Fur or feathers are removed and flesh made into a ball as food for female. Eggs laid nearby in tunnel, and grubs fed at first by mother from regurgitated food. Are powerful enough to drag a corpse to place where soil is workable.

Beetles contd

1 Longhorn Beetle length ¼-1½in, 6-38mm

Wood-feeding beetle with long antennae. Rather shortlived. Whitish grub lives in rotting wood, but may attack various living trees, taking two or more years to mature. Many foreign species imported into Britain. Eggs laid in bark crevices. Larva bores under bark and may penetrate heartwood. Has been known for beetles to emerge from wooden furniture many years later.

2 Glow-Worm length ½in, 13mm

Name derived from the female of the species (2a), which is grub-like and produces a pale, yellow-green glow from a luminous organ under her tail. Glow is produced by oxidation of a substance called luciferin, and can be stopped when required by cutting off oxygen supply. Males (2b) and larvae also produce light, but much weaker. Males are normal-looking beetles and have sensitive eyes for detecting female's glow during mating season. Adults feed little but larvae hunt slugs and snails which they bite, paralyse with digestive juice, then suck out the contents. Glow-worms are localised in distribution, mainly in chalk districts where snails occur.

3 Colorado Beetle length ⅜in, 9mm

Conspicuous beetle introduced originally from America, and marked in longitudinal stripes of black and yellow. A serious pest on potatoes, multiplying rapidly. Turns up in Britain now and then. Larva (3a) resembles ladybird grub — red with black spots. First outbreak noted in 1901. Under strict control by Ministry of Agriculture, Fisheries and Food, and public asked to report discoveries.

4 Bark Beetle length ¼in, 6mm

Small, dark-coloured beetle of serious economic importance due to boring activities of grubs in trees. Cylindrical in shape with clubbed antennae. Male enters through hole made in bark, then excavates a chamber for mating with one or more females. Females then tunnel away from mating chamber below bark, laying eggs at intervals. Hatched grubs then tunnel away at right angles to each 'mother' gallery. This produces a characteristic pattern according to species of beetle. Also known as engraver beetles. Usually attack conifers which are already weakened due to damage or fire. Grubs eaten by woodpeckers. The related ambrosia beetle or pin-hole borers bore deeply into tree along tunnels coloured black due to presence of fungus which is introduced as food. In case of Dutch elm disease, fungus may kill tree.

5 Weevil length ¹⁄₁₆-½in, 1½-13mm

Sometimes called snout-bearers, having head extended into a beak or rostrum which carries mouth-parts at end and clubbed and elbowed antennae half-way along. The family is said to be the largest in the animal kingdom, and there are more than 500 species in Britain. Weevils are plant eaters and can cause harm to crops, fruit, stored grain, nuts, trees, etc., according to species. Some roll up leaves in which they lay their eggs, and are called leaf-rollers. White grubs are legless.

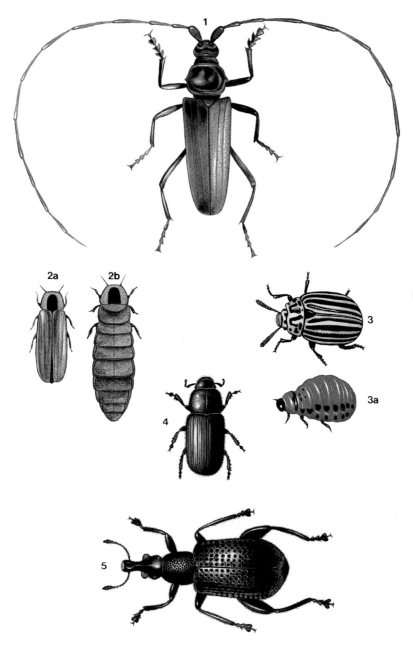

Soil Animals

A vast assembly of small animals live in or on the soil, under logs, and in leaf litter, and are usually hidden by day. This is to avoid light and the danger of desiccation. Known as the litter fauna, they combine with bacteria and fungi in the process of decay and manufacture of fresh soil.

1 Millepede length variable

Resemble centipedes but with more cylindrical body, two pairs of legs per segment, no poisonous jaws. Vegetarian or scavenger, especially of rotten wood. Legs move in series of waves. Slow-moving, protected by an oily secretion. May curl up when disturbed. Lives in hidden places under stones, logs, leaf-litter. Eggs laid in soil and protected with hard covering. Can live many years. Can cause damage in gardens and allotments.

2 Centipede length variable

Single pair of legs per segment, variable in number according to length. Brownish body more or less flattened, moves fast with rhythmic, lateral movements of body. Carnivorous. Small prey caught with sickle-shaped jaws which inject paralysing poison. Eggs laid on soil. Useful to gardener.

3 Pill Millepede length ½in, 13mm

May be confused with pill woodlouse, which has more shiny skin and broad shield on hind end. When unrolled it can be seen that pill millipede has more legs.

4 Woodlouse length ½in, 13mm

Small, mainly terrestrial crustacean related to crab. Slate-grey to brown, oval-shaped with humped back. Quickly dies from exposure due to lack of waterproof skin, and seeks humid surroundings under stones, logs etc., avoiding light. A scavenger feeding on leaves, dead wood, rotting fruit. Eggs carried in pouch under body. Generally useful to gardeners. Lives for about one year. Also called sow-bug. The pill woodlouse or pill-bug rolls up when disturbed.

5 Earthworm

True worms, called Annelids, have body divided into segments clearly seen as rings. British species coloured brownish. (Small white-coloured worms are probably unsegmented nematodes or eel-worms which attack potatoes and other plants). Earthworms have four pairs of bristles per segment, pointing backwards, used to grip sides of tunnel as worm penetrates soil in concertina movement. Eat soil, digesting organic content, leaving remains on surface as familiar worm casts. Also pull fallen leaves into hole. Emerge on summer nights to mate. Each has male and female organs (hermaphrodite) and pair join head to tail to exchange sperm from sex openings. On separation, skin of clitellum (smooth, swollen section near head end) slides off to form a cocoon containing some 25 eggs. Very useful to gardener as they aerate soil. May be extremely abundant (millions per acre).

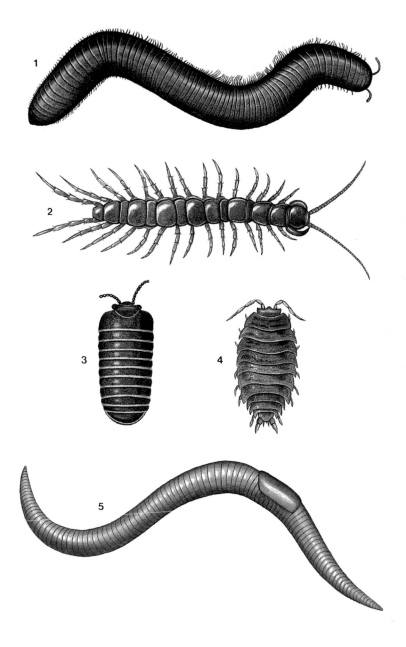

Soil Animals contd

1 Roman Snail length 1¾in, 44mm

Large species of doubtful origin, not necessarily introduced. Very much confined to chalk soil in southern England.

2 Garden Snail length 1½in, 38mm

Called a Gastropod or 'stomach-foot' because it creeps on its belly, really a muscular foot. Paves its way with a trail of slime and can travel over almost any surface, however sharp. Hermaphrodite, a pair can mate and each lay batches of white eggs. Mostly abroad after dark or rain, feeding on plants and fungi. Mouth contains rasp-like tongue (radula). Hibernates under stones, logs, in walls, sealing opening with hardened mucus.

3 Banded Snail length ½-¾in, 13-19mm

A number of species of average size, with darker bands along shell where spirals connect. Commonly seen on chalkland after rain.

4 Garden Slug length 1in, 25mm

Related to snail, but without visible shell. Movement on muscular foot similar. Tentacles used for detecting surroundings and food. Hermaphrodite. A common garden pest feeding on garden plants. Has rounded back, dark-coloured orange foot. More greyish, mottled netted slug climbs plants and is often found inside lettuces and cabbages.

5 Black Slug length up to 6in, 15cm

One of the larger British species. Largest is ash-black slug, up to a foot (30cm). Also in reddish form. Occurs in gardens and hedgerows. Mating is preceded by elaborate courtship when pair encircle, licking one another. In case of great grey slug, pair climb a tree or wall. When tightly joined they lower themselves on thick rope of slime where mating takes place.

Ants

Highly organized, social insects living in colonies, housed in a network of tunnels in soil or wood, or in mounds built of leaves. A single, large queen lays eggs tended by wingless workers. Grubs form pupae, the so-called 'ant's-eggs' used as fish food. Developing queens and males are winged. During summer mating flights take place usually *en masse* on a windless day, causing noticeable swarms. Mated queen returns to start a fresh colony, after biting off her wings. Workers store eggs in chambers, then feed grubs. On finding a meal can leave a scent trail for others to follow. Will collect plant and animal food, preferring sweet things. Some species will 'milk' aphids for 'honeydew' even taking back captives as slaves.

6 Red Wood Ant length ⅜in, 9mm

A large red-coloured species usually found in large nests made of needles in conifer woods. Columns of workers can be seen hurrying to and fro along well-defined pathways, carrying food or nest material. Will attack most things along their path. Can bite or squirt formic acid at enemy.

Arachnids

Not to be confused with insects. Comprise spiders, scorpions (non-British), mites and harvestmen. No antennae, but instead have sensory palps, a pair of fangs, and four pairs of walking legs. Body in two parts. All are carnivorous, taking in pre-digested liquid food. Spiders spin silk from spinnerets at end of body. Silk used for various traps and webs for catching prey. Hunting spiders do not spin. Spiders perform an elaborate courtship of visual displays, touching and vibrating web. After mating male usually dies from exhaustion. One aquatic species (see p.252).

1 Harvestman body ¼-½in, 6-13mm

Small, eight-legged arachnid with undivided body and long legs. Can shed legs to confuse enemy. Hunts live prey which is seized in pincer-like jaws. Common in woodland, grass, compost heaps, often seen on walls and fences, especially in autumn (hence its name). Eggs laid in soil.

2 False Scorpion body ⅛in, 3mm

Small arachnid resembling a miniature scorpion but without tail or sting. Common under bark, stones and leaf-litter. Feeds on smaller animals which it injects with poison. Silken nest built for eggs shortly before death. Larvae tended by mother who provides food from her dying body. Harmless.

3 Garden Spider body ⅝in, 16mm

Also called orb spider. Builds an elaborate, circular web seen in gardens and hedgerows, especially in late summer when these are covered with dew. It is a masterpiece of design, made by instinct in an hour or less — worth observing. Spider then hides, holding a connecting thread to maintain contact with web. Trapped prey, detected by vibrations, is seized, bitten and wrapped in silk.

4 Money Spider body ⅛in, 3mm

Popularly associated with wealth, and responsible for the clouds of gossamer seen drifting in air. A hammock-shaped web is constructed in autumn in long grass, low undergrowth, etc., and is most readily visible during frost or after heavy dew. Spider may travel long distance, carried aloft on silk by wind.

5 Pursweb Spider body ⅜in, 9mm

Related to tropical trap-door spiders. Makes a tube-like web inside a vertical tunnel between blades of grass, but with top end lying along surface of blade, where it hides. Unsuspecting fly is stabbed through the silk by spider's long jaws, and dragged into tunnel after repairing hole. Found mainly on dry soil in southern England.

6 House Spider body ¾in, 19mm

Long-legged, fast-moving hunter, usually in buildings, sometimes scaring occupants when it appears in the bath or basin. Lives in a funnel at base of triangular-shaped web in some odd corner. Web covered with 'trip-wires' over entrance, the so-called cobweb.

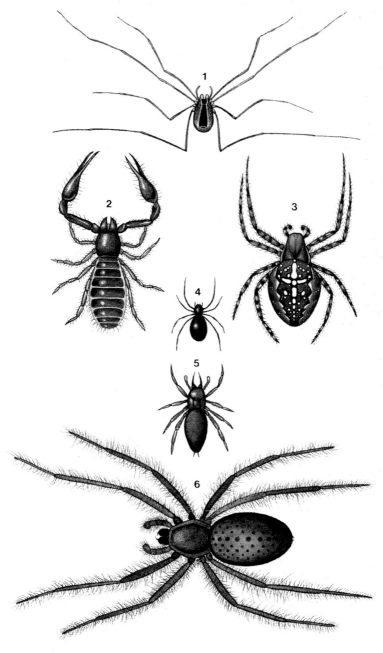

FLOWERS

Flowering plants are the most advanced and colourful members of the plant kingdom. In Britain some 1,300 species range in size from small annuals to the long-lived oak. Known as seed plants, in contrast to the lower plants which produce minute spores (e.g. algae, mosses and ferns), they rely heavily on insects for pollination. Flowers of wind-pollinated species, such as grasses, and those trees with catkins, are usually inconspicuous.

A pollen grain is a flower's equivalent of an animal's sperm cell, and is produced by the male organ, or stamen. These surround the central, female, ovary which is composed of carpels. These occur separately, as in the buttercup, or joined together, as in

to protect the young flower bud. Most flowers are bisexual (hermaphrodite), as in buttercup and rose. Others have separate male and female flowers on the same plant (hazel) or on separate plants (willow). Insect-pollinated flowers stand upright, wind-pollinated flowers hang down, usually in clusters as catkins (hazel, poplar, oak).

Distribution of fruits also requires assistance. Some, like sycamore and dandelion, have wings or parachute-like attachments for dispersal by wind. Hooked fruits are carried on animal fur or human clothing (e.g. burdock and goose-grass). Colourful fruits (berries, hips, and haws) are eaten by birds and mammals, and the seeds passed through their bodies. Nuts and acorns may be stored or buried. Many forms of mechanical dispersal include that of the poppy, which scatters seeds in pepper-pot fashion. Pods of pea

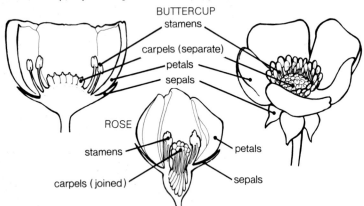

BUTTERCUP
stamens
carpels (separate)
petals
sepals

ROSE
stamens
carpels (joined)
petals
sepals

the rose. A pollen grain carried by a bee is caught on the stigma of the carpel, which it penetrates in order to reach the egg-cell. The result is a seed which contains the embryo plant, surrounded by a supply of food, the endosperm, and encased in a seed coat, or testa (see diagram). Surrounding these sex organs are the colourful petals, which may have scent glands, and both are intended to attract insects.

On the outside of the flower are the green sepals, whose main function is

flowers, such as gorse, explode when ripe.

Originally wild flowers and their fruits were gathered as food. During the Middle Ages great attention was paid to their medicinal properties. Students called herbalists collected and tested their value, at a time when doctors, who were called quacks, relied on herbs for treatment of patients. Many of the fanciful names of flowers were chosen to tell the public which to collect for a specific ailment, though this was not always reliable. Examples include self-heal, nipplewort, eye-bright, fleabane, and feverfew. Sometimes a plant's features acted as an advertisement for its properties, as with lungwort which has spotted leaves resembling a diseased lung.

By the eighteenth century interest in plants led to them being given scientific names following a classification system devised by the Swedish botanist Linnaeus. He gave a double name — first the genus, followed by the species — to each plant (as well as each animal) in his famous *Systema Naturae,* which is still in use today. Latin or latinised names are used, as this is an international language used world-wide.

There are two broad divisions of flowers, recognised in the seedling. The endosperm forms into what is called a cotyledon, or seed-leaf, readily seen in the first shoot. Monocotyledons have a single seed-leaf and long, linear leaves with parallel veins (grasses and bulb plants). They are mostly herbs, whereas the larger dicotyledons with two seed-leaves range from herbs to trees, and have broader leaves with branched veins.

All this information is of use to a trained botanist who studies and classifies plants. In this book, which is mainly concerned with identification, a simplified system is used. The illustrations on the following pages have been grouped according to colour, and the numbers of petals. Thus the five-petalled buttercup is placed with the yellow flowers under the 5-7 petal section. The rose is with the 5-7 petalled red flowers, and so on. In some cases where flowers have joined petals, or the petals are tightly bunched, they are treated as one, and placed in the up-to-4 petal sections. For instance, the bluebell has six joined petals, so appears in the up-to-4, blue section. The gorse, a pea flower, has five petals but with two joined, so is placed with the up-to-4, yellow flowers.

Many of our wild flowers have been introduced from other countries as a food or for medical use, and are now well established. Others are escapes from cultivation. During the days of

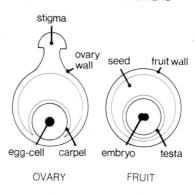

OVARY   FRUIT

Linnaeus, many botanists searched foreign lands to bring back flowers to add to his list, while others collected them to plant in gardens (for example, tulips, dahlias, and rhododendrons).

Flowers, like most living things, require certain conditions if they are to thrive. Some are purely aquatic, others can survive in sand-dunes with a minimum of water. Mountain plants can endure harsh conditions, and sea-shore plants tolerate salt. Flowers of heath and moor are relatively few, limited to those which can grow in acid soil. By contrast, many species occur on chalk and limestone turf, which is rich in mineral salts. A limestone cliff during summer can rival a rock-garden. Woodland flowers bloom mainly in spring when light can penetrate the leafless branches above. They bloom and set seed early. Another large group are the opportunists which colonise waste ground and invade our gardens. They are known generally as weeds — though a flower-lover would prefer to call them flowers growing in the wrong place. Examples are dandelion and daisy, which are well known as lawn-invaders. They both belong to the family Compositae, in which the flower is really a flowerhead, composed of many small florets. The outermost ray florets are female and have a strap-shaped petal. The inner disc florets have tubular petals and are bisexual. Seeds of this family are usually fluffy and windborne, and are carried far in great numbers.

White Flowers, up to 4 Petals

1 Lily-of-the-Valley

Well-known fragrant garden flower which grows as a creeping perennial. A one-sided stem of drooping, bell-like white flowers which produce red berries. Two elliptical glossy leaves arising from base. Grows wild in damp hollows in some woods, though much reduced due to collecting. Shade-loving. Whole plant produces a valuable drug for heart ailments, considered safer than digitalin from foxglove. Lily family. Flowers May-June.

2 Snowdrop

Well-loved perennial with long, linear leaves and drooping solitary flowers. Three large white outer petals and three bell-like, greenish inner ones. Mainly in gardens, appearing early, even through snow. Also grows wild in damp woods. Daffodil family. February-March.

3 Great or Hedge Bindweed

Has large, unscented flowers, sometimes pink with alternate white bands. Sepal-like bracts at base. Leaves arrowhead-shaped. Widespread, common climber over hedges, fences, etc. Pollinated by moths. Smaller field bindweed or convolvulus has more funnel-shaped flowers — white, pink, or both — also widespread as a tenacious garden weed. Grows by twining upwards, or prostrate on ground. Underground stem can penetrate to six feet (1.8m) below and is difficult to eradicate. Bindweed family. June-September. Sea bindweed grows in sand dunes (p.264).

4 Gipsywort

A hairy plant up to three feet (90cm) tall, resembling mint. Numerous leaves deeply toothed and lance-shaped. Small, bell-shaped flowers dotted with purple, in close rings at base of leaves. Produces a strong, black dye once used by gipsies to darken their skins. Labiate family. June-September.

5 Eyebright

Low, hairy semi-parasite attached to clovers or plantain. Small, oval, deeply-toothed, bronze-green leaves. Flowers with petals two-lipped in clusters, normally white, sometimes tinged violet and with purple veining. Widespread in grassy places. Produces a powder formerly used in brightening eyes. Figwort family. June-September.

133

White Flowers, up to 4 Petals contd

1 White Deadnettle

Hairy, slightly scented perennial up to 12 inches (30cm) with square stem. Heart-shaped, toothed leaves resemble true nettle (p.202). Whorls of large, hooded, white flowers with open mouth at base of leaves. Common in hedgerows, more rare in the west. Is attractive to bees. Labiate family. March onwards. Smaller-flowered red deadnettle also common (p.182).

2 Common Whitlow-Grass

Not a grass but a slender, variable, annual herb up to three feet (90cm). A basal rosette of lance-shaped leaves. Terminal flowers with four deeply-cleft white petals on leafless stems, producing round, flattened seed-pods. Common and widespread on bare ground, gravel paths, walls and rocks. Was used to cure whitlows and warts. The rare yellow whitlow-grass now occurs only on ruins and cliffs on the Gower Peninsula, Wales. Cabbage family. March-June.

3 Toothwort

Low, unbranched creamy to pink coloured perennial without leaves; instead, stem covered in broad scales. Grows in groups as a parasite on roots of shrubs or trees such as hazel. Flowers grow in two rows, drooping, open-mouthed, either pink or white. Colour and fang-like shape gave early herbalists the idea that it was good for toothache. Widely scattered in shady hedges and damp woods. Rather similar to broomrape (p.150). April-May.

4 Shepherd's Purse

An annual with heart-shaped seed-pods resembling old-fashioned purse worn by shepherds. Has a rosette of basal toothed leaves; upper ones less toothed and clasp stem. White four-petalled flowers seen at any time of year. Extremely common weed in gardens, on wasteland, world-wide. Wallflower family.

5 Enchanter's Nightshade

A downy perennial not related to true nightshades (pp.140, 198). Up to 12 inches (30cm) tall with opposite leaves oval, slightly toothed and stalked. White flowers on leafless branches. Club-shaped fruits with bristles cling to clothing. A troublesome garden weed, also common in shady woods. Scientific name *Circaea* refers to Circe the enchantress. Willowherb family. June-August.

White Flowers, 5-7 Petals

1 Star-of-Bethlehem

Hairless, bulbous, unbranched perennial up to 12 inches (30cm). Rounded stem with narrow, dark green crocus-like leaves around base. Flowers with six petals in open cluster, white with green stripe on back of each, star-shaped, opening in sun. Common on rock gardens. Widespread but local, mainly in East Anglia in sandy grass, especially on breckland. Abundant in Israel, hence name. Lily family. May-June.

2 Wood Anemone

Low-growing perennial with solitary, nodding, white flowers sometimes tinged red or purple underneath. Leaves three-lobed and much divided. Spreads by underground rhyzome, forming carpets in woodlands and hedge-banks. Name derived from Greek *anemos* for wind. Buttercup family. March-May.

3 White Campion

Perennial up to three feet (90cm), less bushy than bladder campion with large flowers on longer stalks. Rather similar to pink campion (p.188), with which it can hybridise. Has more greenish calyx. Common on wasteland, mainly in south and east, also on arable land. Flowers attract moths. Pink family. May onwards.

4 Bladder Campion

Shiny, greyish-green perennial up to two feet (60cm) with stem swollen at junctions, with opposite pairs of oval and pointed leaves with wavy edges. Flowers white, occasionally pink, with five deeply-notched petals, joined at base to form swollen bladder. Flowering shoots repeatedly forked with flowers in centre of each fork. Scented, and attracts moths. Widespread in grassy places. Pink family. June-August.

5 Yarrow

Downy, scented, dark green perennial with angular stems, up to 18 inches (45cm). Spreads by runners. Numerous long, narrow, bushy leaves. Small flower heads bunched together in a flat cluster and appear as one flower. Once prized as a herb for healing wounds. Scientific name *Achillea* refers to Homer's Iliad, in which Achilles treated his soldiers' wounds with this plant. Very common among grass and neglected lawns. Daisy family. June onwards.

1

2

3

4

5

White Flowers, 5-7 Petals contd

1 Greater Stitchwort

Straggly perennial up to two feet (60cm) tall, growing in conspicuous patches in hedgerows. Clusters of large flowers with five deeply-cleft petals at top of square stems, which bear pairs of narrow, lance-shaped leaves. Plants once used for curing pain in side (stitch), also drunk with wine. Lesser stitchwort similar but smaller, more common on dry, acid heaths and flowers later, June-August.

2 Wild Strawberry

Low, hairy perennial with runners which root and spread, as in garden strawberry. Has smaller, five-petalled flowers with no gaps between, and turned-down sepals on erect stems. Drooping berries have pips protruding. Widespread in open woods and in sand-dunes, especially on lime-rich soil. Rose family. April onwards. Can be confused with barren strawberry, which is smaller with shorter stems, and gaps between petals. Leaves more bluish, and fruit dull and inedible. Earlier growth, February-March. *Note:* garden strawberry occasionally seen growing wild is more tufted with larger flowers. Berries have pips sunk into flesh. Flowers later, May-June. Strawberry so-named from custom of laying down straw to protect fruit from wet soil.

3 Twinflower

An attractive, delicate, creeping, evergreen perennial with small, stalked, oval and toothed leaves on prostrate stems. Funnel-shaped, drooping flowers in pairs on slender, leafless, erect stems. Named by Swedish botanist Linnaeus after himself — *Linnaea borealis*. He discovered it during a journey to Lapland and modestly wrote: 'Lowly, insignificant, disregarded, flowering but for a brief spell, it is named after Linnaeus who resembles it.' Very local in pine woods of eastern Scotland. Worth looking for. Honeysuckle family. June-August.

4 Ramsons

Also called wild garlic, and easily detected by smell. Broad leaves with pointed ends resemble those of lily-of-the-valley (p.132), grow on stalks which are unusually twisted through 180°. Flower stalks three-sided, up to a foot (30cm) tall, bear cluster of starry white flowers with six pointed petals. Widespread, sometimes in masses in damp woods, often together with bluebell. Lily family. April-June.

5 Common Chickweed

Could be confused with stitchworts. A prostrate, rather delicate annual, with stems lined with water-absorbing hairs, soft to touch. Leaves in opposite pairs, oval and pointed, lower ones stalked. Small flowers with deeply cleft petals, as in stitchwort. Once eaten in salads or as a treatment for rheumatism. Seeds readily eaten by wild and cage birds. Very common throughout year on waste ground and in gardens. Pink family. April-September.

1

2

3

4

5

White Flowers, 5-7 Petals contd

1 Sundew

An interesting insectivorous plant. A flat, basal rosette of stalked, rounded leaves in one species, more long-leaved in another, and covered in hairs with sticky glands that glisten in the sun. Leaves curl inwards to trap and digest fly. A central, leafless stalk up to 10 inches (25cm) bears white flowers. Locally common in boggy places on heaths, moorland, usually in company with bog-moss (sphagnum). June-August.

2 Wood Sorrel

Small, delicate, pale green, creeping perennial, has clover-like root leaves which close in dull weather, containing oxalic acid. Solitary flowers cup-like, veined in mauve on leafless stalk up to four inches (10cm) long. Widespread in shady woods, growing in patches, sometimes on fallen logs and tree-stumps. Many garden forms. Fruit explodes when ripe. April-May.

3 English Stonecrop

Commonest of white stonecrops. A creeping perennial, grows in flat patches, the stalks covered with small, stubby, succulent leaves. Star-like five-petalled flowers, tinged pink on short stalks in a cluster. Bears red fruits. Widespread on rocks, shingle, dunes, most common in north and west. June-August.

4 Black Nightshade

Bushy annual up to 12 inches (30cm). Stems often black with oval, toothed leaves. Flowers in bunches with white petals folded back and yellow anthers. Berries green, turning black. Common weed of cultivation including gardens. Nightshade family. June-September.

5 Cow Parsley

One of the commonest white members of the large Umbellifer family. A characteristic growth of flowers arranged on stems like spokes of an umbrella, called rays. A perennial up to four feet (120cm), with large, fresh green, much dissected leaves, which may appear in early winter. Main stem hollow, slightly swollen at joints. Main umbel divides into second umbel terminating in small five-petalled flowers also arranged on umbrella. Abundant and widespread in shady places such as hedgerows. April-June. Similar hedge parsley has solid, rough, hairy stem not swollen at joints. Leaves less divided and frequently pinkish. Flowers in a long-stalked, single umbel. Common along hedgerows and woodland borders. Flowers later, July-September.

141

White Flowers, 8 or more Petals

1 Daisy

Well-known composite. A downy perennial with rosette of spoon-shaped leaves. Flower heads with conical base solitary on leafless stalks. Outer ray florets white tipped with crimson, inner disc florets yellow. Sensitive to light, closing in dull weather, hence name from Anglo Saxon 'daeg's eage' — the 'eye of day'. Widespread on short grass from lowland to mountain, common on lawns, where admired by some. Can withstand mowing. Seen throughout year.

2 Ox-Eye Daisy

A large unbranched perennial up to two feet (60cm). Small, dark, glossy green leaves; upper leaves narrow and lance-shaped, slightly clasping stem, lower leaves long-stalked, spoon-shaped and toothed. Flower heads single, outer ray florets white, inner disc florets yellow. Widespread and abundant among grass, often early coloniser of newly made embankments and on disturbed ground. May onwards.

3 Pineapple Mayweed

Bushy annual smelling strongly of pineapple, up to 10 inches (25cm). Leaves broken into thread-like segments. Flower heads in bunches contain only yellow-green disc florets. Introduced probably from Asia and now common on waste ground and along footpaths. Can withstand trampling. See also scentless mayweed (p.144). Daisy family. June onwards.

4 White Clover

Low, creeping, hairless perennial with trifoliate, finely-toothed leaves. Flowers white, sometimes pinkish, in bunches forming rounded head. Very common and widespread in grass and on lawns. The so-called Dutch clover used as an intermediate crop to restore nitrogen to farm soil, also as fodder for cattle and sheep. Pea family. June onwards. Occasional four-leaved clover considered lucky, and it could have been a clover leaf that St Patrick picked rather than a shamrock. More upright alsike clover introduced from Europe as fodder crop, has flowers first white then turning rose-red, is commonly established along roadsides and on waste ground.

5 Mountain Avens

Creeping perennial, often on bare rock, where roots penetrate cracks and form a dense mat. Large, anemone-like flowers, usually with eight petals and golden stamens, occur singly on erect stalks. Leaves small, evergreen, with wavy border. Fruits in cluster of nutlets with feathery plumes. Grows on limestone pavements on Irish Burren and Pennine Craven districts. At sea-level in north Scotland. A common plant of rock gardens. Rose family. May-June.

White Flowers, 8 or more Petals contd

1 Chamomile

Strongly aromatic perennial, prostrate and turf-forming, with divided leaves. Daisy-like flower heads. Once widely grown on lawns to produce pleasant scent when trodden on, also made into tea for digestive complaints. Extracts from flowers distilled into tea have tonic and sedative value. Grows wild on some grassland and sandy areas. Daisy family. June-August.

2 Sneezewort

Greyish perennial up to two feet (60cm) with stiff, angular, hairy stems. Dark green leaves, narrow and pointed, saw-toothed and partly clasping stem. Flower heads in clusters resemble yarrow (p.136) but larger. Widespread in damp surroundings on heavier clay or acid soils. Can cause sneezing if powdered and dried. Daisy family. July-August.

3 Scentless Mayweed

A scentless, hairless, half-prostrate annual up to 18 inches (45cm). Finely toothed leaves and rather large daisy-like flower heads. The most common mayweed on farmland. Troublesome and resistant to chemical weedkillers. Daisy family. June onwards. *Note:* chamomiles and mayweeds look similar, both with daisy-like flower heads, but chamomiles have scales between the disc florets.

4 Cotton Grass

A sedge, not a grass. Grass-like perennial up to 18 inches (45cm) with purplish green, grooved and grass-like leaves. Flowers small, brownish with yellow anthers in a cluster of nodding heads at top of stem. These develop into fruits with conspicuous white threads in appearance like a ball of cotton wool. Widespread on swampy ground and in bogs on acid heaths and moors, seen as large white patches. Contributes to peat formation, mainly in west and north. April-May.

5 Feverfew

Downy perennial up to 18 inches (45cm) with scented, yellowish leaves. Flowers in loose clusters, daisy-like with yellow central disc florets, short and broad ray florets outside. Name derived from 'fibrifuge', i.e. putting fever to flight. Introduced from south-east Europe and cultivated for use in curing headaches. Now common on walls of gardens, churchyards and along roadsides. Daisy family. June-July.

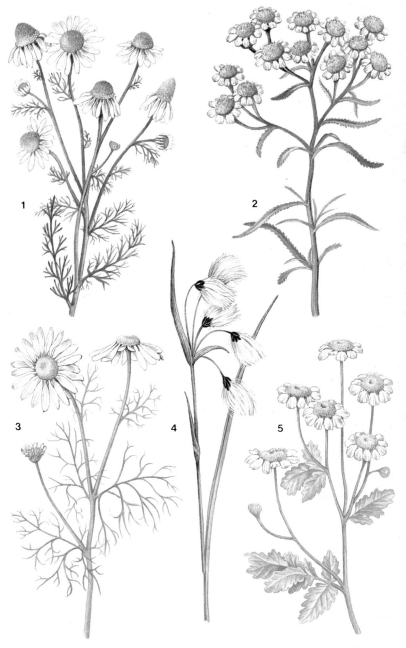

145

Yellow Flowers, up to Four Petals

1 Broom

Deciduous shrub, up to six feet (1.8m), resembling a spineless gorse with angled stems and more willow-like leaves, some small and lance-shaped, others longer, stalked and trefoiled. Large pea-shaped flowers, golden yellow, sometimes tinged with red. Pods somewhat hairy. Widespread, sometimes massed, on drier acid soils on heaths. Flowers have no nectar but are visited by bees for pollen. A trigger mechanism releases this when bee alights. Gave its name (originally as a nickname) to the royal family of Plantagenets, from the Latin *planta*, plant, *genista,* broom. Dried branches tied together once used as a broom. Pea family. May-June.

2 Gorse

Also called furze and whin. Thick-set, spiny evergreen bush up to eight feet (2.5m). Has furrowed stems bearing leaves in shape of rigid spines which help the plant to reduce water loss. Flowers pea-like, a deep golden yellow, almond scented, bloom throughout year, but mainly April-June in a fine display. Year-round flowering gave rise to the saying that 'kissing's out of season when gorse is out of bloom'. Found in dry places on heaths and downs. Greatly impressed Linnaeus, who fell on his knees in admiration when he visited England.

3 Evening Primrose

Downy, variable, erect plant with many hybrids grown in gardens. Robust growth with rigid stems up to four feet (120cm), covered with swollen, reddish hairs. Unstalked leaves, lance-like, slightly toothed and crinkly, spiral up stems. Large, four-petalled flowers slightly scented with reddish sepals. Opens on summer evenings, pollinated by moths. Locally widespread on waste ground and in sand-dunes. Willowherb family. June onwards.

4 Yellow Archangel

Resembles white deadnettle (p.134) in appearance, but less hairy, leaves darker and narrower. Yellow flowers with reddish-brown centres, acting as 'honey-guides', grow in whorls around stem. Has unpleasant smell when crushed, deterring plant-eating animals. Widespread in woodland on heavier soils. Mint family. May-June.

5 Tormentil

Small, slender, low-growing, creeping, downy perennial. Slender stems bearing three toothed leaflets with stipules at base. Four-petalled flowers on long stalks. Related to cinquefoil (p.154) with which it hybridises. Once used to cure the torment of stomach-ache, hence name. Common on moors, heaths and grassy places on acid soil. Rose family. May onwards.

Yellow Flowers, up to 4 Petals contd

1 Wallflower

Familiar garden plant, introduced from southern Europe. Biennial, up to 18 inches (45cm), grown as bedding plant in spring. Bushy growth with stiff, narrow, untoothed, lance-shaped leaves covered in hairs. Flowers scented, usually yellow, also orange or brick-red. Cylindrical pods. Wild plants always yellow, established on cliffs, walls and railway banks. Cress family. March-June.

2 Henbane

Unpleasant, somewhat ominous-looking, evil-smelling perennial up to four feet (120cm) with stout, hairy stem. Leaves sticky, covered in down, lower ones broadly toothed, upper ones narrow with more teeth. Groups of large, terminal, tubular flowers, creamy brown with network of purplish veins, and purple inside; outer calyx green. Once widely used for its sedative properties, derived from the alkaloid hyoscayamine. Local near sea, mainly in south. Nightshade family. June-September.

3 Common Melilot

Hairless biennial up to four feet (120cm) with slender stems bearing narrow, clover-like trefoil leaves. On top a long, terminal row of small, canary-yellow flowers producing brown, wrinkled pods. Common on waste ground. Pea family. June onwards. Similar white melilot grows later, has larger leaves but smaller flowers. Also common on waste ground and by roadside. Is grown as a form of clover for fodder. July onwards. Melilots introduced from Europe as medicinal herbs. Attractive to bees. Name comes from *melilotos,* Greek for 'honey clover'.

4 Wild Cabbage

Stout perennial. Woody stem covered in leaf scars when mature. A rounded mass of broad, fleshy leaves, wavy and greyish, stand free from stem, unlike cultivated forms. Buds forming on terminal branches open into pale yellow, four-petalled flowers. Occurs as native on chalk and limestone cliffs in parts of Wales and southern England. Escapes from gardens and allotments found on waste ground here and there. Is also ancestor to cultivated sprouts, cauliflower and broccoli, going back some 2000 years to Mediterranean origin. Cabbage family. May-August.

5 Yellow Rattle

Erect, stiff, hairless annual up to two feet (60cm), with opposite pairs of leaves, lance-shaped and toothed. Stem may show purple stains. Flowers surround upper stem with canary-yellow petals tinged with violet. Develop into swollen capsules when ripe, containing seeds which rattle when shaken, hence name. Frequent in grass as a semi-parasite connected to grass roots. Figwort family. May-July.

Yellow Flowers, up to 4 Petals contd

1 Bird's-Foot Trefoil

Attractive yellow pea flower. Rather prostrate perennial. Slender stems and unstalked trifoliate leaves with further pair of small, oval leaflets at base. A head of yellow flowers on a long stalk, often suffused with red or orange. Pods in a bunch resemble a bird's foot. Abundant and widespread in grassland, mainly on chalk or limestone, and in sand-dune slacks near sea. Pea family. May onwards.

2 Greater Celandine

Bushy perennial up to 18 inches (45cm) which contains an orange juice. Leaves fleshy and divided into irregular, round, toothed shape. Orange-yellow flowers in umbel-like bunches on stalks produce elongated seed-pods. Juice is said to act as a purgative and is also used as eye-lotion. Once commonly grown in gardens, is widespread along hedge-banks, on walls and around dwellings, preferring sandy or chalk soils. Not related to lesser celandine (p.156), but given same name because they both bloomed when the swallow arrived (Greek *chelidon,* swallow); or may refer to the myth that mother swallow used plant to restore eyesight of young which are blind at birth. Poppy family. April-October.

3 Common Cow-Wheat

Slender annual, a semi-parasite up to 12 inches (30cm), attached to roots of host plant. Leaves in pairs, lance-shaped, lower ones untoothed. Flowers in pairs and face same direction, arise from base of upper leaves, vary from pale to deep yellow. Black seeds resemble wheat grains. Widespread in woods and on moorland. Figwort family. May-September. Much rarer crested cow-wheat has more purple flowers with long, purple, toothed bracts in between. Local on edges of woods in eastern England.

4 Horseshoe Vetch

Similar to bird's-foot trefoil but has leaves with narrower and more numerous leaflets, bunches of smaller flowers without red colouring, and a darker outer calyx. Pods slender and wavy, said to resemble minute horseshoes strung together, hence name. Occurs mainly on chalk and limestone turf in north. Pea family. May-July.

5 Common Broomrape

The five broomrapes in Britain are all parasitic on other plants, and devoid of chlorophyll. Colour is some shade of yellow, brown or reddish. No proper leaves, instead the upright stem is covered in fleshy, pointed scales. Flowers same colour as plant, in rows forming a club-shaped head (more to one side in toothwort (p.134). Egg-shaped fruits produce dust-like seeds. Common broomrape, up to 15 inches (38cm), grows on various hosts but usually clover. Frequent in grassy areas, mainly in south and east. Broomrape family. June-September.

Yellow Flowers, 5-7 Petals

1 Cowslip

Familiar spring flower, scented, five petals orange at base, in bunches drooping to one side at top of stalk. Basal leaves similar to primrose but narrow abruptly at base. Name is a corruption of cow-slop because of its appearance on pasture with cattle. Other names: paigles, St Peter's keys and Our Lady's keys. Made into wine and used as a sedative. Less common than formerly in fields due to ploughing and herbicides, occurs more along hedge-banks and lanes, mainly on chalk soil. Will hybridise with primrose to form false oxlip. Primrose family. April-May.

2 Rock-Rose

Popular as rockery plants in various forms. Not a rose but a small, prostrate shrub with narrow, lanceolate leaves, downy white underneath, with narrow stipules at base. Flowers usually yellow on leafy, erect stalks. Widespread on chalk and limestone grassland. Rock-rose family. May-September.

3 Primrose

Favourite spring flower. A perennial up to 8 inches (20cm) with a rosette of crinkly, bright green leaves, somewhat downy, tapering towards base. Single flowers on stalks, pale yellow with deep yellow centres. Common and widespread in woods and hadgerows, less so near towns because of vandalism. Other name is primerole, derived from Latin and meaning 'little firstling'. In East Anglia is largely replaced by oxlip which has one-sided flowers in drooping head like cowslip. Flowers more like primrose. Up to a foot (30cm) tall. Leaves broad but narrow abruptly at base. Locally common in damp woods and pastures on clay on borders of Essex, Suffolk and Cambridgeshire.

4 Agrimony

Soft, hairy, unbranched perennial known as church steeples. Grows up to two feet (60cm), smells faintly of apricot. Large leaves in pairs with many-toothed leaflets, mixed with smaller leaves in between. Small flowers on a tall, narrow, tapering cluster. Fruits are oval with hooks and readily cling to clothing. Made into herb tea, and used for liver complaints. Gerard, the famous Holborn herbalist, said 'a decoction of the leaves is good for them that have naughty livers'. Widespread along roadsides and hedge banks. Rose family. June onwards.

5 Yellow Pimpernel

Slender, creeping perennial with opposite, oval and pointed leaves. Pairs of five-petalled flowers arise from leaf base on long stalks, opening in bright weather. Widespread in damp woodland. Similar-looking creeping Jenny, common in gardens, has blunter leaves closer together and larger flowers on shorter stems. Primrose family. May onwards. Other pimpernels are scarlet pimpernel (p. 190) and bog pimpernel. Latter is mat-forming with attractive bell-shaped pink flowers. Widespread on damp turf, fens and bogs, sometimes among moss.

1

2

3

4

5

Yellow Flowers, 5-7 Petals contd

1 Creeping Cinquefoil

Similar looking to tormentil (p.146) but with five petals and three to five large, toothed, palmate leaves (hence cinquefoil). Flowers much larger on long, thin stalks. A low, creeping perennial widespread on waste ground and roadsides. Rose family. June onwards. The marsh cinquefoil has large, dark purple, erect flowers and grows in marshy places.

2 Wood Avens

Hairy, erect perennial up to two feet (60cm). Much-divided, dark green leaves have rounded stipules at base. Small yellow flowers with space between each of five petals. Fruit burr-like, hooked and clings to clothes and animals. Also called herb bennet *(herba benedicta)* and said to ward off unholy spirits if worn. Scientific name *Geum* from Greek 'I taste'. Prized as a herb which 'comforteth the heart'. Also used as an astringent for colds. Widespread in woods and on hedge-banks. Rose family. June onwards.

3 Common Mullein

All species of mullein are biennial, with leaves in a rosette at the base, then alternating up unbranched main stem. Up to four feet (120cm). Terminate in elongated cluster of large, yellow, somewhat globular flowers. Many garden escapes. Common mullein or Aaron's rod is covered thickly with hairs. Leaves soft and lance-shaped, the base running down stem. Flowers close fitting, large, with five incurved petals and orange anthers. Widespread on dry banks. Figwort family. June-August.

4 Bog Asphodel

Creeping perennial with tufts of small, sword-shaped, often orange-tinged green leaves. Stiff, erect flowering stems up to six inches (15cm), bearing bright yellow six-petalled, star-shaped flowers, having orange anthers with white hairs. Fruit a conspicuous orange. Widespread in bogs and wet heaths, mainly in north and west. Once thought to affect sheep with foot-rot, hence scientific name *Narthecium ossifragrum* (bone breaker). Lily family. July-August.

5 Silverweed

Related to cinquefoil. Creeping habit and flowers similar looking, but different leaves which are toothed and alternate, large or small, along stem. Have a silvery appearance. Widespread in damp, grassy places and along pathways. Rose family. May-August.

Yellow Flowers, 5-7 Petals contd

1 Seaside Pansy

Member of violet family. Somewhat compact and tufted, with small, numerous, always yellow, five-petalled flowers. A local variety of the wild pansy or heartsease (p.170). Confined to sandy soil, in dunes and on East Anglian breckland. April onwards. Mountain pansy has larger yellow or violet flowers; occurs in hilly districts in north and Scotland; May-August. Heartsease resembles the latter but is taller and leafier, with small flowers and no runners; petals are purple, yellow or both; common in grassy places; April onwards. Field pansy has very small, creamy yellow flowers with patches of orange and streaks of violet. Found in arable fields; April onwards. *Note:* pansies related to violets but differ as follows: pansies usually annuals, with toothed, lance-shaped leaves with stipules, flowers variable, some have 'face'; violets perennial with toothed, more heart-shaped leaves and spring flowering, in shades of blue, sometimes white.

2 Tutsan

Bushy shrub up to three feet (90cm), with reddish stem bearing broad, oval, paired leaves ending in a cluster of five-petalled flowers with numerous stamens, giving a furry appearance. Fruit a juicy berry, first green, then red, and finally black. Local and widespread in shady woods and on cliff ledges. Leaves once used for healing wounds. Name derives from Norman *toute-saine*, all healthy. St John's wort family. June-August.

3 Common St John's Wort

Erect perennial up to two feet (60cm) with regular pattern of angled stems in pairs. Small oblong leaves in opposite pairs covered in transparent glands. Golden yellow flowers with many stamens. Widespread in hedge-banks, along paths and among scrub. St John's wort family. July onwards.

4 Goldenrod

Rather variable, unbranched, downy perennial up to two feet (60cm), bearing oblong, toothed leaves at base and slender, lance-shaped, unstalked leaves higher up. Separate clusters of small flowers with short ray florets and greenish-yellow sepal-like outer bracts. Locally frequent in dry woods and on heaths, dunes and also among rocks. Once prized for healing wounds. The much taller garden goldenrod from Canada has creeping rootstock, downy stems and longer leaves. Flower heads are smaller and a darker yellow, one-sided, forming dense clusters. A common escape on waste ground. Daisy family. July-September.

5 Lesser Celandine

Very early spring flower, unrelated to greater celandine (p.150). Low perennial with tubers. Long-stalked, heart-shaped, dark green leaves. Star-like, golden flowers on long stalks resemble buttercup but with narrower petals which close up in dull weather. Common in damp and shady places, especially in woodland. Wordsworth's favourite flower, engraved on his tomb. Also called pilewort for its reputed efficacy against haemorrhoids. Once a recommended cure for King's Evil or scrofula. Buttercup family. March-May.

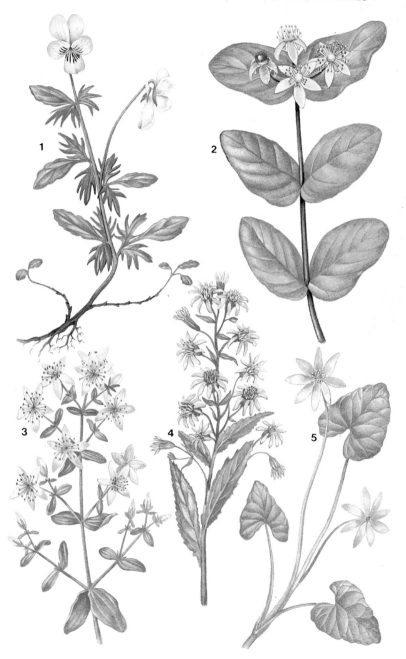

157

Yellow Flowers, 5-7 Petals contd

1 Creeping Buttercup

Rather low-growing, up to two feet (60cm), recognised by creeping runners. Troublesome weed in gardens. Common on waste ground, roadsides and in woods. Buttercup family. May onwards.

2 Tulip

Familiar spring flower in gardens. Introduced from Turkey during the seventeenth century and caused such a sensation that bulbs were bought and sold for ridiculous prices throughout Europe, and many fortunes were lost during this 'tulip mania'. Grows best on light, sandy soils and main growing areas are Holland and East Anglia. Wild tulip naturalised and occurs in meadows and orchards, mainly in lowland England. Grows up to two feet (60cm) and has yellow, fragrant flowers and narrow leaves. Name comes from Persian word for turban. Lily family. April-May.

3 Bulbous Buttercup

Recognised by down-turned sepals and swollen base to flower. Smaller more hairy flower than meadow buttercup, with ribbed stem and palmate leaves less deeply divided. Widespread on drier grassland. Buttercup family. Early March-June.

4 Daffodil

Many importations of foreign wild species cultivated into a bewildering variety of garden plants in many shapes and colours. Escapes seen in a number of places. Native wild daffodil has small nodding flowers with trumpet-like tube of inner petals, darker yellow than more open outer ones. Still widespread but local in damp woods and meadows. Scientific name *Narcissus* based on Greek myth of youth who saw his reflection in water, fell in love with it, jumped into the water and drowned. The flower appeared where he died. Daffodil family. March-April.

5 Meadow Buttercup

Tallest of buttercups, up to three feet (90cm). Smooth stem with deeply cut, palmate, stalked leaves. Rich yellow flowers with cup-shaped, outspread petals with upright sepals. Common in damp grassy places. Has suffered due to loss of meadows. May onwards. Buttercup family. *Note:* all buttercups have glossy yellow five-petalled flowers which produce nutlets (one-seeded fruits) in a tight-fitting head. Most have an acrid taste and are poisonous to varying degrees, have been known to harm farm animals. The wood goldilocks is non-acrid, smaller than meadow buttercup, with fewer flowers, sepals purple-tipped, leaves more kidney-shaped. Local in woods. The buttercup family also includes the spearworts, marsh marigold and water crowfoot, growing on or near water (see Pond and River Life, pp.236, 240, 242).

Yellow Flowers, 8 or more Petals

1 Coltsfoot

Early flowering perennial with leafless, white to purplish flower stems covered in overlapping purple scales. Flower head resembles small dandelion but contains both ray and disc florets, orange on outside. Head remains fairly closed, drooping after flowering, then rising to fruit and form 'clock'. Large leaves, heart-shaped (or horseshoe-shaped) and polygonal, appear much later and are covered in white down with black teeth along border. Dried leaves were used as herb tobacco to relieve asthma and coughs. Common on bare ground, especially clay. Daisy family. February-April, leaves appear in May.

2 Dandelion

Well-known, attractive composite, widely unpopular with gardeners, though admired by some. Rosette of basal leaves deeply toothed (French *dent-de-lion*) and pointing backwards. Large flower head with bright yellow ray florets only, on a hollow, leafless stem. A globular head of parachute seeds with beautiful symmetry. Sharp points on seeds help in clinging to soil. A milky fluid or latex, in all parts, used as laxative, tonic for liver complaints and for making crude rubber. Plant also made into wine and young leaves used in salads. Roots powdered for making coffee. Common on lawns, waysides, meadows, etc. Daisy family. March-October, mostly in May.

3 Mouse-Ear Hawkweed

Hairy perennial up to 15 inches (38cm) with basal rosette of elliptical, untoothed leaves covered in hairs above, white underneath. Single flower head on long, leafless stalk. Lemon yellow outer florets, reddish underneath. Has long creeping runners. Because seeds can ripen without fertilisation there is a great variation among hawkweeds. Parachute seeds non-feathery. Contains latex. Common on grassy turf. Daisy family. May onwards.

4 Greater or Rough Hawkbit

Hairy perennial up to 18 inches (45cm) with a rosette of erect, many-toothed leaves covered in forked hairs. Unbranched flower stem densely haired. Golden yellow dandelion-like flower head with swollen base, drooping in bud stage, closes in dull weather. Produces a fruiting 'seed clock' with feathery parachutes. Widespread among grass, especially on chalk soil. Daisy family. July onwards. *Note:* hawkweeds and hawkbits look superficially similar. The following identification points may help. Hawkweeds: contain latex; leaves more linear, less toothed in basal rosette; non-feathery parachutes; flower heads mainly yellow, seldom orange-red. Hawkbits: no latex; all leaves basal in rosette, toothed; feathery parachutes; golden yellow flower heads.

5 Common Fleabane

Woolly perennial up to 12 inches (30cm), with erect stem bearing alternate, lance-shaped, somewhat wrinkled, slightly-toothed leaves half clasping stem. Flat-topped flower heads in clusters, daisy-like with long outer rays golden yellow. Common in damp places, wet meadows, ditches. Supposed to drive away fleas, hence name. Daisy family. July-September.

Yellow Flowers, 8 or more Petals contd

1 Groundsel

A downy annual composite with many narrow, much-toothed leaves. Flower heads in clusters. Small yellow flowers without ray florets, rather cylindrical in shape, enclosed in tight-fitting bracts and on short stems. Seeds with hairy parachutes. Scientific name *Senecio* (from Latin *senex,* an old man) after white, hairy 'seed clock'. Very abundant on waste ground or neglected land, a nuisance to farmers, but a popular food for rabbits and cage-birds. Daisy family. All year round.

2 Common Ragwort

Hairless biennial up to four feet (120cm), stem branched at top. Closely related to groundsel. Deeply lobed, slightly sticky leaves. Lobes toothed. Flower head in dense clusters, flat topped, with downy disc florets and outer rings of yellow ray florets. Widespread and abundant on sandy and chalk grassland, also neglected pastures, often around rabbit warrens (but rabbits avoid it). Daisy family. June onwards.

3 Carline Thistle

Stiff, spiny biennial up to 12 inches (30cm). Rather low-growing with prickly, thistle-like leaves. Flower heads in groups. Flowers unusual yellow-brown colour without ray florets. Instead, spiny, leaf-like outer bracts and narrow sepal-like inner bracts with purple base. Close in dull weather. Locally common in grass, mostly on chalk and limestone. Daisy family. July onwards.

4 Oxford Ragwort

Branched annual up to 12 inches (30cm). Hairless with glossy leaves, lobed and toothed, lower ones stalked. Large flower heads, outer ray florets notched. Bracts tipped in black. Fruits with downy parachutes. An interesting history. Originates from volcanic soils in Mediterranean, introduced into Oxford Botanic Gardens during seventeenth century. Escaped onto walls of town, then onto cinders of railway tracks and carried in stages by passing trains to most parts of the country. Became a spectacular invader of bombed sites after Second World War as has a tolerance of burnt soil. Still common and seen on waste ground, waysides and along railway lines. Daisy family. April onwards.

5 Corn Marigold

Hairless, greyish annual up to 18 inches (45cm) with fleshy, pointed and toothed leaves clasping stem. Flower head golden yellow with conspicuous yellow ray florets, singly on stalks swollen underneath. Related to chrysanthemum. Locally common on arable land with sandy soil, a weed of cornfields but decreasing due to herbicides. Probably named after Virgin Mary. Daisy family. June onwards.

1

2

3

4

5

163

Blue Flowers, up to 4 Petals

1 Bluebell

Familiar scented spring flower, known as wild hyacinth in Scotland. Hairless, bulbous perennial, with fleshy, leafless stem up to 12 inches (30cm) tall. Leaves long and narrow, keeled, somewhat curled at tip, arise from bulb. Petals joined into a bell-shaped tube, forming blue, sometimes white, drooping flowers hanging one-sided along stem. (Garden form is a larger species native to Spain). Widespread, sometimes in large carpets, in woods and along hedgerows, also cliffs and mountains. The name hyacinth commemorates a Greek youth mourned by Apollo, the sun-god, when he was killed by a discus thrown by the jealous Zephyrus, god of the west-wind. Lily family. April-May.

2 Harebell

Rather slender creeping perennial, up to 12 inches (30cm), with small, rounded leaves near base and more slender stem leaves. So named because it occupies open ground where hares occur. Called bluebell in Scotland. Flowers tubular and nodding, blue, in loose cluster. Widespread on drier grassland of both chalk and acid soils. Bellflower family. July onwards.

3 Bugle

Perennial up to six inches (15cm), with hairy, square stem and runners. Leaves bronze-tinged in opposite, unstalked pairs, oval-shaped and somewhat crinkly. Flowers tubular, deep blue, sometimes pink or white, in angles of leaves and in cluster on top of stem. Once made into an ointment for wounds and ulcers. Widespread in damp woods and grass in shady places. Labiate family. April-June.

4 Brooklime

Spreading, fleshy perennial with rooting stems. Opposite pairs of oval, toothed, stalked leaves. Flower stems arise from these, bearing deep blue, sometimes pink flowers. Once used in salads to cure scurvy. One of the speedwells (p.166). Common in wet places. Figwort family. May-September.

5 Selfheal

Short, prostrate, downy perennial up to eight inches (20cm). Resembles bugle but with more pointed leaves; stalked leaves at base of stem. Flowers more purple in a squarish bunch. Common among grass. Labiate family. June onwards.

Blue Flowers, up to 4 Petals contd

1 Ivy-Leaved Toadflax

So-called 'mother of thousands'. Trailing, hairless perennial with rounded, alternate, ivy-shaped leaves. Flowers solitary, lilac, spurred with yellow honey-guide, resembling miniature snapdragon flower, arising on long stalks from base of leaves. Introduced from Europe. Seed pods curve away from light and deposit seeds in crevices. Common on walls and can spread up to three feet (90cm) across. Resistant to drought. Figwort family. April onwards.

2 Buddleia

So-called butterfly bush, attractive to butterflies and bees. A deciduous shrub up to ten feet (3m). Leaves long and pointed, somewhat wavy, in opposite pairs, downy underneath. Small mauve flowers in dense, elongated clusters at ends of long branches. Heavily scented. Introduced from China, now widespread in gardens, on walls, waste ground, quarries and railway lines, mainly in south. July onwards.

3 Ivy Speedwell

Prostrate annual bearing opposite pairs of stalked, ivy-shaped leaves, three to five lobed. Solitary pale lilac flowers arise from base of leaves. Common on disturbed ground. March-August. Other common speedwells: birdseye speedwell, also called germander speedwell, a weak perennial with bright blue flowers containing white 'eye' in centre; toothed, oval, pointed leaves. Common in hedge-banks and in grass. April-July. Water speedwell, a somewhat erect annual with long lance-shaped leaves and dense clusters of pale blue flowers. Common in wet places. June-August. Heath speedwell, a hairy perennial with creeping and rooting stem bearing pairs of toothed, oval leaves. Long side stems arising from base of leaves have clusters of deep blue flowers. Common in dry, heathy places. May-August.

4 Sea Stock

Very similar to garden stock. Grey perennial up to 15 inches (38cm) with rather woody stem bearing stiff, narrow, lance-shaped leaves. Large, fragrant, four-petalled flowers on stalks, white to purple Seed pods long and cylindrical. Established locally on sea cliffs in south. Cabbage family. May-July. Much larger great sea stock more brownish, downy and bushier with smaller flowers on short stalks. Very local on cliffs and dunes of north Devon. Cabbage family. June-August.

5 Common Field Speedwell

Also called Bauxam's speedwell. Commonest of the speedwell or veronica species. Low, sprawling, pale green annual with stalked, oval, toothed leaves. Long-stalked, sky-blue, four-petalled flowers with dark veining arise singly from base of leaves. Common on disturbed ground and in gardens. Figwort family. Flowers throughout the year.

Blue Flowers, up to 4 Petals contd

1 Ground Ivy

Low, soft, hairy perennial up to 12 inches (30cm). Strong-smelling and attractive to cats. Rooting runners with square stems bearing long-stalked leaves, kidney-shaped with blunt teeth. Flowers, in loose clusters at base of leaves, violet-blue, occasionally white, can be mistaken for violet flower. Common in woods and hedge-banks. Has no connection with ivy. Once used in brewing, before introduction of hops, to clear and flavour beer. Known as ale-hoof and included in Old Cries of London. Helps in digestive complaints. Labiate family. March-June.

2 Grape Hyacinth

Hairless, bulbous perennial up to nine inches (23cm), similar to garden plant, with long, narrow, rather limp leaves arising from bulb. Flowers small, egg-shaped and tubular, deep blue, in dense cluster on leafless flower stem, resembling bunch of small grapes. Local on dry grassland in breckland, Norfolk. Lily family. April-May.

3 Skullcap

Downy creeping perennial up to 12 inches (30cm) with short, stalked, lance-shaped, bluntly-toothed leaves in opposite pairs. Flowers in pairs in angles of leaves, bright blue with hooded shape. Scientific name *galericulata,* after Latin *galerium,* a Roman leather helmet, Common in wet places in grass and by streams. Labiate family. June-September.

4 Common Milkwort

Low, prostrate, slender perennial, up to 12 inches (30cm) with unstalked lance-shaped leaves, lower ones shorter and broader. Flowers along top of stem, mainly blue but can be mauve, pink or white. Five outer sepals, the two inner ones large and wing-like, enclose the five small true petals. feathery stamens in two groups joined in a Y pattern. Said to increase the milk yield of cattle. Common on heaths, dunes and in grass on acid soils. Milkwort family. May-September.

5 Thornapple

Stout annual up to three feet (90cm), with an unpleasant scent. Glossy, pointed, oval leaves, sharply toothed, resembling holly. Large purple or white trumpet-shaped flowers which produce prickly, green, chestnut-like fruit containing dark seeds. Introduced from Peru and grown for medicinal use. Cigarettes made from leaves to alleviate asthma. Seeds contain narcotic which acts on the nervous system causing dilation of pupils and hallucination. Occurs locally on waste ground here and there and appeared on bomb sites after the Second World War. Has caused harm to children. Nightshade family. July-October.

Blue Flowers, 5-7 Petals

1 Common Dog Violet

One of the commonest violets, best identified by the sepals, which are pointed. Stalks do not arise from the base of the plant and are only slightly downy. Leaves heart-shaped, as broad as long. Flowers violet-blue with five overlapping petals and a creamy spur. Common in woods, grassy places and mountains. Violet family. April-June. Similar-looking wood dog violet less robust, with smaller, paler and more upright flowers and dark spur. Petals do not overlap. Leaves paler, longer than broad. Early flowering by end of March. The sweet violet, only scented species, has long runners. Leaves and flower stalks arise in tufts along stem. Leaves heart-shaped, flowers violet, occasionally white, with blunt sepals. Hedge-banks and shady places. March-May.

2 Heartsease or Wild Pansy

Somewhat variable annual, resembling mountain pansy (p.156) but is taller, more leafy, has no runners and smaller flowers coloured blue, white and yellow. Locally common in grassy areas and cultivated ground. April onwards.

3 Pasque Flower

Low perennial up to nine inches (23cm), related to anemone. Hairy stalks with rings of leaves divided into silky strands. Flowers with five rich violet petals, silky underneath, and golden anthers. Produces head of seeds with silky plumes which last well into summer. Named after French word *Pâques,* Easter, which is when it flowers. Also called danesblood. One of our most beautiful flowers, now rare and local on chalk and limestone grassland; should not be disturbed. Cultivated plants readily available from nurseries. Buttercup family. April-May.

4 Columbine

Popular in gardens, in many colours. Perennial up to three feet (90cm). Trifoliate leaves at base of flowering stem. Flowers drooping, five-petalled, each with a spur, said to resemble a group of doves (Latin *columba,* a dove). Genuine wild specimens blue with short curved spurs, local on lime-rich soil in wet woodlands and fens. Buttercup family. May-July.

5 Greater Periwinkle

Creeping evergreen shrub, often in gardens. A trailing stem which roots at tip. Leaves broad, lance-shaped, stalked, leathery, dark green, in opposite pairs, persist through winter. Flowers violet, solitary and stalked on erect stems. Leaves once made into ointment for healing skin complaints. Usually an escape when found outside gardens. Periwinkle family. May-July. Lesser periwinkle, smaller in all parts, occurs more wild in woods and shady banks away from habitation, flowering later. May not be native.

Blue Flowers, 5-7 Petals contd

1 Clustered Bellflower

Stiff perennial up to 12 inches (30cm). Upper leaves alternate, narrow and pointed, clasping stem, lower ones broader and stalked. Flowers at top in a cluster, bright violet, trumpet-shaped. Locally frequent in chalk or limestone grassland. Bellflower family. June onwards. Related to garden Canterbury bell, which itself may be found wild where seeds have blown out of gardens.

2 Viper's Bugloss

Rough and hairy perennial up to six feet (1.8m). Long narrow leaves with prominent mid-rib. Flower buds at top drooping at first in bunches, pink then turning a vivid blue on opening. Trumpet-shaped with pink stamens. Outer sepals hairy. Name derives from belief in it as antidote for snake-bite, because seeds resemble shape of a viper's head; bugloss comes from Latin *buglossa,* ox-tongue, after rough, tongue-like leaves. Common in dry places on chalk, cliffs and in dunes, mainly near sea. Borage family. June-September.

3 Autumn Crocus

Bulbous perennial with lilac flowers resembling garden spring crocus but leaves appear in spring, then die before autumn flowering. Has only three short, pale stamens and a feathery orange stigma. Very local in grass, mainly north-west England. Iris family. September-October. Much larger meadow saffron also flowers in autumn after leaves have died. Rose-mauve, crocus-like flowers have six stamens (not three) with orange anthers on slender stems. Also called naked ladies. Bunches of lance-shaped leaves and egg-shaped fruits seen in spring. Poisonous to livestock. Drug colchinine extracted for relief of pain, such as gout. Localised mainly in East Anglia, in woodland. Lily family. August-September. *Note:* cultivated saffron crocus, *Crocus sativus,* of unknown origin, grown today in gardens and in the past to produce a valuable dyestuff and spice — a flourishing industry, once centred around Saffron Walden in Essex, survived for 500 years.

4 Cultivated Flax

Slender, hairless, cultivated, grey-green annual up to 18 inches (45cm). Upright stems with narrow, close-fitting, lance-shaped leaves. Bright blue, five-petalled flowers with pointed sepals. Widespread on waste ground as escape from cultivation. Flax has been grown for centuries for its fibre for making linen, one of the first fabrics. Also produces linseed oil. Flax family. June-October. Fairy flax, up to two feet (60cm), is a more bushy, slender annual with small, oval, pointed leaves in opposite pairs. Much smaller white flowers. Also called purging flax, and used for that purpose. Widespread in grassland on chalk and limestone. May onwards.

5 Monkshood

Dark green perennial up to six feet (1.8m). Fan-shaped leaves deeply divided. Terminal cluster of helmeted, deep blue or violet flowers resembling garden monkshood. A strong poison extracted from roots was once used on arrows for hunting, giving alternative name of wolfsbane. Wild plants localised along streams in shady places. Buttercup family. May-June.

Blue Flowers, 5-7 Petals contd

1 Borage

Robust, upright, roughly hairy annual, up to two feet (60cm). Grey-green oval leaves with prickly hairs have a cucumber flavour. Wide open, loosely grouped flowers, bright blue and star-like, with five pointed petals spaced out so that narrow sepals show in between. Column of deep red anthers in centre. Popular in herb gardens, widely used in salads and for flavouring drinks. Introduced by Romans, much praised by herbalists (as Pliny wrote: 'I Borage, bring always courage'). An escape, usually near gardens, on banks and hedgerows. June onwards.

2 Larkspur

Popular summer garden plant, up to 30 inches (75cm). Violet flowers, sometimes pink or white, made up of large outspread sepals. In centre, two small petals jointed in a spur and enclosed by upper sepal. Leaves finely divided. Attractive to bees. Occasional escapes along roadsides. A native of Mediterranean. Buttercup family. June-September.

3 Forget-Me-Not

Soft, hairy annual, up to nine inches (23cm), with hairy, oblong leaves bunched around upright stem. Flower stem arises above with rows of rather flat, saucer-shaped, grey-blue to pinkish flowers. Stem slowly uncurls as flowers open. Outer sepals have hooked hairs. Common in disturbed places, roadsides, woods and dunes. Borage family. April onwards. Wood forget-me-not, a creeping perennial, up to 12 inches (30cm), has larger, more pale blue flowers. Common in gardens as border plant, also in damp woodland as garden escape. May-June. Water forget-me-not, a creeping perennial, up to 12 inches (30cm) has angular stems and oblong, unstalked leaves. Flowers blue, or pink as in garden form. Common in wet places. June onwards.

4 Marsh Gentian

Weak-stemmed perennial with slender leaves in opposite pairs, and bearing at top a large, striking, azure-blue flower, trumpet-shaped and tinged with white. Local on damp, acid soil on heaths, not marshes, England and Wales. Gentian family. July-September. Taller, bushier field gentian has paler, lilac flowers, usually with only four petals, larger pair overlapping two smaller inner ones. Locally frequent in grassland on hills and in dunes, rare in south. July onwards. Gentians named after Gentius, a pirate king of Hungary (Illyria) who discovered the tonic properties of the root.

5 Stinking Iris

Also called gladdon and roast-beef plant, up to two feet (60cm). Long, slender, dark evergreen leaves grow in clusters. Flattened flower stem bears short-lived, neat-looking bloom, a slaty purple-grey with dark veining. Bright green fruit opens to reveal round, bright red-orange, fleshy seeds. Leaves produce upleasant, sickly smell when crushed. Poisonous to livestock. Local in woods on chalk and limestone, also cliffs nea. sea. Iris family. June-August. Closely related to yellow flag iris and to white Florentine lily (fleur-de-lys). Latter grown in herb gardens to produce orris powder for cosmetics.

Blue Flowers, 8 or more Petals

1 Michaelmas Daisy

Familiar garden perennial introduced from North America. Various species, commonest has blue flowers. Related to aster. Tall plant, up to five feet (1.5m), with daisy-like flower heads in thick clusters. Propagated by cuttings in spring and divisions in autumn. Attractive to late-flying butterflies and bees. Discarded garden plants may turn up on railway banks and rubbish tips. So named because it flowers around Michaelmas (September 29). Daisy family. September-October.

2 Spear Thistle

Commonest thistle. A downy biennial up to five feet (1.5m), with sharply-pointed, narrow-toothed leaves running down stem. Flower head usually solitary, reddish-purple, surrounded by a collar of prickly, sepal-like bracts. The emblem of Scotland. Very common on waste ground and grassy places. Popular food plant of goldfinches. Daisy family. June onwards. (See also pp.194 and 196).

3 Teasel

Unmistakable biennial, up to six feet (1.8m), with prickly, conical flower head surrounded by small, narrow leaves; flower head persists through winter on dead stem. Oval, pointed, prickly leaves on prickly stem, forming rosette at base. Leaves cupped and hold water. Small purple flowers surrounded by spines. Popular with goldfinches and used as decoration, also in teasing newly-woven cloth to raise nap. Locally common in rough grass and bushy undergrowth. Teasel family. July-August.

4 Field Scabious

Hairy perennial, up to three feet (90cm), with elongated, lobed leaves. Flower head button-shaped, lilac-blue with pink anthers standing up in pin-cushion fashion. Two rows of outer, lance-shaped bracts. Common in dry, grassy areas, meadows and hedge banks. Teasel family. June onwards. Much smaller, more slender, small scabious has more finely cut leaves and pink, more rounded flower heads. Local on chalk grassland and in dunes. July onwards. The devilsbit scabious is shorter with short root (bitten off by the Devil?), has undivided leaves and deep blue flower head with single row of bracts. June-October. Scabious roots once used for treating skin complaints.

5 Cornflower

Greyish, downy annual, up to two feet (60cm), with thin, elongated, bristly leaves. Large single flower heads, rich blue in swollen stem apex, with large disc florets spreading outwards. Many garden varieties. Old name of hurt-sickle refers to damage it once caused by blunting reaper's sickle. Fairly common in grassy places, chalk and limestone but much decreased in cornfields due to herbicides. Daisy family. July onwards.

Red Flowers, up to 4 Petals

1 Hemp Nettle

Stiff, hairy annual, up to two feet (60cm). Square stem with swollen joints. Opposite pairs of broad, toothed, lance-shaped leaves. Flowers pale pink-purple in whorls around stem at base of leaves. Sepals have bristly teeth. Resembles red dead-nettle (p.182). Common in damp woods, fens and on arable land. Labiate family. July-August.

2 Betony

Unbranched perennial, up to 12 inches (30cm). Leaves stalked, oblong with rounded teeth, placed some distance apart on square stem; basal leaves somewhat arrow-shaped. Flowers mainly terminal, brightly coloured reddish-purple. Once a remedy for digestive and liver disorders. Locally frequent on heaths and in bushy places. Labiate family. June-September.

3 Foxglove

Handsome, downy perennial, unbranched, up to four feet (120cm), well-known in gardens. Forms a rosette of leaves in first year, flowers and seeds in next. Leaves large, broad, lance-shaped and wrinkled. Long, downy flowering stem with rows of large, hanging, pink-purple, bell-shaped flowers, paler and spotted inside. Lower flowers open first. Numerous minute seeds produce drug digitalin, a heart stimulus (Latin *digitalis*, a finger). Other names are 'fairy thimbles' and 'dead men's bells'. Common in woods, heaths and hedge-banks, mainly on acid soil. Figwort family. June-September.

4 Common Calamint

Hairy perennial smelling of mint, up to 18 inches (45cm). Sharply angled flower branches in opposite pairs on square main stem. Pale pink-violet flowers with dark spots, stalked on side branches, arising from base of small, slightly toothed leaves. Local on dry chalk and limestone grass, mainly south England and Wales. Labiate family. July-September.

5 Corn Poppy

Well-known flower, commonest in south. Annual, up to two feet (60cm) with hairy stem. Large flowers with four deep-red petals, often with dark patch at base, loosely crumpled and drooping in bud stage. Two green sepals fall off as bud opens. Numerous blackish stamens. Leaves deeply branched. A hairy seed-case with ring of holes scatters seeds in pepper-pot fashion. Produces milky white juice. Widespread along roadsides, railway banks and on arable land, especially on disturbed ground. Poppy family. Flowers June-October. Long-headed poppy commonest in north. Flowers paler red, without dark patch, more compact. Seed-case hairless, more elongated. Juice may turn yellow. Opium poppy is more greyish, up to four feet (120cm), with roughly-toothed, triangular leaves, flowers large, lilac with purple patch at base of petals. A garden escape. June-August. Welsh poppy in gardens, up to 12 inches (30cm), a perennial with pale green, lobed leaves and contains yellow juice. Uncommon escape among damp, shady rocks, mainly Wales. June-August.

Red Flowers, up to 4 Petals contd

1 Fuchsia

Well-known garden and pot plant, named after the botanist, Dr Fuchs. Introduced from North America. Deciduous shrub up to six feet (1.8m) in wild form. Paired opposite leaves pointed and toothed. Hanging funnel-shaped flowers with deep, plum-red petals, bulbous base and prominent stamens. Mainly a hedgerow plant, often mixed with wild rose, in south-west England and west Ireland. Willowherb family. June onwards.

2 Cross-Leaved Heath

Downy, greyish, low shrub, up to 12 inches (30cm), with leaves in whorls of four (i.e. cross-shaped), their margins rolled inwards. Clusters of small, drooping, bell-shaped flowers, rose pink in colour. Mostly on wetter parts of heaths and in bogs. Heath family. June onwards.

3 Himalayan Balsam

Tall handsome plant up to five feet (1.5m). Has reddish grooved stems, lance-shaped leaves bordered with red teeth. Large pink-purple flowers arranged in a broad lower lip, small upper hood with spur behind, on long stalks, resembling a lantern. Also called jumping jack, as ripe seed pods burst at slightest touch. Well established, sometimes in large masses, along borders of rivers and streams. Balsam family. July onwards. The native balsam, or touch-me-not, has yellow flowers and is localised in damp woods in north-west England and North Wales, rare elsewhere. July-September.

4 Heather

The true heather, also called ling. Familiar low evergreen, up to 18 inches (45cm), which turns vast areas of moorland purple in late summer — hence the 'bonnie blue hills' of Scotland. Numerous small leaves in two opposite rows overlapping. Small flowers, occasionally white (lucky heather), hang along numerous side branches. Old Norse name *lyng.* Attractive to bees, and hives taken on to moors by bee-keepers. Also favourite food of red grouse. Often set on fire to encourage young shoots on grouse moors. Heather contributes to peat formation. Abundant on moors, heaths, bogs and mature dunes. Heath family. Late flowering, August-September.

5 Bell Heather

Low evergreen shrub with whorls of short, elongated, dark green or bronze leaves, down-curved, interspersed with bell-shaped, red-purple flowers. Abundant, mainly on drier parts of heaths and moors. Heath family. June onwards.

Red Flowers, up to 4 Petals contd

1 Great Willowherb

Tallest and largest species of willowherb, up to six feet (1.8m), very hairy. Leaves in opposite pairs, unstalked, half-clasping stem. Purple-pink flowers stand erect with long female stigma. Abundant in wet places alongside ditches and streams. Also called codlins-and-cream. Willowherb family. July-September.

2 Red Deadnettle

Related to white deadnettle (p.134) but smaller in all parts, up to nine inches (23cm). Rather prostrate downy annual with square stem tinged purple when damaged. Stalked leaves oval, pointed, wrinkled and toothed. Flowers pale pink or darker, small upper lip hooded, in angles of upper leaves. Common weed of cultivation. Attractive to bees. Labiate family. Flowers all year round.

3 Rosebay Willowherb

Handsome strong-growing perennial, up to five feet (1.5m), with narrow lance-shaped leaves, rather curly. A long, open cluster of pink-purple, four-petalled flowers, sepals more reddish at ends of branches. Lower flowers open first. Four-sided pods split open to scatter numerous silky-haired seeds. Once rare, now widespread on waste ground, woodland clearings, railway lines, on walls, and especially where fire has occurred. Made a spectacular invasion of bombed sites after Second World War. Called by Londoners the bombweed, and in America, where sheets appear after a prairie fire, fireweed. Willowherb family. June-September. *Note:* There are various other species of willowherb in Britain with smaller flowers. All are hairy, often with reddish stems, and spread by shoots from base of main stem. Named after their willow-like leaves.

4 Snapdragon

Familiar garden plant in various colours, mainly red in wild. Bushy perennial up to 15 inches (38cm). Leaves narrow and lance-shaped. Flower has petals forming upper and lower lobes which open when squeezed or entered by a bee. Once considered a protection against dragons and witches. Naturalised on walls, railway banks, mainly in south. Figwort family. July-September.

5 Common Lousewort

Low creeping perennial, up to 12 inches (30cm), a semi-parasite on other plants. Many-stemmed with leaves separated into toothed leaflets. Terminal flowers bright pink, petals in two lobes, upper one longer. Sepals with swollen base and toothed border. Once believed to rid sheep and cattle of lice. Common on heaths, moors and bogs. Figwort family. May-September.

183

Red Flowers, up to 4 Petals contd

1 Henbit

Closely related to red deadnettle (p.182), up to 12 inches (30cm), with more rounded, deeper-toothed leaves without stalks, clasping stem. Flowers brighter, more upright, in whorls around stem, more widely separated. Local weed of cultivated ground. Labiate family. April-August.

2 Squinancy Wort

Small, low, slender perennial, thin-stemmed with whorls of four thin elongated leaves. Flowers in clusters at tips, pinkish white and veined, tubular with four lobes, tinged pink. No outer sepals. Name a corruption of quincy, a throat infection, for which it was used as a soothing gargle. Local on chalk and limestone turf, also dunes, mainly in south. Bedstraw family. June-September.

3 Hedge Woundwort

Dark green, hairy, creeping perennial, up to three feet (90cm). Strong-smelling. Leaves hairy, heart-shaped, toothed and stalked. Flowers at top of square stem beetroot-coloured with whitish markings, in ascending whorls. A bristle-like bract at base of each. Once used in dressing wounds. Common in hedge-banks and shady corners. Labiate family. June onwards. Similar looking marsh woundwort has narrower leaves often without stalks. Flowers more pale purple, also less aromatic. Widespread near water and along ditches. Hybridises with hedge woundwort. July onwards.

4 Marjoram

Downy, aromatic perennial, up to two feet (60cm). Slightly reddish, slender, twin-branched stems at top of plant arising from base of oval, pointed leaves. Heads of small, pale purple flowers enclosed in purple bracts. Used as culinary herb. Widespread in grassy places on chalk and limestone. Labiate family. July-September. *Note:* Many varieties in cultivation, long-prized for oil used in perfumery, also added to mixed herbs to improve flavour. Enjoys sunshine. Originally from sunny slopes of southern Europe. Scientific name *Origanum* from Greek *oros,* mountain, and *ganos,* joy.

5 Whortleberry

Southern name for bilberry. Erect, woody plant, up to 18 inches, (45cm), with angled twigs bearing oval, pointed leaves. Flowers single or in pairs, globe-shaped, hanging, a dull greenish-pink. Fruit an edible berry, first green turning black with grape-like bloom. Gathered for making jam or pies. Important food for grouse. Abundant on heaths, moors, conifer woods, on acid soil, also in mountains. Heath family. April-June. Will hybridise with cowberry, which has groups of white or pinkish, open-mouthed flowers at end of stems. Fruit red and bitter. Local on moors in north and west. May-June. Cranberry has thin, creeping stems with small oval leaves in pairs. Flowers bright pink with petals bent backwards, at end of each branch. Acid fruit pear-shaped, whitish, spotted red. Used as sauce with venison and turkey. Local in wet places in bogs and between sphagnum moss. June-July.

Red Flowers, up to 4 Petals contd

1 Rest-Harrow

Woody, downy perennial, up to 12 inches (30cm) with tough stems creeping and rooting along ground. Small, toothed, oval and trefoil leaves with pronounced teeth and leaf-like stipules at base. Pink, pea-like flowers, hooked on more reddish lower lobe. In earlier days a nuisance to farmers because it 'arrested the harrow'. Common on dry grassland on chalk and limestone, also dunes. Pea family. July-September.

2 Cuckoo Flower

Also called milkmaid and lady's smock. Unbranched perennial, up to 15 inches (38cm). Leaves divided into leaflets along stem forming a rosette at base. Flowers on top large with four petals, white to deep lilac, yellow anthers. Said to bloom when cuckoo arrives. Name also possibly due to presence of cuckoo spit, actually a frothy protection of the frog-hopper nymph. Common in damp places in meadows, woods and along ditches. Cabbage family. April-June.

3 Common Vetch

Somewhat sprawling, variable annual grown as fodder plant. Leaves with four or more leaflets ending in a branched tendril. Solitary purple flowers on short stalks along stem. Common as escape from cultivation in grass and along roadsides. Pea family. June-September.

4 Thyme

Commonly grown in rock gardens. Prostrate, aromatic perennial forming a dense mat with creeping and rooting runners. Opposite pairs of oval leaves, small and short-stalked, twisted into a flattened position along ground. Small reddish-purple flowers in bunches at end of square stems. Attractive to bees. Once used as insect repellent, also well-known culinary herb. Widespread in dry grass, heaths and dunes, also rock ledges, in south-east England, mainly on chalk downs. Labiate family. June-August.

5 Fumitory

Somewhat variable annual, low and bushy or climbing up to three feet (90cm). Leaves much divided, feathery, a smoky grey giving plant its name (Latin *fumus terrae,* smoke of the earth). Four-petalled, pink-purple flowers, outer pair enclosing inner ones. An 'official' herb once used for many ailments. Widespread weed of waste places and cultivated ground. Fumitory family. May onwards.

Red Flowers, 5-7 Petals

1 Dovesfoot Cranesbill

Small, low and somewhat prostrate, hairy annual, up to 8 inches (20cm). Flowers often in pairs, pinkish-purple, petals notched and narrowing at base, sepals pointed. Fruit wrinkled. Commonest of small-flowering species, in dry fields, waste ground and dunes. Geranium family. April-September.

2 Common Storksbill

Small, prostrate annual, up to 12 inches (30cm), somewhat hairy with sticky leaves to which sand grains may stick. Leaves divided into leaflets. Flowers in loose clusters with deep pink petals and a black spot at base. Flowers soon fall off. Is self-pollinating. Common in dry and sandy places, especially in dunes and near sea. Geranium family. May-September. Sea storksbill (p.266) is smaller.

3 Herb Robert

Hairy, variable, strong-smelling annual up to 15 inches (38cm). Rather reddish, especially on stem. Leaves triangular, deeply lobed, fern-like. Flowers pink with pale lines, anthers orange. Common in shady places, on walls and rocks. Geranium family. April onwards.

4 Pink Campion

Hairy perennial, up to two feet (60cm). Leaves oval, pointed, lower ones clasping stem. Clusters of large flowers with rose-pink, notched petals, bulbous sepals more reddish and toothed. Male and female on separate plants, as with white campion with which it hybridises (p.136). Common in woodland, hedge-banks, cliffs, mountains. Pink family. April onwards.

5 Bloody Cranesbill

Very striking, hairy, spreading perennial, up to 12 inches (30cm). Leaves small and deeply cut. Large, handsome, purple-crimson flowers singly on stalks, petals with shallow notch. Local in dry grassy areas, among rocks on limestone, also dunes. Geranium family. June-August. Meadow cranesbill has bright blue flowers on long stalks, up to two feet (60cm), with deeply-lobed, long-stalked leaves. Local in grassland. June onwards.

Cranesbills and Storksbills

Non-woody plants of geranium family. Cranesbills have deeply-cut, lobed leaves with stipules at base. Flowers with five mainly pink to purple petals, five sepals with sharp tips. Fruit uncurled with long, pointed beak, i.e. like a crane's bill. Storkbills have leaves divided into toothed leaflets (pinnate). Fruit has a spiral twist to its beak. Flowers pink to purple.

Red Flowers, 5-7 Petals contd

1 Scarlet Pimpernel

Rather prostrate annual with oval, pointed, unstalked leaves in pairs on square stem. Also called poor man's weatherglass as reacts to weather, closing when sun goes in. Flowers mainly bright red with purple centres, petals fringed with hairs on drooping stalks. Common on bare ground, ploughed fields and dunes. Primrose family. June onwards. See also yellow pimpernel (p.152).

2 Dodder

A leafless parasite without roots which twines its thin, red and wiry stem anti-clockwise around other plants, especially clover, gorse and heather. Sends in suckers to tap nourishment. Small flowers tinged white in unstalked clusters. Small, bell-shaped, pointed and waxy petals are pinkish, pointed sepals more reddish. Mainly found in England and Wales. Bindweed family. July-September.

3 Redleg

Also called persicaria or redshank. Somewhat sprawling annual, up to 18 inches (45cm), with reddish dividing stem. Leaves lance-shaped, silky white underneath with darker patch in middle. Oblong cluster of pink flowers at top of erect branches. Common weed on bare wet earth and along ditches. Dock family. June onwards.

4 Common Centaury

Rather stiffly erect, variable perennial, up to 12 inches (30cm), with a rosette of pointed, oval, veined leaves in pairs up the stem. Open cluster of pink flowers on short branches. Sepals strongly toothed. Locally common in dry grass on chalk, limestone and dunes. Gentian family. June onwards. Yellow-wort, also in dunes, looks similar but has yellow flowers.

5 Red Valerian

Greyish perennial, up to three feet (90cm), with upright stem bearing tufts of oval, pointed leaves, lower ones stalked. Red, sometimes white, flowers in dense cluster at top of stem, narrowly tubular with spur at base. Single stamen. Locally frequent on walls, cliffs, quarries, mostly in south and west. Valerian family. May onwards. Larger common valerian, up to four feet (120cm), with similar flowers but more pale pink with three stamens, leaves with toothed leaflets. Common in woods and rough grass. June-August.

191

Red Flowers, 5-7 Petals contd

1 Common Bistort

Unbranched perennial, up to two feet (60cm). Strongly triangular leaves abruptly narrowing into leaf stalk. Lower leaves arrow-shaped on short stalk. Small flowers pink in compact spike, rather similar to redleg (p.190). Latin *bistorta*, twice twisted, referring to contorted roots. Common in wet pastures in hilly country, especially north. Dock family. June-August.

2 Houndstongue

Soft perennial, up to two feet (60cm), with mousy smell when leaves crushed. Greyish leaves lance-shaped and downy, alternate along stem. Small, deep maroon flowers with five close-fitting petals and outer, pointed sepals. Four flattened, hooked fruits. Leaves said to resemble a dog's tongue and once used to cure dog bites. Local on bare soil and sandy turf, in dunes and quarries. Borage family. May-June.

3 Butterwort

Unusual insectivorous plant (see also sundew, p.140). Sticky, hairy perennial with flat rosette of leaves around base of stem, yellow-green with incurved edges and a sticky surface. Margin rolls inwards to digest trapped insect, extracting nitrogen, enabling the plant to grow in acid and peaty, nitrogen-deficient soil. Flowers single on leafless stem, deep violet with long spur. Common in bogs, on wet heaths, moors and between rocks on mountains. Butterwort family. May-June.

4 Soapwort

Somewhat resembles garden sweet william. Creeping perennial with thick and brittle stem, up to two feet (60cm). Lance-shaped leaves in opposite pairs. Bunch of rose-pink, fragrant flowers, occasionally double. Originally introduced from Europe and grown near woollen mills as leaves were formerly crushed and boiled to produce lathering liquid used for washing cloth. Occurs widely by roadsides and streams. Pink family. June-September.

5 Common Mallow

Rough, hairy perennial, up to three feet (90cm), with leaves crinkly and ivy-shaped. Handsome, pink-purple flowers, the five-lobed petals marked with darker lines. Fruits disc-shaped, resembling small cakes, hence country name of cheesecake. Common on waste ground, roadsides and near houses, especially by the sea. Mallow family. June-October. Marsh mallow more greyish, has soft feel, paler pink flowers, leaves broad and pointed. Roots used in marsh mallow confectionery. Local on salt marshes, along ditches and dykes by the sea. Becoming rare due to drainage. August-September. Tree mallow, a well-branched perennial, up to eight feet (2.4m), more woody and downy. Ivy-shaped leaves somewhat crinkly. Flowers pinkish, darker at base. Sepals cup-shaped, forming three broad lobes. Local on cliffs and rocks by sea, mainly in south-west. July-September.

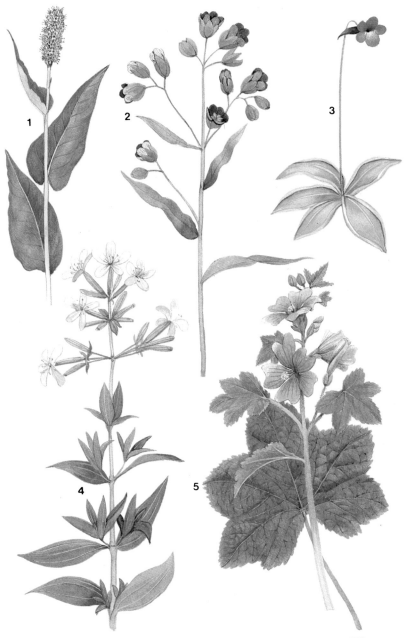

193

Red Flowers, 8 or more Petals

1 Greater Knapweed

Attractive perennial, up to two feet (60cm), with stiff, grooved, wiry stems. Elongated, lobed leaves, similar to thistle but lacking bristles. Flowerheads large, purple with many elongated, spreading outer disc florets with pointed petals. Head enclosed in compact, globular base of dark green, scaly bracts. Avoided by cattle and can become a serious weed. (See also hardhead, p.196). Common in grassy places on chalk and limestone. Daisy family. July onwards.

2 Scotch Thistle

Also called cotton thistle. Tall, stout biennial, up to four feet (120cm). Stem whitish with cottony down and winged with raised triangular spines. Spiny, oblong leaves. A globular, solitary flowerhead pale purple without ray florets, enclosed in sepal-like bracts with yellow spines. Local on waste ground and roadsides, rare in Scotland despite its name. Daisy family. August-September. The large, handsome woolly thistle has grey, woolly stem, deeply cut leaves cottony underneath. Large, globular, purple flowerheads with spiny bracts thickly mixed with white woolly hairs. Local on chalk and limestone grassland, chalk-pits and open scrub in England and Wales. July-September.

3 Amphibious Bistort

Similar to common bistort (p.192) but found in different habitat. Creeping and rooting perennial, up to three feet (90cm), with thick, long-stalked, lance-shaped, blunt-based leaves which float in aquatic forms, more short-stalked and rounded in land forms. Small pink flowers in compact head, more so than in common bistort. Frequent close to, or standing in shallow water. Dock family. July-September.

4 Butterbur

Conspicuous perennial, up to 12 inches (30cm), with thick, hollow stem covered in pointed bracts. Huge leaves up to three feet (90cm) across, long-stalked, heart-shaped and toothed, resembling rhubarb leaves, appear after flowering, in thick patches. Sexes on separate plants. Female flowerheads pale lilac without ray florets form dense clusters. Male flowerheads with white anthers, more separated. Frequent on damp soil along ditches, streams and in water meadows. Named after shape of bur-like flowerheads. Visited by bees. Daisy family. Flowers March-May, before leaves appear.

5 Red Clover

Perennial up to 18 inches (45cm), with oval, trifoliate leaves bearing a pale patch. Flowerhead densely globular, varying from pink to purple. Used in wine-making and by bee-keepers. Cultivated forms, as with white clover (p.142). Pea family. May onwards. Very similar zig-zag clover has zig-zag stems and flatter, more reddish flowerheads.

1

2

3

4

5

Red Flowers, 8 or more Petals contd

1 Creeping Thistle

Hairless, creeping perennial with few branches, up to five feet (1.5m). Only British thistle with flowerheads clustered together at top of stem. Rather small, pale lilac heads, sexes on separate plants. Close-fitting, conical base of more purple bracts. Prickly leaves on spineless stem. A weed of fields, roadsides and waste ground. Daisy family. June-September.

2 Stemless Thistle

Also called dwarf thistle. Very low perennial, up to six inches (15cm), with basal rosette of shiny curled leaves, deeply cut into prickly side leaflets. In centre a single, unstalked flowerhead with wide crown of reddish-purple disc florets. Below, a tight conical base of compressed bracts. Frequent locally in turf on chalk and limestone, mainly in south. Daisy family. July onwards.

3 Burdock

Stiff, downy perennial, up to three feet (90cm), many-stemmed with broad, oval, pointed leaves alternating, lower ones up to 12 inches (30cm) long with hollow stalks. Flowerheads thistle-like on short stalks in open clusters between leaves and without ray florets. Outer bracts purple-tipped and hooked, closing up to form the fruit (bur), which readily sticks to clothing and animal fur. Roots and leaves once used in treatment of skin complaints and leprosy, also the 'bite of serpentes and madde dogges'. Common along roadsides, in woods and waste ground. Daisy family. July-September.

4 Musk Thistle

Stately, somewhat downy biennial with solitary, drooping, scented, reddish-purple flowerheads without ray florets, on stalks without spines. Purplish bracts below, large, spreading and spiny tipped. Stem prickly with very spiny leaves. Locally frequent on grassland, in quarries and on waste ground on chalk and limestone. Daisy family. June onwards.

5 Hardhead

Also called lesser knapweed or black knapweed. Similar but smaller than greater knapweed (p.194). Stem ribbed and leaves lance-shaped. Has more compact, hard, purple flowerhead. Bracts overlap, dark brown to black with fine teeth forming hard base. Common in grassy areas. Daisy family. June onwards.

197

Green or Inconspicuous Flowers

1 Dog's Mercury

Hairy, creeping perennial, up to 15 inches (38cm), with unpleasant smell. Unbranched stem with broadly lance-shaped, dark green and toothed leaves in opposite pairs. Small, greenish flowers on stalks from base of leaves, sexes on separate plants. Male flowers in rows along branches, female more hidden in groups of two to four. Large patches occur, usually of plants of one sex. Very common in woods and shady places, from lowland to mountains, especially in beech woods. Spurge family. February-May.

2 Herb Paris

Easily recognised perennial, up to 12 inches (30cm), with unbranched stem. Usually four unstalked, oval and pointed leaves at top of stem only, veined underneath. In centre unusual flower with very narrow, pointed, pale yellow-green petals and four lance-shaped sepals, anthers yellow. Produces a black berry. Lily family. May-June.

3 Deadly Nightshade

Stout, bushy, downy perennial, up to six feet (1.8m). Broad, oval, pointed, stalked leaves. Solitary, drooping, dull purple, bell-shaped flowers arise slightly from base of leaves. fruit green turning to glossy black, cherry-sized berries with brown, lobed sepals still attached. Whole plant poisonous and has caused death. Local among bushes and in quarries, mainly on chalk. Nightshade family. June-August.

4 Ratstail Plantain

Coarse, stout perennial, up to 15 inches (38cm). Rosette of broadly oval, stalked, toothed, wavy leaves, strongly veined underneath. Small, tightly fitting flowers with purple anthers in long greenish row up to six inches (15cm), tail-like, at top of central stem. Very common weed on bare ground, footpaths and waysides. Plantain family. June onwards. Ribwort plantain, up to two feet (60cm), has long-stalked, slightly-toothed, lance-shaped leaves, ribbed underneath. Flowers in dense, oval cluster on furrowed stalk, green turning dark brown, with prominent pale yellow anthers. Abundant in grass, waste ground and on lawns. April onwards. Hoary plantain, up to 12 inches (30cm), has flat rosette of elliptical leaves narrowing into short stalk, prominently ribbed. Dense cluster of greyish flowers with purple stamens on unfurrowed stalk. Locally common in grass and lawns, on chalk and limestone. May-August.

5 Sedge

Sedges are grass-like flowering plants, differing from true grasses in having three-sided, never hollow, stems and no leaf junctions. Separate male and female flowerheads in most species, on same stem, males above, all without petals or sepals. Anthers bright yellow and hanging. Fruit a nutlet. About 80 British species, mostly in damp and marshy surroundings. Example shown is pendulous sedge, one of the largest, up to five feet (1.5m), with drooping flower branches. Widespread in woodland, especially on clay. May-June.

Green or Inconspicuous Flowers contd

1 Common Sorrel

Unbranched perennial, up to two feet (60cm), with long-stalked, arrow-shaped leaves, upper ones clasping stem. A head of tightly-packed, dull green flowers, turning crimson when fruiting. Once used in salads and as a drink to aid digestive complaints. One of the commonest grassland plants, can be a troublesome weed. Old French *surelle*, little acid plant. Dock family. May-August. Sheep's sorrel is smaller, more slender, with more strongly arrowed leaves. Small flowers more widely spaced. Common on heaths and grassland on acid soils. Dock family. May-August.

2 Mistletoe

Well-known Christmas decoration. Woody, yellow-green evergreen. Semi-parasitic perennial with regular branching, terminal leaves in pairs, narrow and leathery. Small, inconspicuous, greenish flowers, female producing sticky white berries eaten by birds such as mistle thrush, which wipes its beak on branch to which seeds adhere and may germinate. Host trees mainly apple and poplar, rarely oak as recorded in Celtic mythology. Kissing under mistletoe may be connected with fertility rite. Plant cut down by Druids with golden knife as a magic ritual. Widespread, in woods, orchards and old gardens in England and Wales. Mistletoe family. Flowers March-May.

3 Moschatel

Small perennial, up to four inches (10cm), with long-stalked, trifoliate leaves arising from base on long stem, somewhat similar to wood anemone. Small greenish flowers at top of stem in bunches of five, four being arranged like the four faces of a tower clock, the fifth pointing to the sky, hence other name of town-hall clock. A spreading undergound stem. Has musky smell after rain. Widespread, easily overlooked, in woods, hedge-banks, also mountains. Moschatel family. April-May.

4 Butcher's Broom

Unusual, stiff evergreen, up to two feet (60cm). True leaves minute at base of stem branches which are modified into flattened, oval leaf-shape with sharp spine at tip. In centre of leaf surface a minute, white flower, male and female on separate plants. Fruit a red berry. Used in decoration and grown in gardens. Supposedly tied in bunches and used as broom by butchers. Locally widespread in woodland in south. Lily family. March-April.

5 Fat Hen

Unattractive, much branched, upright annual with stiff stems, up to three feet (90cm), streaked reddish. Leaves lance-shaped, toothed with whitish mealy surface on young shoots. Leafy flower branches with numerous, small, dull green flowers without petals, producing black seeds. A nuisance to farmers. Once eaten as spinach. Widespread on waste and cultivated ground. Goosefoot family. June onwards. Good King Henry similar, but perennial, up to 12 inches (30cm), with larger, more triangular leaves. No leaves on flower stalks. Henry from German Heinrich, name of a woodland elf.

Green or Inconspicuous Flowers contd

1 Stinging Nettle

Unbranched perennial, up to four feet (120cm). Heart-shaped leaves on stalks in opposite pairs, covered in efficient, stinging hairs. Small catkins of tiny green to purple flowers in angles of leaves, male and female on separate plants. A tenacious weed, unpopular in gardens but important food for caterpillars of butterflies such as peacock, red admiral and small tortoiseshell. Made into nettle tea and beer, and a green dye extracted. Widespread on waste ground, hedgerows, etc. Nettle family. June onwards.

2 Wood Spurge

One of a number of Euphorbias (spurge family), all yellow-green. Stems exude sharp-tasting, milky fluid. Flowers of unusual design, separate male and female. Male a single stamen and female a single ovary, all in a close cluster surrounded by a cup of petal-like bracts. Wood spurge is a downy, unbranched perennial, up to 12 inches (30cm), with narrow, untoothed, lance-shaped leaves tinged reddish. Common in woods, mainly in south. Sun spurge has broader, toothed leaves. Flowers yellowish in an umbrella-like cluster. Common as garden weed. April onwards. Dwarf spurge is small and slender, with short leaves and yellow flowers. Common on culitivated chalk soils. May onwards.

3 Salad Burnet

Slender, rather dainty perennial, up to 12 inches (30cm). Rows of opposite, paired leaflets, sharply toothed. Small green flowers in a globular head, males without petals but with yellow stamens, females below with reddish styles. Wind-pollinated. Has a cucumber smell. Once common in herb gardens, formerly used in salads and added to drinks. Taken by Pilgrim Fathers to New World. Burnet from early French *brunet,* mahogany, after colour of flowerhead. Locally abundant in grasses on lime-rich soil, mainly in lowland England and Wales. Rose family. May-August.

4 Common Figwort

Perennial, up to two feet (60cm), with unpleasant aroma. Opposite pairs of oval, pointed, well-toothed leaves. Side branches bear open clusters of small, globe-shaped, greenish flowers, hooded above, with three lower lobes, open-mouthed and tipped reddish-brown. Tuberous roots, once used as remedy for piles, have resemblance to small figs. Common in woods and hedge banks. Figwort family. June-August.

5 Pellitory-of-the-Wall

Spreading perennial, up to two feet (60cm) long, with reddish-brown hairy stems bearing alternate, stalked, lance-shaped, glossy leaves. Separate, minute, greenish-brown flowers, males with pale yellow anthers, in bunches along branches. Anthers, when touched, spring open to scatter pollen. Old name paritarie, from Latin *paries,* a wall. Common on walls and brickwork. One of the official herbs used in treating sore throats and bruises, also a laxative. Nettle family. June onwards.

Green or Inconspicuous Flowers contd

1 Wild Arum

Called variously cuckoo-pint, parson in the pulpit, and lords and ladies. Easily recognised perennial. Leaves stalked, arrow-shaped and net-veined, sometimes spotted in black, arising from base of flower stem, appearing early in year. Minute flowers, male above female, in whorls around base of club-shaped stem, or spadix, coloured purple. A broad and pointed, pale green overhanging hood forms a lower chamber enclosing flowers. Small insects attracted by scent push past a ring of hairs around spadix, and enter chamber to assist in pollination. Hood later withers, releases insects and exposes ripe, orange-red, poisonous berries. Common in hedgerows and woodland borders. Arum family. April-May.

2 Lady's Mantle

Low-growing perennial, somewhat hairy. Stalked leaves rounded and palmate, up to eight lobes, strongly toothed. Small yellow-green flowers without petals in loose clusters at top of terminal branches. Leaves said to resemble a cloak, hence name. A very variable species in size and leaf shape especially in mountain forms. Common in grassland mainly in north and west. Rose family. May-September.

3 Sweet Flag

Stout iris-like perennial, up to three feet (90cm). Long, sword-shaped leaves, swollen down middle, crinkly edges. Minute brown-yellow flowers, densely packed in a stiff, pointed shoot arising halfway up stem. Crushed leaves emit aromatic scent, once strewn on floors of halls and castles as rush matting. Introduced from Middle East. Root-stock provides extract used in tonics. Local by fresh water, mainly in south. Arum family. June-July.

4 Hop

Rough, hairy, climbing perennial with angled stems twining up bushes, or on poles where cultivated, up to 12 feet (3.6m). Coarse, toothed, ivy-shaped leaves. Green male and female flowers on separate plants. Males form catkins, females globe-shaped, enlarging into cone-like fruits with resinous glands. Used in clarifying beer and imparting bitter flavour. Mainly in hop-fields since sixteenth century, but could be an original native. Occurs in hedgerows and thickets. Hemp family. July-August.

5 Stinking Hellebore

Foul-smelling perennial, up to three feet (90cm). Dark, evergreen, palmate leaves, the leaflets lance-shaped and toothed. Above, a cluster of bell-shaped, greenish-yellow, long-stalked flowers with purple edges. Local in woods, on chalk and limestone in England and Wales. Buttercup family. March-May. Smaller green hellebore, a perennial up to 12 inches (30cm), leaflets more toothed, no scent. Flowers greenish, more open, shaped like white-flowered Christmas rose, to which related. Local in woods on chalk and limestone in southern England. Both plants poisonous and dangerous to children and cattle.

Orchids

About 50 British species, all terrestrial. Many prefer chalk and limestone soil, others found in meadows, marshes, woods and heaths. Leaves flat, spear-shaped, or oval with parallel veins, and arise mainly from base of flower stem. Roots fleshy or tuber-like, associated with micro-organisms and difficult to transplant. Some very rare and should not be disturbed. Flowers twisted upside down. Three petals alternate with three sepals. Sepals same colour as two upper petals. Lower petal has swollen lip (labellum) variable in colour and shape, with a spur, giving distinctive appearance to flower and fanciful names such as bee, frog, man and spider orchid. Small bract at base of each flower whose stamens and stigma are joined by a central column. Pollen contained in sticky sacs (pollinia) which stick to heads of visiting bees and wasps who mistake them for mates (see bee orchid, p.208). Enormous numbers of minute seeds produced. Colour in orchids can vary, and hybrids are common. Note that spotted orchids have solid stems, marsh orchids hollow ones.

1 Early Purple Orchid

Early flowering, up to 12 inches (30cm), smelling of tom-cats. Long, linear leaves mostly arising from base, blotched purple. Flowers in open cluster, rich purple, well hooded, the labellum broad and wavy with long, central lobe, spur long. Locally widespread, mainly in woodland. April-June.

2 Common Spotted Orchid

Variable, up to 12 inches (30cm). Leaves narrow, spotted, deep purple. Flowers in long, pointed cluster, mainly pink, varying from pale to dark. Sepals spreading like bird's wings. Labellum wavy-edged, 3-lobed on each side, with central notch, spotted crimson. Widespread, mainly in south and east, in woodland, glades, downs, marshes, avoiding acid soil. June-August.

3 Early Marsh Orchid

Somewhat slim build with hollow, stout, green stem, leaves pale green, spotted, keeled. Flowers mainly pink but can vary. Sepals erect. Labellum with wavy edge, tapering spur. Widespread but local in peaty marshes, fens and dune slacks. May-August.

4 Scented or Fragrant Orchid

Graceful species, up to 12 inches (30cm). Leaves long and narrow, keeled, unspotted, arising along stem in two rows. Flowers rather closely packed, sweetly scented, with short three-lobed labellum. Long, slender spur can be confused with pyramid orchid. Locally frequent on chalk and limestone grassland. Attractive to moths. June-July.

5 Pyramid Orchid

A foxy-smelling species, up to 12 inches (30cm). Narrow, unspotted leaves attached close to stem. A dense pyramid-shaped cluster of deep pink flowers with hooded sepals, a deeply three-lobed labellum and long slender spur. Attractive to moths. Locally widespread in dry grassland, dunes, usually on chalk or limestone. June-August.

Orchids contd

1 Birdsnest Orchid

Rather colourless, honey-brown all over. Pair of broad, oval, unstalked bracts arise from stem. Long, leafless stalk bears small, dull flowers with long labellum divided into two outwardly curved lobes. Named after shape of roots. Widespread in shady woods, especially beech, in south. A semi-parasite, sometimes in rows following roots of beech tree. June-July.

2 Twayblade

Inconspicuous orchid, up to 12 inches (30cm) or more. Single pair of broadly oval, opposite leaves from base of stem. Flowers small, yellow-green, labellum with long, twin-forked lip, no spur. Widespread but rather hidden in woodland and damp grassy areas. May-July. Smaller lesser twayblade, up to four inches, fewer flowers and heart-shaped leaves. Mainly in north, nowhere common, among moss or under heather, especially in pinewoods. June-August.

3 Bee Orchid

Attractive, readily recognised orchid, up to 12 inches (30cm), has a swollen, furry, brown labellum without spur, marked with a pale U enclosing a yellow patch. Mistaken for female bee by male bumble bee which will visit in attempt to mate. Sepals pointed, bright pink, two green upper petals narrow and blunt-tipped. Locally widespread, some years in large numbers, on chalk and limestone turf. June-July.

4 Common Helleborine

Handsome orchid, up to two feet (60cm). Three or four broad, oval, pointed leaves, dull green to purplish, spiral round stem. Purplish flowers in dense, one-sided row, backed by leaf-like bracts same size as flower. Labellum heart-shaped with spur. Locally widespread in woods, in shade. July-September. White helleborine has flowers which seldom open fully, orange-yellow inside (so-called poached-egg plant). Locally common in beech-woods. May-July.

5 Butterfly Orchid

Attractive orchid with two oval, shiny, unspotted leaves arising from base, and small, lance-shaped, unstalked leaves up stem. Flowers in broad, loose clusters, greenish-white with long down-curved spur. Labellum narrow and long. Locally widespread in woods and chalk pasture in south. June-July. Lesser butterfly orchid similar but smaller in all parts, up to 10 inches (25cm). More usual on moist heaths and bogs, mostly in north. June-July.

Lower Plants

Ferns

One of the flowerless plant groups which reproduce by spores, not seeds. Non-woody perennials with divided leaves (fronds) which uncurl with growth and are found mainly in damp and shady surroundings. Spores scattered by wind are shed from containers (capsules) gathered together in groups on back or edges of fronds and covered with a hood (indusium). Spore settles and germinates into a small, green, disc-like organ, the prothallus. On this sperms from male organ swim actively towards female organ to fertilise the egg, from which new plant develops. This repeated asexual spore-producing stage, followed by a sexual stage, is called the 'alternation of generations'. Some 50 British species. Prehistoric ferns were the size of trees.

1 Male Fern

Familiar fern grown in gardens. Fronds with lance-shaped side leaves, with further leaflets, widest in middle, arising in a bunch from central root-stock. Stalks covered in brown scales. Capsules in rows either side of mid-rib of leaflets, each group covered by kidney-shaped indusium. Very common in woodland and hedgerow, especially along ditches and in hollows, also among rocks. July-August.

2 Hartstongue

Only British fern with undivided leaves, strap-shaped or tongue-shaped, both short and long, with rounded base on dark brown stalks, arising in clusters. Capsules in diagonal rows along sides of mid-rib of fronds. Common on rocks, walls, along hedge-banks, mainly in west. July-August.

3 Common Polypody

Fronds evergreen. Side leaves have wavy edges instead of leaflets. Leaves arise separately from creeping rootstock covered in brown scales. Capsules in orange groups in rows along sides of mid-rib of side leaves. Common, mainly in west, in woods, frequently in crown of trees, also among rocks and on walls. June-September.

4 Bracken

Very common fern. Fronds divided into side leaves, each with further leaflets, arising from a creeping underground rhyzome. Capsules around borders of leaflets under turned-over edge. Very abundant and widespread, sometimes in large patches, taking over heather and grass, and a nuisance to hill farmers. Has been called 'Britain's worst weed'. Resistant to fire. Fronds turn copper-brown in autumn. Mainly on acid soils. May-August.

5 Wall Rue

Small, tufted fern with distinctive fronds resembling dark green parsley. Fronds fan- or diamond-shape, broadest across middle, toothed along outer edge, on stalks with black base. Capsules cover centre of leaf. Named after the yellow-flowered rue, a culinary herb with similar-shaped leaves. Frequent on rocks and walls. June onwards.

Lower Plants contd

1 Mosses

Primitive group of small, green, flowerless plants, with pointed leaves encircling stem. Sex organs on separate plants. Wind-blown spores germinate into new plants. Grow close together in dense colonies almost anywhere — on ground, walls, rocks, trees, one or two in bogs (e.g. sphagnum), or in water (willowmoss, p.246). Important pioneer colonisers of bare surfaces. An alternation of generations as with ferns. About 600 British species. Species shown is *Mnium hornum,* common in shady woods and hedgerows.

2 Liverworts

Small, spore-bearing, flowerless plants, can be mistaken for mosses. Mostly without upright stem or leaves. A few leafy species have rounded leaves. Most consist of flat fronds with slender rootlets resembling lobes of liver, also similar to prothallus of ferns. Alternate generations as in ferns and mosses. Male and female organs on adult plant. Mostly in damp places: ditches, drains, bogs, rotting wood and by streams and waterfalls. More than 200 British species. Shown here is the common *Pellia,* which grows along ditches, on wet mud and on base of tree-stumps.

3 Clubmosses

Creeping, spore-bearing perennials somewhat moss-like but more robust, with small, pointed leaves which overlap and encircle stem. Spore cases at base of scales in erect cones in most cases. Mainly grow in rough pasture on mountain slopes, moors and heaths. Six British species. Shown here is the stag's horn clubmoss, frequent on moors and mountains, among heather, mainly in north and west. August-September.

4 Algae

Simplest of plants, mainly aquatic, ranging from one-celled forms to large seaweeds. All contain chlorophyll, some masked with other pigments may be brown or reddish. Common one-celled land form is *Pleurococcus* which forms powdery film on wet bark and wooden posts. In fresh water there are numerous microscopic forms, such as *Chlamydomonas* and *Euglena* (4a), which swim actively with whip-like threads. *Volvox* (4b) is a colonial sphere of many linked cells. Others form filamented threads of cells, end to end, as shown here (4c), which sometimes choke a pond or aquarium and are popularly known as blanketweed.

5 Lichens

Actually a combination of two plants, fungus and alga. Former produces fruit, latter provides food. Usually much paler than mosses, more greyish, but some with bright splashes of coloured fruit bodes. Lichens take many forms, some flat and encrusted on rocks, bark and gravestones, others more bushy and attached to branches, some terrestrial on bare soil, among grass or heather. Rootless — water absorbed through surface. Very sensitive to pollution. Slow-growing. Mainly occur in cleaner, wetter west and north.

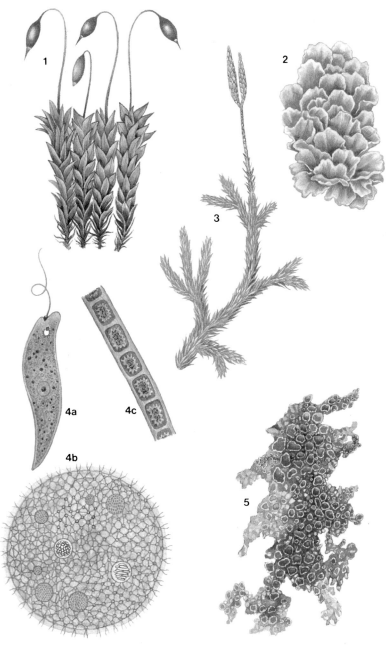

Fungi

Flowerless plants without chlorophyll, living on dead remains of plant or animal (saprophytes) or as parasites on live host. Size varies from small, such as moulds (e.g. pin-mould on cheese) and mildews (e.g. rose-mildew) to large ones like the giant puffball (p.218). Large kinds, popularly known as toadstools, produce a visible fruit body (sporophore) from actual plant hidden in leafmould, dead tree, grass, etc.; sporophore liberates countless spores on wind. Apart from typical toadstool shape (cap on stalk), fruit bodies take many forms, such as puffballs, brackets, fairy clubs, stinkhorns and pixie cups. Most species fruit in autumn in woodland. Commonest examples are the agaric toadstools, with gills beneath the cap. Spores are produced in fours from special cells (basidia) which line the gills. Altogether, some 10,000 British species of fungi.

Warning: Never eat a toadstool without positive identification that it is edible.

1 Oyster Mushroom

Cap dark when young, turns more slaty. Shell-shaped. Lilac gills run down stem. Attached to trees, logs, in woodland, mainly on beech. Edible. Autumn.

2 Sickener

Member of the Russula genus of toadstools. Agaric with firm flesh and white gills which rustle when stroked. No ring or volva. The sickener causes vomiting. Pinkish cap. Other species variously in red, yellow, and black. Under trees in woodland. July-October.

3 Sulphur-tuft

Common agaric, appears in clusters usually around base of tree stumps. Yellowish cap somewhat conical in centre, which is rusty yellow. Gills and spores purple-brown. Conifer and deciduous woods. September-October mainly, but at almost any time.

4 Saffron Milkcap

Agaric of Lactarius group, so-called milky toadstools which exude drops of milky fluid. A carrot-red cap with circular grey rings. No ring or volva. Stem hollow. A delicacy, hence scientific name *Lactarius deliciosus,* but it may temporarily turn urine red. Conifer woods. July-October.

5 Deathcap

Aptly-named agaric, deadly poisonous, causing up to 90 per cent of all deaths from fungus poisoning. Two alkaloids responsible — amanitin and phalloidin. Resembles a mushroom, but fortunately not very common. Member of amanita group of toadstools with a ring on stalk and a sheath or volva around base. Gills white. Cap a pale olive-green with fine, dark, radial streaks. Singly or in small groups in woodland and among bushes. August-October.

6 Wood Hedgehog

Wavy yellow-ochre cap with yellowish spines (not gills) underneath. In woodland, often in rings around beech trees. Edible. October-November.

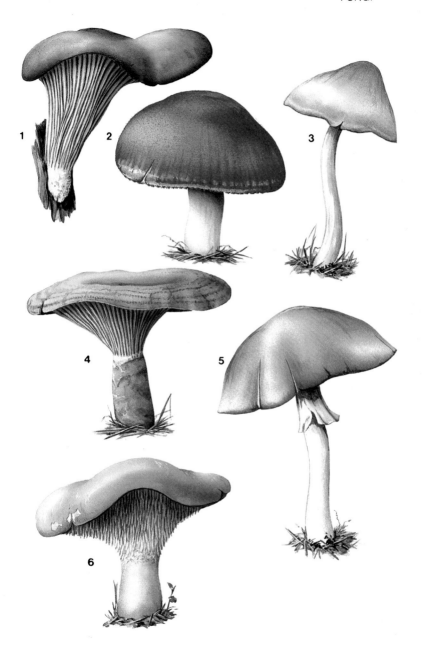

Fungi contd

1 Parasol Mushroom

Handsome species growing up to 15 inches (38cm) with cap 12 inches (30cm) across. Cap covered in grey-brown scales. Stem has circular wavy markings. In small groups in grassy places in woodland glades and parks, often on ant-hills. Edible, a sweet and nutty flavour. Summer-autumn.

2 Fly Agaric

Readily recognised. An amanita agaric with scarlet cap, spotted white. Spots from torn-apart white skin which covers at button stage. Gills white. Highly poisonous. Mainly among bracken and birches, also conifers. October.

3 Field Mushroom

Familiar fungus gathered as food. White to brownish cap, rounded at first then flattens, dry and may be a little scaly. Stem firm, rather short, a ring but no volva. Gills white at first, turning pink then purple-brown. Late summer and autumn. Horse mushroom has a more robust cap, fawn to brownish with incurved margin. Gills white, turning brown. Stem white and hollow. Meadows, often in rings. Also edible. July onwards. *Note.* Yellow-staining mushroom resembles horse mushroom but is mildly poisonous. Turns chrome-yellow when bruised.

4 Blewit

Also called blue-leg. Cap greyish white to brown, regular shape with somewhat arched centre, incurved margin. Stem attractive lilac. Gills white or pale brown, spores dull red. Short stem swells near top. In crowded rings in fields, orchards and cattle pastures. Edible. Late fruiting. October-November.

5 Lawyer's Wig

So-named from shape and appearance, up to 12 inches (30cm). Club-shaped cap covered in white and brownish scales. Gills slowly dissolve into a black, inky fluid from edge upwards, each drop containing spores. Edible when young, common in groups on made-up ground, along pathways, compost heaps and freshly sown grass. May onwards.

6 Chanterelle

Cap funnel-shaped, egg-yolk colour, with navy border. Underside not gilled but veined and branched in ridges running down stem. Grassy places in pine-woods and among moss in beech woods. Edible. June-November.

7 Penny Bun

Member of pored boletus toadstools, also known as cep. Thick and stubby, with spongy surface under cap full of fine tubes. Cap at first white, turning a liver- or nut-brown, up to eight inches (20cm) wide. Skin smooth or wrinkled, slippery when wet, slightly overhanging edge. Brownish stem with pale vertical lines. In woodland, especially sandy soil among conifers. Edible. May onwards.

Fungi contd

1 Stinkhorn

Unmistakable due to shape and smell. Fruit body starts as a soft white 'egg' containing fully-formed stem which emerges and elongates within hours, bearing a cap covered in dark-green slime containing spores. Liberates powerful, unpleasant smell detected many yards away. Attracts flies which feed on slime, picking up spores on feet. Common stinkhorn up to ten inches (25cm), in woodland. May-November. Smaller dog stinkhorn up to six inches (15cm), has reddish cap.

2 Puff-Ball

Rounded fungi, whitish, turning brown with age. A double skin which opens at top when ripe, releasing clouds of spores at the slightest touch, even from a single rain-drop. Occur on tree-stumps in woods, or in grass in meadows, according to species. July-October. Giant puff-ball whitish at first, turning brown with age, up to size of football. In long grass in pastures and orchards. Edible when young. May-October.

3 Fairy Club

Small fungi, also called stags horn or coral fungi. Small fruit body, erect, simple, branched or club-shaped. Spores appear on upper surface of branches. Colours vary with species — white, yellow, orange, brown. Terrestrial or on rotten wood, tree-stumps. August onwards.

4 Cup Fungi

Group of fungi with cup or spoon-shaped fruit bodies, also called pixiecups or elfcups. Variously coloured yellow, orange, red, and black, Spores produced on upper surface. Terrestrial on fallen leaves. Shown here is the orangepeel fungus. Cup shiny reddish-orange, paler on outside, margin turned inwards, thin and soft. In clusters on ground, usually attached to roots. Autumn.

5 Honey Fungus

Parasitic agaric which attacks and kills trees, especially conifers. An established plant produces thick, black strands of fungal threads which penetrate below ground, entering roots of neighbouring trees. Visible signs of disease are fruit bodies appearing in clusters out of bark. Caps are vivid yellow to tawny brown, with downy or scaly surface especially in centre, with thin, curved, striated margins. Gills whitish becoming rufous, run down stem. A large ring. Can produce luminescence seen after dark. Autumn.

6 Birch Bracket

Bracket fungi live on dead or dying trees, producing sporophores in shelf-like formation, singly or in tiers, out of tree-trunk, branches and logs. Underside is lined with small tubes of differing shape — round, oval, angular, sinuate. Usually leathery or woody, some with a stalk, can last for many months. Birch bracket whitish when young, turns brown, often mottled. Tubes white. Flesh white and soft, later becoming corky. Can be used as razor-strop, hence old name razor-strop fungus. May-June, on birch trees.

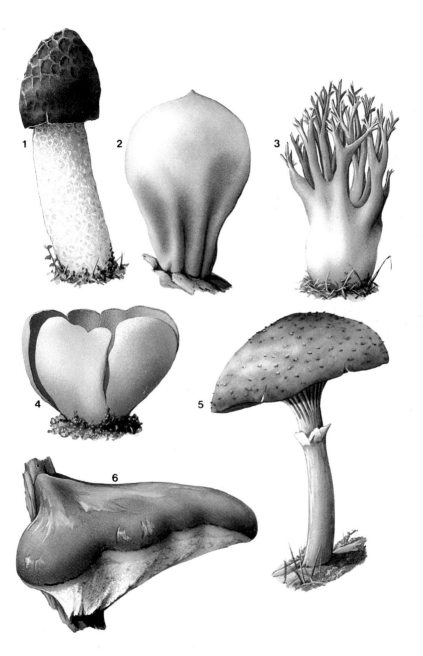

Deciduous Trees and Shrubs

Britain's maritime, temperate climate is mainly suited to the growth of deciduous or broad-leaved trees, which once dominated the landscape, though now greatly reduced. There are many introductions. Trees may be identified by their leaves, flowers or fruits, and in winter by their buds and bark pattern. Shape is not always reliable, since a tree may be damaged by weather or lopped for timber and firewood, either pollarded (beheaded) at crown level or coppiced (cut) at ground level, from where new branches grow. Also, crowded trees grow thin and tall (thus called spear trees).

1 White Poplar

Average size. Smooth, pale, greenish-white bark with many black fissures. Twigs and buds covered in white down. Leaves broadly palmate, roughly toothed, cottony-white underneath reflecting light, hence name. Hanging male catkins green, turning reddish, female catkins green on separate tree. Seeds with parachute hairs, wind-blown, seldom germinate. Reproduces mainly by suckers. Widespread, frequently planted from cuttings. March.

2 Sweet Chestnut

Also called Spanish chestnut. Sturdy tree with furrowed brown bark spiralling up trunk. Stout buds, leaves lance-shaped and sharply toothed. Male flowers stiff, elongated, upright, yellow catkins with sickly smell, females sitting at base. Fruit plump, triangular, brown nuts in green husk covered in tangle of sharp spines. Introduced by Romans. Flowers July, fruits in October.

3 Horse Chestnut

Readily recognised. Large, rounded shape and spreading branches turned up at end. Large sticky buds in pairs. Leaves compound, fan-shaped, palmate, five to seven leaflets. Horseshoe-shaped scars with 'nail' marks where leaf has fallen. Fine display of 'candles' of white blossom, sometimes reddish, pollinated by bees. Large, glossy brown nuts produced in spiky green husk. Introduced from Europe. Flowers May, fruit ripe in October.

4 London Plane

Recognised by patchwork bark which peels off, giving dappled colours of greys and yellows, helping it to breathe and thrive in polluted, smoky atmospheres. Pale green leaves, five-lobed, sycamore-like with long stalks. Separate male and female flowers, in ball-like hanging cluster. Females turn brown, breaking into hundreds of small, hair-tufted seeds, mostly infertile. London plane is a hybrid between Oriental and American planes and propagated by cuttings. Common in town squares and parks. May-June.

5 Common Lime

Stately tree with smooth, dark brown bark, rather spoiled by swollen bosses on trunk and clusters of side shoots around base. Infested with aphids secreting honey-dew on leaves, which turn black from fungus mould. Reddish buds, heart-shaped leaves. Ridged, nut-like fruits in bunches attached to stalk with side wing. A fertile hybrid between small-leaved and large-leaved limes. Common in avenues, streets and parks. Flowers July, fruits in September.

Deciduous Trees and Shrubs contd

1 Pedunculate Oak

Massive trunk with rugged bark, broad crown, and spreading, curved branches. Oval, lobed leaves with two lobes at base on very short stalk. Buds rounded, clustered at end of twigs. Male flowers small, numerous in hanging, slender catkins visited by bees. Females, more hidden among young leaves, develop into acorns in scaly cups on longish stalk (i.e. peduncle). Widespread, mainly in south on heavier clay soils. Flowers March and April. Durmast or sessile oak has acorn cup direct on stalk (i.e. sessile).

2 Ash

Tall tree with olive-grey bark, with network of shallow ridges. Buds black, in opposite pairs, produce compound leaves of separate leaflets late in season. Petal-less flowers in clusters, male, female or mixed, with purple stamens, wind-pollinated. Elongated fruits with long, narrow, twisted wings hang in bunches. Grows best on limestone. Flowers before leaves, April-May.

3 Beech

Tall, handsome tree with solid, round trunk, smooth greyish bark. Leaves oval, pointed, wavy-edged, slightly downy, turning copper-brown in autumn. Buds long and slender. Leaves positioned in mosaic fashion on spreading, often horizontal branches, cutting out much daylight. Male flowers in short-stalked hanging tassel, yellow stamens, wind-pollinated; females unstalked. Fruit called mast, three-sided nutlets; three to four in a tough, bristly husk. Widespread, some natural woods on chalk in south, also planted as hedge. Flowers April-May, with leaves.

4 Mountain Ash

Also called rowan. Small tree with smooth, grey bark. Alternate compound leaves with toothed leaflets (superficially ash-like, hence name). Large, purple buds. Flat bunch of white flowers produce orange to red berries. Hardy mountain tree, mainly in dry woods, among rocks in north and west. Berries enjoyed by many birds. Flowers May-June, berries ripe August.

5 Hornbeam

Somewhat small tree with smooth, grey and fluted bark, can be mistaken for small beech. Leaves oval, pointed and toothed, strongly veined underneath. Loose, hanging catkins (males yellowish, females greenish); females at first erect, then hanging to produce small nutlets with unmistakable, three-lobed wing. Grows mainly with oak, especially in south-east (e.g. Epping Forest), elsewhere in hedgerows and parks. Flowers April, followed in May by leaves.

6 Crack Willow

Familiar waterside willow, often pollarded. Spreading crown, bark green with fissures. Twigs break easily, hence name. Leaves long, narrow, toothed. Catkins slender on short, leafy stalks, on separate trees; male with two stamens yellow when ripe, female green. Flowers April, with leaves. *Note:* many kinds of willow, all with catkins. See also sallow, p.230.

Deciduous Trees and Shrubs contd

1 Common Elm

Tall, handsome tree with upper branches rising almost vertically to form peg-top shape to crown. Suckers freely around base. Twigs slender, leaves oval, pointed, toothed, lop-sided. Early flowers in thick tufts with reddish stamens on bare branches, before leaves. Fruit a small, pale-green rounded disc, deeply-notched, containing mostly infertile seeds. Often called English elm. Widely planted in lowland Britain along hedgerows. Reduced by Dutch elm disease. Probably derived from wych elm, a more woodland tree with rounded crown, larger leaves, and does not sucker. Fertile fruit has seed in centre. More common in north and west. Flowers February-March, fruits May-June.

2 Field Maple

Only native maple. Small tree or shrub. Bark light grey, ribbed, downy twigs becoming corky. Leaves palmate, five-lobed as in Canada's emblem, turning magnificent golden brown in autumn. Flowers separate male and female in erect clusters. Fruits like sycamore in pairs, but with wings in horizontal line. Common in woods and hedgerows on chalk and limestone. May-June.

3 Sycamore

Large tree with rounded crown, smooth, grey bark with tendency to become scaly and flake off with age. Greenish winter buds in pairs. Leaves somewhat palmate with five rounded lobes, resembling plane (p.220), become attacked by black fungus. Greenish-yellow flowers hang in separate loose clusters visited by bees. Pairs of hard seeds, each with efficient propellor-like wing placed at right-angle. Tree resistant to hard weather and pollution. Introduced from Europe into parks and gardens and can take over woodland. Flowers May-June, fruits in October.

4 Silver Birch

Well-deserved name of 'lady of the woods'. Graceful, average-sized. Drooping branches, papery, peeling bark, trunk rough at base. Twigs shiny, warted and hairless. Leaves oval, pointed, toothed. Hanging, yellow male catkins wind-pollinated. Females at first short, scaly, erect, then droop into seed-bearing catkins, releasing numerous winged seeds. Readily colonises cleared or burnt ground. Mainly lowland species in south, on heaths, in woods, preferring sand or gravel. Flowers April-May, shortly after leaves. Can hybridise with downy birch, which has more erect growth, hairy twigs, more greyish bark. Leaves less pointed. More common in wetter north and west.

5 Alder

Common waterside tree, often shrub size, with black, fissured bark. Leaves broad, toothed, more or less rounded, with notched tip, purplish. Yellow, hanging male catkins, at first small and green in autumn, long and ripe in spring. Females short, purple, erect, egg-shaped, develop into cone-like, green structures (5a), which remain on tree, turning black (5b), after releasing wind-blown seeds. Seeds float. Widespread along streams and swampy areas, may form into alder woods. Flowers March-April, before leaves.

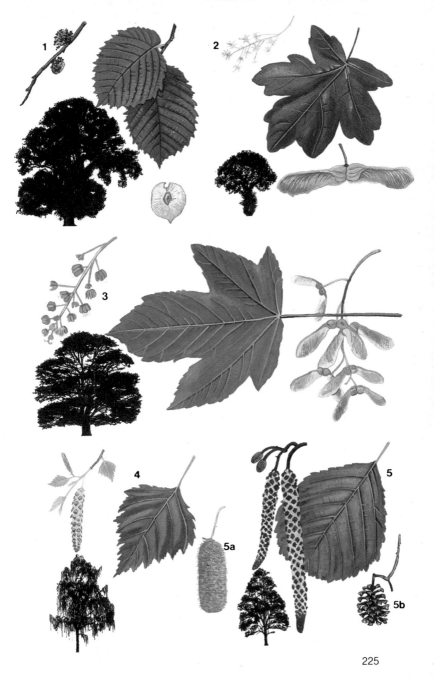

Deciduous Trees and Shrubs contd

1 Holly

Familiar evergreen shrub, but can grow to tree size. Bark smooth and grey. Leaves thick, waxy, spiny on lower branches, usually spineless higher up. Leaves can resist cold and live up to four years before dropping. Small white flowers in bunches, male and female on separate plants, attract bees. Female produces bright red berries eaten by birds, which assists dispersal. Garden strains grafted on to wild stock. Christmas decoration in homes and churches and associated with the crown of thorns. Widespread in woods and hedges. May-August.

2 Hawthorn

Also called may and whitethorn. Thickset, thorny shrub or small tree. Leaves deeply three- to five-lobed, in clusters. Flowers white, sometimes pinkish in bunches, scented. Dull, round, red berry or haw contains one stone in common species. Important winter food for birds and mice. Was extensively planted during eighteenth century land enclosures to contain farm stock, but may go back to Saxon times. Common and widespread along lanes, around fields, in woods and downs. Rose family. Flowers May, fruits in October.

3 Sloe

Also named blackthorn. Thorny, stiff, branching shrub, differing from hawthorn in having blackish bark, longer thorns and flowers appearing before leaves. Leaves oval, slightly toothed, grow alternately. Fruit — the sloe — resembles small, blue-black plum covered with whitish bloom, very sharp tasting. Made into jelly and for flavouring gin. Spreads by suckers. Widespread in hedgerows. Rose family. Flowers April, before leaves, fruits in October.

4 Dog Rose

England's flower emblem, one of many rose species in Britain. Stout bush up to 10 feet (3m), with arching branches which readily layer. Stout, curved thorns. Leaves broken into toothed leaflets. Has largest flowers of British rose species, white or pale pink, scented, yellow stamens. Fruits (hips) red, egg-shaped, without sepals. Used as rootstock for garden roses. Widespread in thickets and hedges, less common in Scotland. Flowers June-July, hips ripen through autumn. Downy rose more common in north, has greyer leaflets and straight thorns. Flowers deeper pink, hips more globular with sepals attached. Field rose more usual in woods as a climber, always has white flowers with prominent female styles fused together in centre.

5 Bramble

Familiar, prickly perennial, variable in growth, prostrate or climbing. Woody branches readily root. Forms dense cover and supports wide variety of wildlife. Leaves prickly, of three to five leaflets. Flowers white or pink. Fruit (blackberry) a rounded cluster of separate fruitlets each containing a pip, green at first turning red, then black, retaining turned-down sepals. Widespread in woods, hedge-banks and open glades. Readily colonises exposed soil. Rose family. Flowers in June, fruits ripe by September.

Deciduous Trees and Shrubs contd

1 Guelder Rose

Shrub or small tree up to 12 feet (3.6m). Leaves three- to five-lobed and toothed, in pairs. Flat, umbel-shaped cluster of white flowers in two forms, outer ones much enlarged but sterile, inner ones small and fertile, with five petals forming tube. Fruits shiny, bitter-tasting red berries. Named after Dutch province of Gelderland. Widespread but local in woods and fens, in damp places. Honeysuckle family. Flowers May-July.

2 Wayfaring Tree

Downy shrub up to 12 feet (3.6m), with hairy surface on twigs, buds, and leaves. Branches supple. Leaves oval, wrinkled, heavily veined underneath, in pairs. Flowers all similar, unlike closely related guelder rose in flat-topped clusters. Fruits green, turning red, finally black. Frequent locally on chalk and limestone, along lanes and among other bushes, mainly in south. Honeysuckle family. Flowers May-June, fruits July onwards.

3 Whitebeam

Shrub or tree size, somewhat variable. Leaves oval, slightly toothed, heavily coated underneath with white hairs. Clusters of white or pink flowers produce light scarlet berries. Widespread along woodland borders, scrub and hillsides, on chalk and limestone. Rose family. Flowers in May-June, fruits September.

4 Common Buckthorn

Also called purging buckthorn. Dense and thorny shrub up to 12 feet (3.6m), spreading branches, greyish bark, can be confused with sloe (p.226). Leaves finely-toothed, oval, pointed, rather long-stalked. Clusters of four-petalled green flowers, male and female on separate plants, on short, ridged projections of old wood, resembling antlers of roebuck. Old name buck's-horn tree. Autumn berries black, once used as purgative. Widespread in bushy areas and hedgerows, on chalk and limestone, rare in north. Flowers May-June, fruits in September. Alder buckthorn a more slender bush, thornless, with alternate, untoothed leaves. Flowers five-petalled. More common in damp woods on acid soils. Used to be much planted for charcoal-making.

5 Spindle

Shrub or tree size up to 12 feet (3.6m). Bark smooth, grey, with greenish, square twigs. Greyish leaves lance-shaped, slightly toothed, in opposite pairs. Small, green-white, four-petalled flowers, male, female, or both, in clusters in angles of leaves. A striking autumn fruit, a bright coral-pink, four-lobed capsule which splits open to reveal four seeds covered in fleshy orange coats. Hard, smooth stem once made into spindle before use of spinning wheel. Locally common in woods, hedgerows, on chalk and limestone. Flowers May-June, fruits September.

Deciduous Trees and Shrubs contd

1 Crab Apple

Average-sized tree of rugged or 'crabby' appearance. Bark purple-brown, spiny, with reddish-brown twigs. Leaves oval, pointed, toothed, on short stalks. Flowers five-petalled in clusters, pinkish-white inside, more reddish on outside, stamens yellow, on short spurs as with cultivated apples. Apples yellow-green, may turn reddish, very tart, made into jelly. Common in woods and hedgerows. Rose family. Flowers May, fruits fully ripe late winter.

2 Pussy Willow

Average-sized willow, mostly a shrub. Leaves lance-shaped or oval, narrowing towards base, turned over along edge, rough to the touch. Catkins on separate plants, yellow males visited by bees. Female green, usually overlooked. Widespread in damp places. Flowers March-April, before leaves.

3 Hazel

Spreading bush rarely more than shrub size, up to 12 feet (3.6m), due to regular coppicing to produce poles, hurdles, etc.; occasionally tree-sized. Smooth bark reddish-brown, peels. Male catkins visible as buds in autumn, develop into much-loved, hanging yellow 'lamb's tails' in early spring, shedding clouds of golden wind-blown pollen. Female flower resembles a leaf-bud with red tassel on top, the stigma, which receives pollen. Develops into nut at first enclosed in thick, green, toothed husk. Leaves oval, pointed, toothed. Hedgerows, open woods. Flowers January-March, before leaves.

4 Dogwood

Shrub up to 12 feet (3.6m), has firm structure, greyish bark, blood-red twigs. Leaves oval, pointed, untoothed and downy, turning red in autumn. Small white flowers with four petals in tubular shape with unpleasant scent. Soft, round, black berry. A vigorous grower, suckering even when cut back, invades downland in absence of sheep. Widespread in hedges, open woods, downs on chalk and limestone. Flowers June-July, fruits September.

5 Elder

Shrub or tree size. Corky yellow-grey bark with stout twigs containing white pith. Dark green leaves with toothed, lance-shaped leaflets. Small flowers in large, flat-topped clusters, creamy white, scented, with pale yellow anthers. Fruit a juicy berry first green, then black. Flowers made into elder tea, berries into wine. Plant distasteful to animals, turns up in hedges, woods, waste ground. Honeysuckle family. Flowers June-July, fruits August-September.

6 Wild Cherry

Also called gean. Tall tree up to 75 feet (22.8m), smooth, shiny bark, reddish brown, showing breathing pores. Peels off when mature. Wounds sealed with sticky brown resin. Pale green leaves hanging, oval, pointed, toothed, turn orange in autumn. Small, white, hanging flowers on separate stalks, short-lived, produce shiny red or black bitter-tasting cherries. Widespread in hedgerows and woods. Rose family. Flowers May, fruits July-August.

Coniferous Trees

Trees with needle-shaped leaves, mostly evergreen, can exist in cold and dry climates, in poor soil and in mountains. Shape symmetrical. Catkins of separate sexes on same tree. Male flowers in small clusters near branch tips shed wind-blown pollen to small, bud-like female flowers which develop into green cones, turning brown when ripe, opening to shed seeds. Three native species — Scots pine, yew and juniper.

1 Scots Pine

Only native pine, has short, blue-green needles in pairs. Flat or dome-topped with reddish bark flaking off in patches. Once widespread, now only truly native in parts of Scotland. Also found in plantations, and as escapes. Mostly on sandy soils and heaths. Flowers May-June.

2 Yew

Stout, broad evergreen, usually has more than one trunk, spreading branches, grows to very old age, 1,000 years or more. Up to 60 feet (18.3m). Scaly, reddish-brown bark. Leaves dark green, glossy, elongated, arranged in rows along separate branchlets. Fruit with bright scarlet cup enclosing seed. Leaves, seed and bark poisonous (though flesh is not). An ancient symbol of life, common in churchyards, also widespread in parks, dry woods, especially on chalk. Flowers February-April, fruits follow.

3 Juniper

Evergreen shrub with reddish bark, up to 12 feet (3.6m). Resembles gorse; blue-green, waxy leaves short and spiny, in whorls of three along branches. Green, round berries, turning blue-black and sloe-like over 3 years, contain black seed. Tree has smell of gin: oil from berries flavours it. Widespread but local, mainly south-east England and Scotland. Flowers April-May.

4 Norway Spruce

So-called Christmas tree, a custom introduced by Prince Albert in 1844. Tall, symmetrical growth, cone-shaped, branches upright and whorled around trunk. Dark green, four-sided needles, singly on small, peg-like stalk, thickly spiralling along branch. Long, narrow, hanging brown cones. Grown widely for timber and Christmas trade. Flowers May-June.

5 Lawson's Cypress

Tall, narrow, pointed growth, bark stringy. Fern-like foliage of small needles thickly clasping and hiding stems and buds. Round, brown, woody cones with triangular-shaped scales. Introduced from Oregon, USA, by Peter Lawson in 1854. Widely planted for decoration in parks, gardens as a hedge, and for florists' decoration. Flowers April-May.

6 European Larch

Tall conifer with somewhat hanging branches, is deciduous, showing knob-like swellings on yellowish twigs. These bear tufts of bright green needles, turning yellow in autumn before leaf-fall. Barrel-shaped, flat-ended brown cones. Introduced from Europe, Pine family. Flowers March-April.

Climbers

Woody perennials which require support and climb up bushes, trees, walls, etc., many producing colourful fruits, a food supply for birds during winter.

1 Honeysuckle

Also called woodbine. Woody climber twining clockwise up bushes and trees for support, up to 20 feet (6m) or more. Firm grip may distort young trees. Leaves in opposite pairs, oval, untoothed, short-stalked, appear during winter. Flowers cream to pinkish, crimson on outside, in clusters of up to twelve. Each has deep, one-sided tube, petals forming long, two-lipped upper lobe. Five protruding stamens. Sweet-scented, attracts night-flying hawkmoths (see p.101). Widespread in hedgerows and woodland. Many garden varieties. Red berries in autumn. Flowers June-September.

2 Ivy

Well-known, woody, evergreen climber with tough main stem, attached to trees, walls, etc. by small roots, also trailing along ground and readily rooting. Leaves dark green to purplish, shiny, of variable shape, some rounded and pointed, others more conventionally ivy-shaped. Flowers small, greenish with yellow anthers, in rounded bunches on stiff, erect stems. Fruit a black berry. Common in woods, hedgerows, on walls and in gardens, sometimes carpeting ground. Flowers September onwards.

3 Traveller's Joy

Related to garden clematis. Woody climber, can reach 50 feet (15.2m) up a tree, even hanging down from branches. Bark of old wood pale brown, fibrous and shredding. Leaves paired, opposite, broken into leaflets on long stalks which curl around supports. Clusters of small, fragrant, greenish-white flowers with prominent stamens produce small, brown seeds with woolly, greyish plumes, (so-called old man's beard). Common in woods and hedgerows on chalk and limestone. Buttercup family. Flowers July-September.

4 Black Bryony

Climbing perennial, up to 12 feet (3.6m), twisting clockwise up support with unbranched stem. Fresh stems arise from tuberous roots. Leaves broadly heart-shaped, shiny, dark green turning black with age. Small, green, six-petalled flowers on side stems in loose groups. Fruit a round, scarlet berry. Hedgerows and copses, mainly in south, absent from Scotland. Yam family. Flowers May onwards. Similar-looking but unrelated white bryony has ivy-shaped leaves, climbs with tendrils. Gourd family, related to cucumber.

5 Bittersweet

Also called woody nightshade. A weak climber up to five feet (1.5m), woody near ground, twining in any direction. Leaves alternate, oval, pointed, often with two narrow lobes at base. Striking flowers similar to potato, in clusters with five turned-back, purple petals forming tube, with central column of yellow anthers. Hanging bunches of poisonous egg-shaped berries, first green, then yellow, turning red. Widespread in hedges, woods and waste ground, also over pebbles on beach. Nightshade family. June-September.

235

POND AND RIVER LIFE

Life in ponds and rivers is adapted to an aquatic existence. Among animals, for instance, streamlining, swimming organs and gills are common features. A natural balance in the community is maintained by a series of food chains which can be traced from microscopic plants and animals through to large creatures like pike and heron. Plants grow in recognised zones ranging from the exposed bankside into open water, while different animals occupy different levels and habitats, some on the surface, some at the bottom, some in open water and others hidden among plants. Due to changes in farming practice and to neglect and pollution, freshwater life has suffered from the loss of habitats and breeding sites, and some species have thus become rare.

Marsh Zone

This outer zone is where plants grow in waterlogged surroundings with their roots in wet soil. Such plants occur in marshes, bogs, ditches, damp hollows, and by ponds and riversides.

1 Ragged Robin

Hairy perennial resembling pink campion (p.188) but with deeply-cleft, ragged-looking petals broken into 3-4 lobes. Leaves lance-shaped. Marshes, fens, damp woods, ditches and waterside. Pink family. May-July.

2 Water Mint

One of several related species. Stiff, hairy, perennial, often with purplish stems. Opposite leaves oval, pointed, toothed, stalked. Flowers reddish to lilac in round, terminal head, with a lower whorl in angles of topmost leaves. Petals form a tube. Wet places. Labiate family. June-September.

3 Meadowsweet

Perennial with stiff stems. Leaves broken into leaflets, slightly toothed, large and small, silvery green underneath. Foamy clusters of small, creamy flowers, scented, with numerous stamens, once used as floor covering. Damp woods, fens, ditches, and waterside. Rose family. June-September.

4 Water Avens

Downy, unbranched perennial. Compound, hairy root-leaves, the end leaflet large and rounded. Flowers drooping, with notched, pink petals and large, purple sepals, not unlike much larger marsh cinquefoil (p.238). Fruit hooked. Ditches and wet, shady places, mainly south-east England. Rose family. April-September.

5 Marsh Marigold

Large cousin of the buttercup. Hairless perennial with hollow stem. Five golden petals, no sepals. Leaves dark green, glossy, kidney-shaped. Also known as kingcup. Wet meadows and waterside. Buttercup family. March-May.

Marsh Zone contd

1 Yellow Loosestrife

Downy perennial, not related to purple loosestrife. Broad, lance-shaped, pointed leaves with dark spots, short-stalked, encircling stem in whorls of 2-4. Yellow flowers five-petalled, in clusters on long stalks arising from angles of leaves. The word loosestrife, literally 'ending strife', derives from an old belief that the plant can calm temperamental farm animals. Widespread by ponds and rivers, Primrose family. July-August.

2 Hemp Agrimony

Downy perennial. Reddish main stem branched above with palmate leaves, leaflets lance-shaped, toothed, somewhat wavy. Dense, terminal flower-head, each flower with pinkish disc florets, outer sepal-like bracts purplish. Resembles valerian (p.190). Common by ponds, in ditches, wet woods. Daisy family. July-September.

3 Purple Loosestrife

Tall, conspicuous, downy perennial, erect four-sided stem. Leaves lance-shaped, untoothed. Row of red-purple, six-petalled flowers in whorls, opening from bottom to top. Resembles rosebay willowherb (p.182), though this occurs in dry situations. Loosestrife family. June-August.

4 Unbranched Bur-Reed

Unusual-looking waterside perennial. Solid stem bearing narrow, stiff, iris-like leaves, strongly veined and keeled, some floating. Round, greenish, compact flowerheads, bur-like, attached closely to main stem. Males above with yellow stamens, green females below. Fruit beaked, and floats. Widespread by fresh water. June-August. Larger branched bur-reed has leaves more three-sided, with male and female flowerheads on separate branches.

5 Marsh Cinquefoil

Perennial, not unlike water avens (p.236). Compound leaves grey-green, palmate shaped with 3-6 toothed leaflets. Large, conspicuous, dark purple flowers, pointed petals, large spreading sepals. Flower held erect (drooping in water avens). Fruit dry and strawberry-like. Locally frequent in swamps and by ponds, less so in south. Rose family. May-July.

Reed Zone

Conspicuous zone bordering ponds and rivers where water meets land. Tall plants dense and crowded, standing in shallow water, mostly with long, narrow, flexible stems and leaves so as to avoid damage from wind. Provides cover and nest-sites for waterbirds and insects.

1 Great Reedmace

Also called false bulrush (though in separate family from true bulrushes) as a result of famous painting of baby Moses in basket hidden among this plant. Easily recognised. Long, greyish, lance-shaped, fleshy leaves, central flower stalk. Has sausage-shaped top composed of densely packed flowers. Males above, fluffy golden when ripe, short-lived; chocolate-brown female flowers below produce tufted, wind-blown fruits. Common and widespread, usually standing in water, may fill entire pond. June-August. Lesser bulrush similar but smaller, has a gap between male and female flowerheads. More local in lowland England.

2 Common Bulrush

One of large family resembling sedges (see p.198) but which differ in having clusters of small, greenish or brown flowers with petals and sepals, six in all. Leaves sheath the stiff, sometimes hollow stem. Common bulrush is a tall perennial, with soft rounded flower stem more or less leafless. Flowers reddish-brown, in egg-shaped terminal clusters on short stalks with leaf-like bracts at base. Common by streams and ponds. Stems used for basket making. June-July.

3 Flowering Rush

Handsome waterside plant. Tall perennial with long, grass-like leaves. Leafless main stem bears umbel of rose-pink, stalked flowers with six similar petals and sepals. Local in or by water, mainly in south. July-September.

4 Spearwort

Greater spearwort has narrow, lance-shaped, toothed leaves, hence name. Flowers twice size of buttercup, on long stems. Local in marshes, ditches, ponds. Buttercup family. June-August. Lesser spearwort smaller but similar, lower leaves more oval. Common and widespread.

5 Bogbean

Also called buckbean. Attractive creeping perennial, easily recognised by large, clover-like, trifoliate leaves rising above water surface. Upright stem bearing conspicuous white flowers, pink outside, the five petals fringed with hairs. Local in shallow ponds, swamps, etc. May-June.

Aquatics

Three kinds of plants which grow in open water. **Rooting aquatics** grow up from bottom each year, with leaves and flowers on long stalks reaching surface, dying down in winter. **Floating aquatics** lie on surface with roots dangling freely. **Submerged aquatics** mainly below surface, leaves small, long or freely divided, flowers small at surface. Commonly spread by fragmentation. Form compact winter buds (turions) which grow out following spring.

1 White Water-Lily

Rooting aquatic producing floating, round leaves (lily pads) on long stems. Large, floating white flowers, fragrant, with bright yellow stamens, short-lived, close up at night. Common in still water or ponds and lakes, more so in north and west. June-August. Yellow water-lily has larger, more flask-shaped flowers with small petals, large sepals. Also called brandy-bottle. Leaves more oval. Widespread. Fringed water-lily has round leaves arising on upper stems near surface, yellow flowers with fringed border to petals. Local in still water. Nor a true water-lily. Bogbean family.

2 Pondweed

Common rooting aquatics. Sometimes cover entire pond with submerged and floating leaves. Surface leaves usually oval or elongated, brownish-green, but vary according to water depth, still or moving. Small, greenish flowers with four sepals, no petals, on upright stalks above surface. Pondweeds occur in fresh and brackish water, in ponds, lakes, ditches, streams. Some 20 species. Three common examples — broad-leaved pondweed has large, elliptical surface leaves, narrow ones submerged; curled pondweed has wavy-edged, submerged leaves; slender pondweed has grass-like, submerged leaves.

3 Arrowhead

Rooting perennial, up to 3 feet (91cm), readily recognised by large, arrow-shaped leaves above water, floating lance-shaped leaves and submerged ribbon-like leaves. Male flowers white, three-petalled with purple centre, grow in whorls on vertical stem. Females separate and without petals. Standing in shallow water. Water-plantain family. July-August.

4 Water Crowfoot

Crowfoots are very variable aquatics. Common species (shown here) rooting with small, lobed, floating leaves, finely divided, submerged ones in clusters. Ivy-leaved crowfoot has only shiny ivy-shaped, floating leaves. River crowfoot has only elongated, submerged leaves. Flowers white. Common in ponds and lakesides, sometimes in profusion. Buttercup family. May-June.

5 Water Violet

Attractive rooting perennial with whorls of submerged, finely divided, feathery leaves supporting an upright flower stem of pale lilac five-petalled flowers with yellow centres in ascending whorls. Local in ponds, rare in north. Primrose family. May-June.

Aquatics contd

1 Frogbit

Floating aquatic. Bronze-green, kidney-shaped leaves in rosettes, with long, hanging roots, reproduces by runners, in strawberry fashion. White three-petalled flowers, male and female on separate plants, appear just above water. May cover entire pond. Local, mainly in south. June-August.

2 Duckweed

Minute floating aquatics with hanging roots in still water, usually in large green sheets which may carpet entire pond, puddle or ditch during summer. Each plant a single frond, no stem or leaf, with minute green flower rarely produced, mainly spreads by budding off new fronds. Common food of water fowl. Can also grow on wet mud. Common duckweed has rounded fronds 1/8 inch (3mm) across with single root. Very common. May-July. Greater duckweed almost twice as large, more roundish fronds, and tuft of many roots. More local, mainly in south. Ivy-leaved duckweed entirely submerged, has lance-shaped translucent fronds each with single root, several fronds attached together at right-angles. Widespread, less so in north. Least duckweed, smallest European flowering plant, minute, rootless, egg-shaped, about size of pin head, feels like a piece of grit, is mixed with other duckweeds. No flowers. Very local in south.

3 Water Fern

Attractive, hairy, moss-like, floating fern up to 3/4 inch (19mm) across, has thread-like roots, each plant with lobed, overlapping blue-green leaves turning red in autumn. Spore cases in pairs under leaves. Local in still water, mainly in south. Introduced from USA, usually an escape from aquaria.

4 Water Milfoil

Long, trailing, submerged aquatic, not unlike hornwort (p.246). Feathery leaves much separated into side branches, in whorls of four to five along main branches. Whorled milfoil has small, unstalked, male and female greenish flowers at base of upper leaves, on short stem projecting just above water. Spiked water milfoil (shown here) rather similar, has flowers on leafless, longer erect stalk well above water. More obvious upper flowers male with yellow anthers and red petals, green females below. Both widespread in still or slow-moving water. Can also grow on wet mud. June-August.

5 Water Soldier

Unusual floating aquatic, may be entirely submerged when not flowering. Dark green perennial of numerous, stiff, lance-shaped leaves with sawlike edges resembling leaves of pineapple, spreading upwards from base out of water, with long, hanging roots. Reproduces by runners in strawberry fashion. Small, three-petalled white flowers, sexes on separate plants, males rare. Seldom seeds. Local in eastern England, mainly East Anglia, in fens, broads, ponds and canals. Frogbit family. June-August.

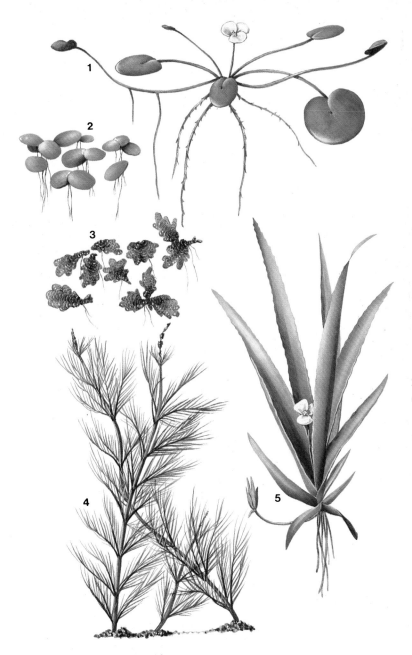

Aquatics contd

1 Canadian Pondweed

Also called water thyme. Submerged aquatic with branched, brittle stems, covered with overlapping whorls of close-fitting, narrow, oblong, dark green leaves. Small, whitish female flowers at surface on long, thin stalks, very occasional. Males on separate plant extremely rare. Reproduction by fragmentation, quickly roots. Rapid coloniser, one of the commonest water plants, introduced from America. A good oxygenator, popular with aquarists. Widespread in still water.

2 Hornwort

Somewhat resembles water milfoil (p.244). Submerged, brittle aquatic, with stiff leaves thinly forked and toothed, branches bushy at tips, rootless. Separate small green flowers at base of leaves. Unusual underwater pollination in which pollen sacs float to surface and pollen then sinks on to female flowers. Flowers occasionally, small fruit reddish. Locally common in England. July-September.

3 Water Starwort

Variable aquatic, mainly submerged, in thick tufts with weak stems. Leaves pale green, oval, in dense clusters, those at surface forming star-shaped rosettes. Small, inconspicuous male and female flowers on same plant without petals. Very common in still and slow-moving water, in ponds, puddles and streams, also on wet mud. May be only colourful patch of green showing in winter.

4 Willowmoss

Submerged, aquatic moss named after shape of leaves, which pack tightly around branches. Is attached to stones in long streamers pulled by current in rivers. Also grows in ponds. Spore capsules rarely produced underwater, but may develop where water dries up.

5 Bladderwort

Floating, rootless aquatic. Leaves feathery, much divided, the toothed segments bearing small air bladders which catch small water animals (e.g. Daphnia). Mouth of bladder triggered by sensitive hairs which release pressure so that victim is sucked inside and digested. Central stalk produces rich, yellow, two-lipped flowers with spur behind. Seldom flowers. Reproduction by fragmentation. Still, often deep, fresh water. June-August. Small bladderwort similar but smaller, sometimes without leaves, only bladders. Local in acid bogs.

Animals

1 Dragonfly up to 3in, 7½cm

Powerful insect with large, efficient eyes. Strong and rapid in flight, hovering and moving in any direction. Prey caught in flight or by darting from perch. Mates during flight, when male grasps female by neck with hind claspers. Eggs laid in plant stems or on surface. Adult life about one month. Larva, called nymph (1a), has powerful jaws fixed to hinged lower lip (the mask) which are shot forward to seize prey. May take five years to mature. Can dart forward by pumping water from hind end. No pupal stage, nymph climbs out of water on plant stem, then changes into adult. Wings held outstretched at rest. Some 27 British species. Harmless. May travel far from water.

2 Damselfly up to 2in, 5cm

Smaller, more graceful kind of dragonfly with more fluttering flight. Keeps close to waterside. Wings held over body at rest. Eyes more widely spaced than dragonfly. Nymph (2a) has three 'tails' acting as gills, and moves with wriggling motion. Colours vary between sexes. About 17 British species.

3 Mosquito up to ¼in, 6mm

Mosquito and gnat are synonymous terms for group of biting insects which grow up in water. Only female bites, with stabbing, needle-like mandibles. Some species feed on blood of animals and man; some may spread disease. Male harmless, does not bite, has feathery antennae. Best known kinds are common mosquito ·or gnat (Culex) and so-called malaria mosquito (Anopheles). Gnat (shown here) rests with body parallel to surface, lays eggs in rafts on water. Larva (3a) hangs from surface by hind end. Anopheline mosquito holds body sharply tilted, lays eggs singly. Larva hangs parallel to surface. Brackish water form of anopheline mosquito used to carry ague, the now extinct British form of malaria. Breed in most stagnant waters.

4 Alderfly up to ¾in, 19mm

Waterside insect seen in large numbers resting on plants, including alder, in May and June. Dark body, long antennae, dull, heavily-veined wings held roof-wise over body. Reluctant to fly, short-lived, does not feed. Batches of eggs laid on plants and stones near water. Larva (4a) has rows of gills along sides of body, may live for two years before leaving water to pupate in bankside. Adult emerges in three weeks.

5 Mayfly up to 1in, 25mm

Recognised by four wings held erect at rest, and long 'tails', three in some, two in others. Eggs, laid or dropped on water, hatch into nymphs (5a) which vary much in colour and shape according to species, but all have three tails. Occur in ponds and rivers, those in fast water clinging to stones. Nymph stage lasts up to two years. Nymphs much eaten by fish, copied as artificial flies by anglers. Adult emerges from nymph at surface as a sub-imago with clouded wings, the 'dun' of anglers, then changes to true adult or 'spinner'. The latter occur in large swarms, do not eat and are short-lived. About 46 British species. Start to appear in May.

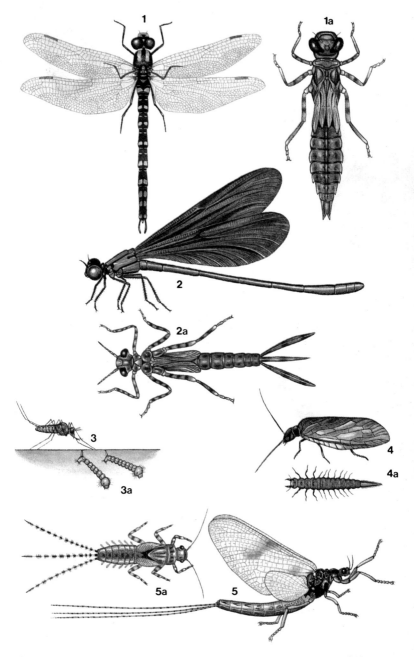

Animals contd

1 Caddis-Fly up to ¾in, 19mm

Somewhat moth-like, usually on wing at dusk. Dull-coloured wings mottled in browns and greys, covered in fine hair, long antennae. Adult has short life spent near water, lacks jaws, hardly feeds. Eggs laid in jelly mass fixed to plant or stone. Larva (1a) of two kinds. Most species spin tube of silk to which is attached case of twigs, leaves, stones, shells, according to species and habitat. Larva grips end of case with hooks on tail; protrudes head to crawl or feed. Other kinds, mainly in running water, build silken net attached to a stone. About 180 species, in ponds and rivers.

2 Great Diving Beetle up to 1½in, 38mm

One of the largest water beetles. Streamlined body, olive-brown with orange border to wing case and thorax. Powerful swimmer and ruthless predator. Rises to surface to collect air under wing case through hind end. Case smooth in male, furrowed in female. Male (shown here) has large suckers on front legs used for gripping female when mating. Eggs laid in stems of water plants. Elongated larva (2a), equally ferocious with powerful jaws, also rises for air. Prey seized and contents sucked out. After one year larva pupates in a cell on bankside, emerges as adult after three weeks. Adult can fly, usually at night. Found in ponds and lakes.

3 Whirligig Beetle up to ¼in, 6mm

Small beetle which spends much of its time gyrating in circles on surface in small groups. Dives when disturbed. Eyes divided, upper half sees above water, lower half below. Elongated larva (3a) hatches from egg laid in spring, has outer gills on each segment. In July climbs up water plant at pond-side, builds cocoon of mud to pupate. Adults appear in August. Common in ponds.

4 Water Boatman up to ⅜in, 9mm

Group of brown to yellowish water bugs with long, oar-like hind legs. Swim in jerky movements, rising to surface for air. Piercing mouthparts used for spearing prey and sucking out contents. Eggs laid in water plants hatch into wingless nymphs. Adults can fly. Common large species (shown here) swims upside-down and is called backswimmer.

5 China-Mark Moth up to ¾in, 19mm

Moth whose caterpillar lives in water. Adult has greyish wings with fanciful markings like those a potter makes on china. Eggs laid on floating water leaves, especially lily-pads and pondweed. Larva cuts oval pieces from leaf and attaches to underside with silk as protective cover. Feeds on leaf. Is covered with hair to remain dry. Pupates in silken cocoon covered with pieces of leaf attached to plant stem above water. Moths appear around ponds and lakes in June-July.

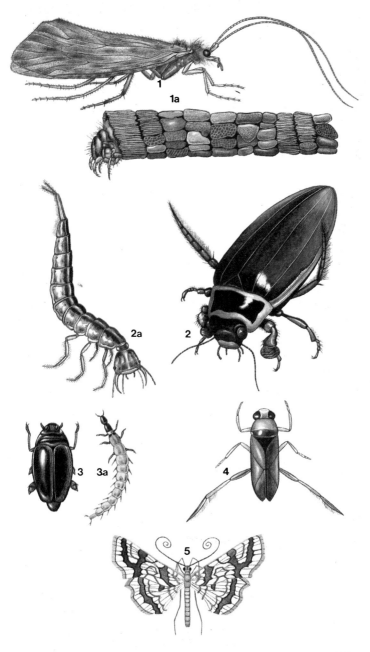

Animals contd

1 Water Spider up to ¼in, 6mm (female)

Only British spider which lives in water. Male larger than female (unusual for spiders). Recognised by silvery appearance underwater due to light reflection from film of air on body. Spins a horizontal platform among plants. Collects air bubbles from surface (in its body hairs) with repeated visits, releases them under web to force it upwards into bell-like shape (1a). Inside bell spider can breathe, lay eggs, feed, even hibernate. Up to 100 eggs sealed off inside bell. Young spiders disperse to live separate lives. Mainly in ponds.

2 Great Pond Snail up to 2in, 5cm

Largest of group of pulmonate snails, which rise to surface for air. Shell brownish, spiralling to a point. Flat, trianglular tentacles with eyes at base. Eggs laid on plants in sausage-shaped jelly coat. Feeds on plants, also scavenges on newts and small fish, using horny tongue (radula) like land snail. Common in ponds, canals, slow-moving rivers.

3 Ramshorn Snail up to 1in, 2½cm

Another group of pulmonates with flattened spiral shell resembling sheep's horn. Long thin tentacles. Blood containing haemoglobin gives flesh reddish-brown colour which shows through in occasional albino. Much prized by aquarists. Eggs laid in roughly circular jelly mass. Somewhat local in ponds, canals, lakes.

4 Swan Mussel up to 4in, 10cm

Large species of freshwater mollusc with oval shell hinged at top. Moves over bottom by protruding tongue-like foot in mud or sand, holding like an anchor, then pulling body forward. Feeds on microscopic life, which it filters from water passing in one opening and out of another (the siphons). Numerous eggs, fertilised by nearby male and kept in brood pouch, develop the following spring. Ejected as tiny larvae (glochidia) which attach to passing fish, especially stickleback, and live on host for a while as parasites. Pearl mussel, long, oval and dark, can produce pearls and once supported a flourishing fishery in Roman times. Now confined to swift rivers in the north.

5 Horse Leech up to 6in, 15cm

Annelid worm related to earthworm. Brownish-green body segmented but without bristles. Suckers at both ends. Larger hind one for gripping perch, front one for gripping prey and feeding by sucking out contents. Feeds on fishes, frogs, snails, storing food in internal pouches, one meal lasting several months. Harmless to man and horse, despite name. Graceful swimmer with undulating movement, also crawls in looper fashion. One inch (2½cm) long when at rest but can expand to six inches (15cm). Medicinal leech, now rare, the only British species capable of piercing human skin. Once used by doctors for blood-letting.

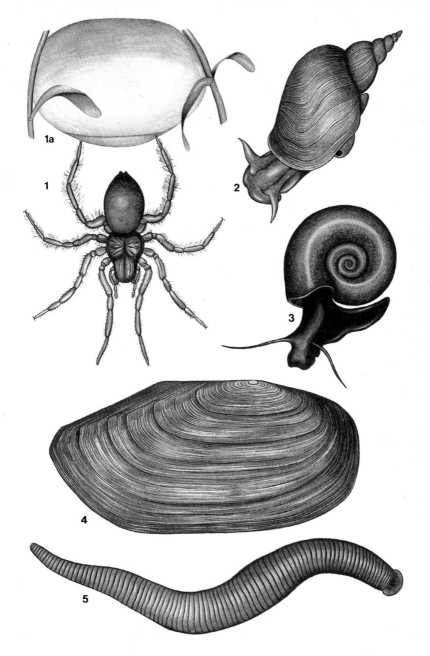

Freshwater Fishes

1 Pike up to 4ft, 122cm

Large carnivorous hunter, can weigh 30 pounds (13.5kg) or more. Torpedo-shaped, with duck-bill-shaped snout and sharp, recurved teeth. Dorsal fin lies far back. Blends well with reeds where it hides in ambush. Darts forward at speed to catch prey — other fish, frogs, young waterfowl. Spawns in early spring, when two or three small males follow female into shallows. Eggs scattered among plants. Young pike called jack. Larger ponds, lakes, slow-moving rivers. Widespread, but not north Scotland.

2 Atlantic Salmon up to 4ft, 122cm

Large, migrating game fish of clean rivers, weighing up to 100 pounds (45kg). Blends well with river bed. Spends most of its life at sea in North Atlantic, until finally swimming up river, often to birth-place, possibly detecting it by smell, and overcoming obstacles with spectacular leaps. Stops feeding. Hen fish excavates shallow nest (redd) on river bed with flapping tail in late November. Eggs fertilised by cock which has hooked lower jaw (kype). Further flapping of tail covers eggs. Fry (alevins) hatch in March with yolk-sac attached, turn into bright-coloured young parr which stay in area for two to three years. These turn into smolt with silvery coat and move down to sea. May return in a year, or later. After spawning and without feeding spent adults (kelts) usually die.

3 Common Carp up to 2ft, 61cm

Large, strongly built, weighing up to 40 pounds (18kg). So-called old English carp imported by monks in fourteenth century. Barbels on mouth. Dorsal fin concave. Two varieties — leather carp has thick skin without scales, mirror carp has a few large scales along flanks. Widely kept as a food fish. Can withstand stagnant water. Mainly plant-eater, in ponds, lakes, slow-moving rivers.

4 Brown Trout up to 18in, 46cm

Game fish, life history similar to salmon. Moves into shallows to spawn during winter. Very variable in colour, size and habits. Small, speckled brook trout, a few inches long, in clear moor and hill streams. Large sea trout, up to 2½ feet (75cm), migratory; smolts move down to sea. Trout feed throughout life.

5 Eel up to 18in, 46cm

Easily recognised, long, sinuous body with long dorsal fin. Eggs laid in Sargasso Sea, hatch into leaf-like larvae (Leptocephalids) carried on Gulf Stream across Atlantic, taking 2-3 years, then change into baby glass eels or elvers around European and British shores in shoals in early summer. Ascend rivers to grow up in any water, even polluted. Mature eels turn silvery, move down to sea but never return.

6 Perch up to 2ft, 61cm

Carnivorous fish with two dorsal fins, front one spiny, lower fins reddish. Hunts in pike fashion, blending with water plants, waiting in ambush. Eggs laid in lace-like strings attached to plants and exposed tree-roots. Widespread in ponds, lakes and slow-moving rivers.

Freshwater Fishes contd

1 Roach up to 12in, 30cm

Silvery fish with bluish back, belly fins reddish, iris red. Weighs up to three pounds (1.4kg). Spawns April-May in vegetation near waterside. Occurs in large shoals in ponds, lakes, rivers, can tolerate stagnant water. Widespread, introduced Ireland, common in built-up areas, popular with anglers. Very similar rudd has dorsal fin well behind pelvic fin (directly above in roach), fins redder, iris orange. Both mainly plant-feeders.

2 Bullhead up to 4in, 10cm

Small with thick, broad, spiny head, tapering body, fanlike front fins. Other name miller's thumb after old custom of kneading flour grains by hand, giving the miller broad thumbs. Mainly shallow water of streams with stony bed where eggs are laid and guarded. Hides by day. Widespread.

3 Gudgeon up to 6in, 15cm

Average-sized bottom-dweller. Slender shape, drooping mouth, barbels hanging from lips used to detect food. Rivers, lakes, and ponds with sandy or gravel bottom, eggs attached to stones. Feeds on water insects. Mainly England, introduced Ireland.

4 Stone Loach up to 6in, 15cm

Slender body, barbels round mouth. Widespread in shallow stony streams, hiding under stones by day, emerging at night to feed on water insects. Sensitive to pollution. Spined loach, up to four inches (10cm), paler colour, has spine below each eye. Mainly eastern England in deeper water of rivers. Hides among plants.

5 Minnow up to 4in, 10cm

Small, lively fish, dark vertical bands along flanks. Breeding male colours up with golden flanks, red belly and bright, white mark on front fins. Common and widespread in shallow water of streams and rivers, living in shoals. Inquisitive, attracted to bright objects. Smallest member of carp family, and favourite bait for anglers.

6 Three-Spined Stickleback up to 3in, 7½cm

Familiar schoolboy's quarry. Three spines in front of dorsal fin. Blue-black above, paler below. Breeds in May-July when male (shown here) colours up with red throat and stomach and bright, emerald-blue eyes. Establishes a territory between water plants, drives away intruders. Red throat a warning (as with robin). Builds nest of plant material on bottom, weighed down with small stones and bound with sticky secretion from kidneys. Courts swollen, egg-bound female with a zig-zag 'dance' leading her to nest to lay eggs. Male fertilises then drives off female. Guards nest, fans eggs, and protects young for about a week. Widespread in most ponds, lake-sides, also around coast in sea-water. Ten-spined stickleback slimly built, dark olive. Breeding similar, nest built above bottom among plants. Mainly southern England.

1

2

3

4

5

6

COAST AND SEASHORE

The shores of Britain vary according to the nature of the coastal rock, direction of sea-current, and presence of river mouths. Tall cliffs of hard rock with small, sheltered bays and rock-pools occur mainly along the Atlantic coast and around Scotland. Open, sandy beaches occur along the North Sea and Channel coast. Rivers deposit silt to form mud flats and salt marshes, the wind builds up sand dunes, and sea currents deposit stones on shingle beaches. Each of these habitats supports its individual community of wildlife, most abundant on rocky coasts.

Shoreline

Plants on shores periodically covered at high tide consist mainly of seaweeds, which tend to occur in zones — green on upper shore, brown on middle, and red on lower shore. Seaweeds are algae which reproduce by spores.

1 Wrack

Familiar, brownish, leathery seaweeds attached to stones, groynes, rocks, pier supports by organ called a holdfast, grow at various levels. Channelled wrack at top of shore has grooved fronds with divided tips, hangs downwards, turns black and brittle if exposed. Flat wrack, a little lower on upper shore, has branched fronds ending in granular fruit bodies. Middle shore contains most familiar bladder wrack (shown here), which has fronds with prominent mid-rib, and bladders in pairs. Egg or knotted wrack, also middle shore, has single, egg-shaped bladders in middle of thin, branched fronds. Serrated wrack on lower shore has toothed fronds, no bladders. Wracks secrete an oily substance, giving protection against exposure when out of water.

2 Eel-Grass

Also called grass-wrack. Flowering plant which can live submerged in seawater. Rooting, green perennial resembling patches of grass. Long narrow leaves up to three feet (91cm), alternate along stem. Minute flowers without petals, reduced to one male anther, one female style, at base of leaves. Local and much decreased (see brent goose p.32). June onwards.

3 Tangles

Large, brown to reddish seaweeds, up to three feet (91cm) or more, also called kelps. Tangles have smooth, flattened stalk and strap-like blade slit into several finger-like sections which grow up round, smooth stalk, up to two feet (61cm). Both are attached to stones or rocks by holdfast, sometimes forming large underwater forests, only exposed at very low tide.

4 Sea Lettuce

Flat, blade-like green seaweed, fronds resembling lettuce leaves, up to one foot (30cm), grows on upper shore washed by freshwater streams.

5 Enteromorpha

No English name. Common green seaweed of thin, unbranched, tubular straps constricted at irregular intervals. In pools on upper shore, also in great masses as early colonisers of mud in estuaries, seen at low tide.

Saltmarsh

Areas of silt or mud deposited by rivers in estuaries and bays and periodically covered by sea. Plants which tolerate salt help to consolidate ground which eventually becomes a saltmarsh, then a salt pasture where sheep can feed and bulbs and root crops are grown, such as on Romney Marsh, Kent, and Lincolnshire and Norfolk coasts.

1 Cord Grass

Also called rice grass. A fertile hybrid between an American species and small, now uncommon, British grass, first detected in Southampton Water in 1870. Stiff, erect, hairless perennial up to three feet (91cm). Leaves yellow-green, tough, grooved, tapering to a point. Elongated flowerhead of closely packed spikes pressed against stem. Locally common on estuarine mud and lower saltmarsh in south England, but is spreading. Often planted to bind mud. July onwards.

2 Glasswort

Also called marsh samphire. Succulent, salt-loving flowering plant which can withstand seawater. Stiff, erect annual up to six inches (15cm), with fat, cylindrical sections of jointed stem, yellow-green. Similar-looking opposite branches, actually leaves, with blunt ends. Minute flowers without petals visible between joints as 1-2 stamens. Seen at low tide. Once used to produce soda for making glass, hence name. Widespread on bare mud of saltmarshes, estuaries. Goosefoot family. August-September.

3 Sea Lavender

Hairless perennial, up to one foot (30cm), resembling true lavender only in colour. Branched, rounded stems, broad, lance-shaped leaves forming rosette. Small blue flowers, closely packed on leafless, curved stalk, rise above leaves. Local but widespread on mud, saltmarshes in England and Wales, rare in Scotland. Sometimes seen in large colourful sheets. Lasting colour makes it popular in flower decoration. Sea lavender family. July-October.

4 Seablite

Much-branched, low-growing, succulent annual, up to nine inches (23cm) wide, dark blue-green or reddish, with numerous, cylindrical, pointed, alternate leaves. Small unstalked, greenish flowers at base. Common in saltmarshes between tides, usually growing higher than glasswort. July-October.

5 Sea Aster

Stout, fleshy, erect perennial, up to three feet (91cm), much branched. Dark green, lance-shaped, alternate leaves with strong mid-rib. Flowerheads resemble Michaelmas daisy, yellow disc florets, pale purple ray florets, in loose clusters. Locally common on saltmarshes along borders of muddy salt creeks. Daisy family. July-October.

Cliffs

Sea cliffs, as well as those inland, support plants which can withstand exposure and which obtain a foothold on bare surfaces by penetrating cracks with a long tap-root, growing in mat or rosette formation. Humus from dead plants, washed into cracks by rainwater, provides nourishment. Limestone cliffs, in particular, rich in calcium salts, can support a wealth of plants of varied colour and form. Lichens are common as colonisers. Plants higher up depend on nature or rock, those lower down tolerate sea-spray. Leaves tend to be fleshy.

1 Thrift

Also called sea pink, Tufted perennial with thick cushion of small, fleshy, elongated leaves. Leafless stalk arises from centre, bearing round head of pink flowers with brownish bracts underneath. Common on sea-cliffs, also saltmarshes, inland on mountains. Familiar in rock gardens. Sea lavender family. May-August.

2 Sea Campion

Low-growing perennial, up to six inches (15cm), forming mat of shoots with small, pointed, oval, waxy leaves, and white flowers. See also bladder and white campions (p.136), which grow inland. Widespread on sea cliffs, also shingle, inland on mountains. Pink family. June-August.

3 Wall Pennywort

Also called navelwort. Distinctive, fleshy perennial, varies in height up to one foot (30cm) or more. Disc-shaped, wavy-edged leaves, size of old penny, hollowed in centre with stalk underneath, mainly around base of flower stalk. Hanging, greenish, tubular flowers. Locally common on cliffs, rocks and walls in west, near sea. Stonecrop family. June-August.

4 Spring Squill

Also called vernal squill. Attractive small bulb plant. Perennial up to eight inches (20cm). Narrow, linear, twisted leaves arise from base. Leafless flower stalk bears short column of star-like, six-petalled, bluish flowers interspersed with blue bracts. Locally common in grass on cliffs near sea, mainly in south-west England. Lily family. April-June. Similar-looking autumn squill has deeper blue flowers on longer columns, no bracts. More widespread, very local. Lily family. July-September.

5 Maidenhair Fern

Attractive, easily-recognised fern. Fronds broken into fan-shaped leaflets on thin, wiry, black stems. Spore-cases below, under inrolled edges of leaflets. Native species very local, easily overlooked, in moist, sheltered cracks in cliffs or caves, mainly in south-west and north-west England, also south Wales and Ireland, especially on limestone. Polypody family.

Sand Dunes

Dune formation occurs where sand is washed on to the beach and blown inland, usually on to a shingle bank, and is slowly fixed by plant growth. Front dune nearest sea is unstable and subject to 'blow-outs', and is mainly colonised by sand-binding plants. Behind this is a hollow or dune slack, usually well watered, with carpet of drought-resistant plants (xerophytes). Features to avoid wilting are reduced leaf surface and thick, rolled up, hairy or spiny leaves. Behind this is a more permanent or 'fixed' dune, well turfed, often used for golf. Old inland dunes occur on Suffolk and Norfolk breckland.

1 Marram Grass

Important sand binder. Stout, creeping perennial, up to four feet (1.2m), broad, sharp-pointed, shiny, greyish-green, stiff leaves with inrolled edges, arise in rows from underground stem of considerable length. Long flowerhead of closely-packed, silky flowers. Sends up fresh plant every year at higher level where sand accumulates. Often planted to fix dune. The principal plant in young dunes. July-August.

2 Burnet Rose

Low, bushy perennial, readily suckers to form extensive patches, up to two feet (61cm) high. Stems thickly covered in long and short straight spines. Leaves with small, toothed leaflets. Flowers on separate stems, creamy white, scented. Sepals remain on deep purple hops. Widespread on dunes, also heaths and downland. Rose family. May-July.

3 Sand Sedge

Perennial with far-creeping, underground stem, bearing rows of grass-like leaves in tufts. Surface stems up to nine inches (23cm), somewhat curved, bearing clusters of short-stalked flowers, male above, female below. Widespread in dunes, similar in habit to marram grass as a sand binder. June-July.

4 Felwort

Small, hairless annual or biennial, up to nine inches (23cm), also called autumn gentian. Elongated, oval leaves in pairs on stem. Flowers on single stem, dull purple, bell-shaped, sepals and petals in fives, hairy white inside. Local in dunes where soil is alkaline, more common on chalk and limestone turf. Gentian family. August-September.

5 Sea Bindweed

Attractive convolvulus. Hairless, prostrate, creeping perennial. Fleshy, kidney-shaped leaves. Large open flower, pink with white stripes; large, green outer bracts. Local on sand dunes. Bindweed family. June-August.

1

2

3

4

5

Shingle

Coastal areas where water-worn, smooth and rounded pebbles accumulate, sometimes along main shore, or sometimes as shingle spits parallel to coast, as at Chesil Bank, Dorset. Seaward side mostly barren due to constant battering and shifting of stones. Landward side supports limited plant-life, mostly perennials which penetrate stones with deep roots to reach fresh water.

1 Sea Holly

Distinctive, stiff, hairless, creeping perennial, thick and bushy, up to one foot (30cm). Spiny, blue-green leaves with white veins and border. Clusters of powder-blue flowers with spiny bracts in thick flowerheads. Local on shingle, also sand. An umbellifer, not a holly. Carrot family. July-August.

2 Sea Pea

Low, mat-forming, fleshy perennial, three feet (91cm) across, with curved stems, blue-green. Leaves short-stalked, with numerous oval leaflets ending in tendrils. Bunches of large, purple pea flowers, pods swollen. Local on shingle, mainly in east and north. Pea family. June-August.

3 Yellow Horned Poppy

Conspicuous perennial, up to two feet (61cm), contains yellow juice. Leaves silvery grey, deeply lobed, clasping stem. Orange-yellow, four-petalled flowers with upstanding female organ which develops into long, curved seed-pod (i.e. horn). Local on shingle. Poppy family. June-September.

4 Sea Storksbill

Small, compact, downy annual usually in rosette form. Leaves small, oval, toothed. Small, pale petals soon fall off, often in one day. Fruit beaked. Shingle, sand dunes and dry turf near sea, mainly in west England and Wales. Geranium family. May-August.

5 Sea Kale

Only white crucifer (with four petals). Cabbage-like leaves in large mass up to two feet (61cm). Thick-set, woody base. Leaves waxy, grey, thick, fleshy and crinkled. Flowers in large cluster, resemble cauliflower. Local on shingle. Cabbage family. June-August.

Rock Pools

Apart from various seaweeds which cling to the rocks, a wealth of animal life can survive in this natural aquarium. Dislodgement by the battering waves and exposure to the air and hot sun are avoided by clinging tightly to the rocks, or living within cracks and among seaweeds.

1 Common Prawn

Elongated shape, up to four inches (10cm), with a long projection of thorax between eyes and pair of long antennae. Second pair of legs with pincers. Colour transparent grey, dotted purple. Crawls, burrows, swims backwards with flapping tail. A scavenger. Edge of sea and in rock pools, among seaweeds, mostly south and west coasts.

2 Shrimp

Smaller cousin of prawn, up to three inches (8cm). General habits similar. Somewhat flattened body, first pair of legs short and heavy. Variable colour yellow to dark brown, dotted red by day, more transparent at night, red when boiled. Eggs carried by mother. Swims with paddle-like limbs (swimmerets), also burrows. Lower shore on sand, also rock pools and estuaries.

3 Lobster

Familiar, large, walking decapod, up to twenty inches (51cm), has powerful pincers for crushing crabs, molluscs, etc., feeding at night. Colour blue, red when cooked. Walks on sea-bed, also swims backwards with flapping tail. Large numbers of eggs (berries) carried by female, hatch in about ten months. Lurks among rocks, young lobsters sometimes trapped in rock pools. Mainly west coast. Spiny lobster or crawfish more reddish-brown, without large pincers, has spiny body, up to two feet (61cm). Mainly below tide mark, south and west coasts.

4 Hermit Crab

Abdomen soft, protected by occupying empty shell of sea-snail such as whelk. Enlarged right pincer used to cover opening. Body up to five inches (13cm), red to yellow foreparts, abdomen brown. Very common on most shores, in rock pools. Can burrow.

5 Shore Crab

Shell four inches (10cm) across, dark green with pale markings. Last pair of walking legs flattened. front border of shell (carapace) serrated. Middle and lower shore in pools under rocks. Commonest crab.

6 Edible Crab

Up to ten inches (25cm) across, can weigh up to ten pounds (4.5kg). Oval shell pinkish-brown, dark claws, front of carapace deeply indented. Middle and lower shore, under stones, in seaweeds and in rock pools, around rocky coasts. Widespread. Also fiddler crab or velvet crab, up to eight inches (20cm) across, reddish-brown, shell covered with fine hair. Blue lines on legs, eyes red. Lower shore, mainly in south and west.

Rock Pools contd

1 Sea Anemone

Resembles a flower in appearance. A hollow, tubular body with single opening at top, surrounded by stinging tentacles. Related to jellyfishes and corals. Sedentary on rocks and seaweeds, sometimes on shells of hermit crabs. Traps small animals. Retracts body when exposed. About fifteen British species, coloured variously cream, brown, orange, blue, green. Two common examples in rock pools are the blood-red anemone, and the largest species, the dahlia anemone (shown here).

2 Starfish

An echinoderm (spiny-skin), radially built with five arms joined at base which can be regrown if lost. Firm skin, mouth underneath. Many suckers (tube-feet) under arms used in crawling and gripping objects, also burrowing. Can force open shell of mollusc such as mussel and feed by protruding stomach through mouth to digest contents. Common starfish reddish-brown, about ten inches (25cm) across, produces large numbers of eggs shed into sea. Common on rocky shores and in pools. Sunstar has eight to thirteen arms, occurs mainly on lower shore.

3 Brittlestar

Similar build to starfish, but with five thin, long, spiny arms clearly separated at base, brittle, easily broken off. Numerous species of various colours, some living in rock pools, others on sea bottom buried in sand. Moves in jerks.

4 Sea Squirt

Also called tunicate. Sedentary, bag-like shape with two openings (siphons) through which water passes to filter plankton. Water squirts out if squeezed. Adults attached to rocks, shells and seaweeds. Some species single, others colonial. Larva is tadpole-shaped, free-swimming, and has affinities with backboned animals. Star seasquirt is colonial, several joined together in jelly coating, about six inches (15cm) across with yellow fringed siphons, attached to boulders, buoys, breakwaters.

5 Sea Urchin

Echinoderm related to starfish. Globular, brittle shell, round, oval or heart-shaped, up to six inches (15cm) across, marked on surface in sections corresponding to arms of starfish. Covered in spines moveable on ball-and-socket joints, also rows of tube-feet. Coloured reddish to purple. Sexes separate. Feeds on seaweeds. Shells sold as ornaments. Common urchin six inches (15cm) across, deep reddish, spherical with blunt spines, in lower rock pools. Heart urchin up to one and a half inches (4cm) across, heart-shaped with yellow spines directed backwards, burrows in sand. Sea potato shaped like heart urchin, smaller, up to three inches. Brittle spines easily break off. Sandy coloured shell often washed up on beach. Burrows in sand.

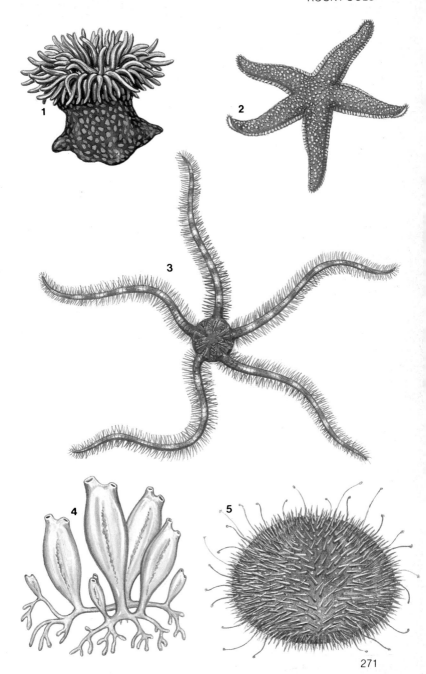

Rock Pools contd

1 Barnacle

Small crustacean cemented to rocks, breakwaters, piers, boats, by secretion from head. Lives upside down, covered by series of plates. Through these, six pairs of forked limbs fringed with hair sweep in and out through gap to trap plankton food. Bisexual. Common acorn barnacle shown here, about half an inch (13mm) in diameter, encrusts rocks in millions. Goose barnacle hangs from thick stalk and resembles goose head, attached to floating weeds, sometimes washed ashore. Mainly south-west shores.

2 Limpet

Mollusc with conical shell, clings to rocks with sucker-like foot, difficult to dislodge. Keeps to a home base which may show as a scar on the rock surface where it fits tightly. Makes circular forays up to three feet (91cm) around home, browsing on film of algae when tide is in. Returns to same spot at ebb tide. Common limpet, shown here, has oval shell two and a half inches (6½cm) long with pale foot. Occurs widely on middle and lower shore, in rock pools. Breeds late summer, shedding eggs into sea.

3 Topshell

Molluscs with distinctive, cone-shaped shell, straight sides, broad base, revealing mother-of-pearl where shell is worn. Variously coloured white, pink, streaked with darker red or purple. Also occurs in zones from middle to lower shore. Common in rock pools.

4 Dog Whelk

Common sea snail. Thick, sculptured, spiral shell, one and a half inches (4cm) long, has hinged doorway (operculum). Long breathing tube (siphon) extends above, used to detect food and clean water. A flesh-eater, can extend mouth to feed, boring into shells of barnacles, mussels, etc. Eggs laid in small sacs attached to rocks on stalks. Very common in rock pools. Larger common whelk or buckie, up to six inches (15cm), lives more offshore, and is gathered commercially for food. Eggs laid in sponge-like mass of pale yellow capsules, often washed ashore when empty.

5 Periwinkle

Group of small molluscs with solid, smooth, rounded shells pointed to one side, variable in colour. Long tentacles. Door sealed with operculum. Plant feeders. Examples are: **a, rough periwinkle.** Quarter-inch (6mm) across, deeply ribbed, rough to touch, yellow, orange or brown. Lower down in upper to middle shore. Produces live young. **b, small periwinkle.** Quarter-inch (6mm) across with small, pointed, smooth, fragile shell with a dark-coloured bloom. Mainly upper shore in splash zone, in rock crevices, often exposed. Feeds on lichens. Lays eggs. **c, edible periwinkle.** Up to one inch (25mm), pointed, with surface pattern lined dark red or grey. Middle and lower shore among seaweeds, in crevices, rock pools, among stones, even in sand or mud.

Rock Pools contd

1 Mussel

Familiar bivalve mollusc, elongated blue-black shell pointed at tail end where growth centre (umbone) occurs. Shows curved growth rings. Frilled edge of mantle appears when shell opens. A filter-feeder through two openings (siphons). Strap-like foot used for fixing sticky threads to rock, secreted from a gland. Bisexual, eggs fertilised in water. Young mussels occur in masses in nurseries on lower shore. Adults up to four inches (10cm) long, very common on rocks, in rock pools, etc., on middle shore. Large horse mussel up to nine inches (23cm), deep blue to purple, does not show mantle when open. Lower shore or offshore, usually on gravel bottom and among kelp.

2 Chiton

Also called coat-of-mail. Small, flat mollusc, up to one inch (25mm), dull-coloured, reminiscent of a wood louse in build. Easily recognised by eight, articulating plates on shell, arranged one behind other along back. Can curl up. Gills arranged under border of shell. Habits similar to limpet, clings to rocks, feeds on seaweed. Not always easy to find.

3 Blenny

Small fish, long dorsal fin whole length of back, pectoral fins fan-shaped, pelvic fins much reduced. No spines on gill covers. Heavy head and large eyes. Common blenny or shanny, up to five inches (12½cm), olive or dark green, blotched with black, feeds on barnacles bitten off rocks. Adult guards eggs.

4 Goby

Small fish with pelvic fins modified into a sucker for clinging to rocks. Two dorsal fins, front one spiny. Large protruding eyes. Common goby up to two inches (5cm), dark sandy or grey, freckled. Breeds in empty shell or under stone, male guards eggs, aerates them with fins.

5 Butterfish

Also called gunnel, related to blenny. Slippery, elongated, eel-like body flattened sideways, tapering to round tail. Up to seven inches (18cm). Pelvic fins minute. Yellow-green to bronze, fins reddish, with about twelve black spots along back. Guards eggs.

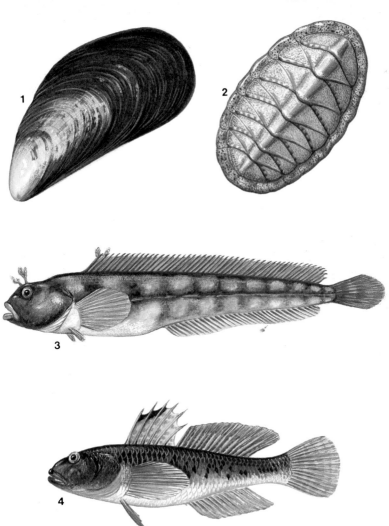

Mud-Flat

Shores and estuaries where mud accumulates, carried down by rivers and exposed at low tide. A stable environment where shore animals can make permanent homes in burrows. Favourite feeding ground of waders and gulls.

Bristle Worms

Bodies segmented with pairs of paddles and projecting bristles used for burrowing or swimming. Some species free-living, others sedentary in tubes hardened with mucus which binds the sand or mud. Examples include:

1 Ragworm

A number of similarly-built species ranging in size up to the large green ragworm, twelve inches (30cm). Has a pair of paddles with bristles on each segment. Large head has two antennae, numerous feelers, and a pair of large, black jaws. Head can be contracted or extended. Teeth show as black dots. Swims well, can burrow.

2 Lugworm

Also called lobworm. Bristle worm which lives in U-shaped tube in coastal mud. Presence can be recognised by a hollow depression at surface (head end) adjacent to a worm cast, sometimes in large numbers. Feeds by swallowing mud. Common lugworm nine inches long (23cm), thick as a man's finger, brown to greenish-black, has reddish, plume-like gills along middle region. Popular as fisherman's bait.

3 Sand Mason

Bristle worm up to twelve inches (30cm). Body pink with a fringe of numerous thread-like tentacles and dull red gills at head end which projects from tunnel. Widespread in sand and tidal mud. Tube built vertically, rather fragile, with mud or sand cemented with small stones, as shown here.

4 Gaper

Bivalve mollusc which burrows in muddy sand, Large, oval shell which gapes widely behind due to massive siphons. Sand gaper is the 'soft-shelled clam' popular as food. Shell five inches long (13cm), olive-brown. Burrows deeper with growth, down to one foot (30cm), as siphons lengthen to reach surface. Has a fringe of tentacles at head end, with minute eyes for detecting surroundings. Widespread on sand and mud in estuaries.

5 Cockle

Solid, rounded bivalve with circular, brown markings on pale background. Common cockle, up to two inches (5cm) across, has globular, ridged shell. Lives near surface on muddy, tidal shores and estuaries, breathing and feeding with short siphons. Popular food, easily gathered by raking mud.

6 Razorshell

Easily recognised mollusc. Elongated, tubular bivalve open at both ends. Short siphon with divided tip at one end, foot at other. Shell straight or curved, up to eight inches (20cm). Burrows vertically. Common pod razorshell has curved shell. Hinge is close to food end, which protrudes into sand or mud to hold and pull shell downwards. Expels water to facilitate movement. Can burrow rapidly. Siphons open at surface. Empty shells common.

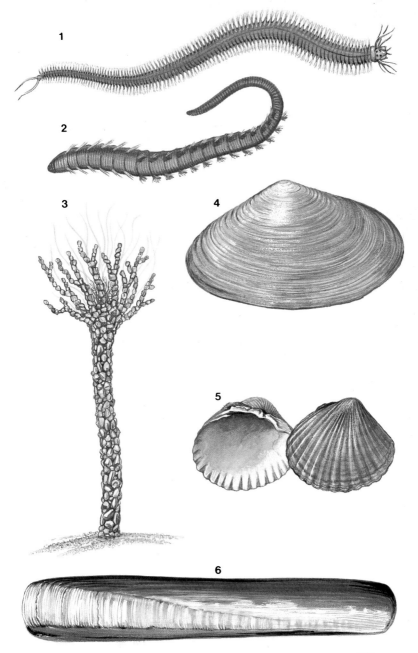

277

Cattle

Western breeds of cattle are descended from the aurochs or urus, a black woodland giant up to six feet (1.8m) tall which survived until the early seventeenth century in Poland. The famous white cattle kept in various parks in Britain closely resemble it in size, build and temperament, but their origin is uncertain. Early records of domestication are mainly from the Middle East, going back some 6,000 years. Various invaders brought cattle to Britain, from which some 20 modern breeds have developed, consisting of long-horned and short-horned cattle. Some, such as the British white, Galloway and Aberdeen Angus, have their horns removed (polled), a practice carried out mainly in eastern Britain and introduced by the Vikings. Beef cattle are fleshy, stocky, broad and short-legged. Dairy cattle are longer, more wedge-shaped, with narrow hind quarters and large udders. They range in size from large Friesian to small Jersey. All British cattle are now tested for tuberculosis. Cattle are bred for meat, milk and hides, largely by factory farming methods. The male is called a bull and becomes a bullock when castrated; the cow is a heifer until her first calving.

1 Hereford

Most abundant of beef cattle, originating from Welsh border. Pure breed deep red with white face and fore-quarters, the result of importing the Blaaskop (white head) from Netherlands. Heavy, deep body with short, broad head, usually polled. Bull shown here.

2 Highland

Hardy mountain breed, small and shaggy, hair falling in thick fringe over face. Head short and broad, long horns sweep upwards and outwards. Mainly in Scottish Highlands. Usually black but may be red or brindled. Good but slow-maturing beef breed.

3 Friesian

Also called Holstein, originally from Jutland. Large, heavy breed easily recognised by black and white colour. Horns curl forwards and inwards. Introduced from Netherlands (Friesland) in 1909. A dominant Dutch breed. Large and heavy build, most numerous in England and Wales. A dairy cow with high yield of milk and butterfat.

4 Jersey

Lean, dainty, fine-boned dairy breed, only one allowed on island, now common in mainland Britain too. Of mixed origin, from Asia and Northern Europe. Colour light fawn or darker reddish, pale around snout and undersides. Short-legged, curved face, short horns, and large udder. Rich milk-producer, high in butterfat.

5 Guernsey

Only breed allowed on the island. Originates from France. Small dairy cow, lean-shaped, fawn to reddish, or black and white. Long head with short, curved horns, large udder. Excellent milker, especially for making butter.

279

Cattle contd

1 Dexter

Smallest British breed, somewhat localised, native to mountains of western Ireland. Heavy head, usually horned. Deep, compact body, short-legged, mainly all-black. Can subsist on poor grazing. Good for meat and milk.

2 Ayshire

Second most numerous breed in Britain and native to south-west Scotland. Hardy dairy cow of typical wedge shape, has mixed brown and white coat. Slender, erect horns grow outwards and forwards. Produces high-quality milk.

3 South Devon

Largest British breed, native to Devon and Cornwall but now widespread throughout Britain. Massive build, short-legged, deep-bodied, broad head carries short, down-curved horns. Colour sandy-red. High butter-fat yield, produces well-known Devonshire cream. Also reared for beef.

4 Aberdeen Angus

Breed native to Scotland but widespread throughout Britain. Squat, long-bodied build, short-legged, broad, polled head, coat black. Good meat producer, matures early. Bull shown here.

5 Charolais

Recent French introduction. Massive, short-horned breed, heavy-boned, short legs, bull (shown here) has powerful neck crest. Colour creamy white. Used at first for all-purpose milk and meat production, and as a draught animal on farm. Crossed with dairy breeds to produce beef calves. An indifferent milk producer.

Dairy Farming

Dairy farming has become intensely mechanised since the Second World War and now produces some 30 million pints a day for British householders. One cow produces an average of three gallons (can reach six) during the 300 milking days after calving. Cows are artificially inseminated, bulls are kept at breeding centres. Cows are put out to summer grass and in winter are fed on hay and silage mixed with barley grain, plus straw as roughage. Dairy cattle consist of Friesian, Ayshire, Jersey, Guernsey and South Devon.

Pigs

Domestic pigs are descended from the wild boar, which still survives in scattered forests and parks across Europe, Asia, and North Africa. Formerly hunted in India as a sport called pig-sticking with lance and horse. European breeds tend to be long-bodied and lop-eared, those from Asia short and fat, short-legged, and with erect ears. Influence from both is seen in Britain, mainly from Chinese imports, apart from so-called Landrace pigs native to Northern Europe, which are lean-bodied and directly descended from European wild boar. Early pigs in Britain had a dirty yellow colour, with darker markings and coarser coat, and roamed streets during Middle Ages cleaning up litter. Were also released onto common land to feed on acorns and mast, an ancient commoner's right still practised in New Forest. During nineteenth century native pigs were crossed with more docile forms from Asia, from which modern breeds developed. Despite their reputation pigs are clean and intelligent, and useful providers of bacon, ham and pork. They are susceptible to cold and exposure, and can suffer from sunburn because of their thin coat of bristles. Usually kept in sties or on factory farms. A sow can produce two litters (farrows) a year, of up to 15 young.

1 Large White

Largest, most numerous and most prolific breed, originates from Yorkshire. Is basis of many crosses, such as with Chester White, which originated in Pennsylvania in the United States. Both have white colour with occasional darker markings. Head of medium length with curved, upturned snout, ears pricked. An excellent bacon producer.

2 Saddleback

Hardy, all-purpose breed developed from East Anglian and Dorset strains. Colour black with white 'saddle' over shoulders and down front legs. Ears loose and hanging.

3 Welsh

Hardy breed popular in Wales. Body somewhat lean and long, rather weak limbs and flop ears. Colour white. Has close resemblance to the Landrace breed from north-west Europe, from which it is derived. Good bacon producer.

4 Gloucester Old Spot

A small, localised, all-purpose breed from the Severn Valley, descended from a hardy, foraging type of pig capable of subsisting on fallen fruit, etc., such as windfalls in apple orchards. Colour white, marked with black spots in various patterns.

5 Large Black

Large breed similar in build to Large White, with which it is frequently crossed. Originally from West Country and East Anglia. Heavy coat of black hair. Long, hanging ears impede vision and may be cause of its docile habits. Hardy pig which can subsist on poor diet.

Horses

The evolutionary history of the horse is well known through whole series of fossils which originate with the minute, terrier-sized, four-toed dawn horse *(Eohippus)* of Eocene Period, 70 million years ago. Immediate ancestor of modern horse *(Equus)* is the tarpan (p.286) of Europe and Asia, now probably extinct. Domestication began in Bronze Age. Two types developed — the slender, lively racing horses of warmer countries, such as Arab and Thoroughbred, also various pony breeds, and heavier, more robust horses used in farm work and labour in colder climates, such as Percheron and Clydesdale. Height of a horse is measured in 'hands' (four inches/ten cm) behind shoulders to ground. Horse brasses, now used for decoration at shows, were once worn as charms to ward off evil spirits.

Draught Horses

1 Shire

Powerful breed, up to 17 hands, originates from Belgium. Once used as war horse by knights. With change from heavy armour to light cavalry, the breed was used more for farm work, then went into decline with arrival of mechanisation. Still retained for pulling brewers' drays, for appearance at shows, in ploughing competitions. Colour brown, bay or black, usually with white on face and legs, which are well feathered. Heaviest of draught breeds.

2 Suffolk Punch

Mixed ancestry of Belgian heavy horse and trotting horse. Broad, deep-bodied, short mane, unfeathered legs. Colour always chestnut. Powerful breed, up to 16 hands, was used for pulling gun carriages during First World War. Moves well at a trot. The heavy horse of East Anglia.

3 Percheron

Most common heavy breed, originates from France (La Perche). Introduced into Britain during First World War. Rather small draught horse, up to 16 hands, refined by Arab blood. Deep, compact body, small head, short legs, no feathers. Colour a dappled grey and black, is in much demand at agricultural shows, also as dray horse for breweries.

4 Clydesdale

Like the Shire, is descended from old Flemish stock first established in Lancashire during eighteenth century. A cross between native Shire and Flemish stallion. Less massive than Shire, up to 16 hands. Feathers at back of legs. Colour brown, bay or black, with occasional greys. White on face and legs. Rather temperamental. Less powerful than other heavy breeds.

Horses and Ponies

Note: the horses and ponies listed on this page are domesticated animals rather than farm animals, but are included here for convenience.

1 Cob

Cobs and hacks are not breeds. Cob is an all-purpose horse, strong and short-legged, up to 15 hands, often used as riding horse, especially the Welsh Cob. Hacks were once used for pulling light vehicles (e.g. hackney carriage) before the motor car, and trained to trot with high-stepping action. Now seen mostly in show-ring.

2 Exmoor

One of a number of small horses (ponies) which roam semi-wild on open commonland, on heaths, moors and mountains in Britain and Europe. Nine breeds in Britain — Exmoor, Dartmoor, Fell, Dale, Connemara, Highland, New Forest, Welsh, Shetland. Exmoor is considered closest in appearance to early Celtic horse already in existence before Roman arrival. Exmoor is coloured bay or brown without any white, broad head and nostrils, short ears, up to 12 hands. Hardy breed formerly used as pack animal, now popular as children's pony.

3 Arab

Small horse with good staying power. Head with small muzzle on long, arched neck. Strong, straight back with broad, deep chest. Is descended from Libyan horse about 600 AD. Skin is black with variable hair colour — black, brown, grey, white. Up to 15 hands. The Thoroughbred is descended from three Arab stallions brought to England during eighteenth century, and is bred and trained for racing. Racing is now a flourishing industry, first inspired by Charles II, who frequented Newmarket, the present headquarters of British horse racing. There are some 10,000 race-horses in Britain today, and 18,000 in Ireland.

4 Tarpan

Ancestral wild horse, now probably extinct, which once roamed the open steppes and forests of Europe and Asia. Steppe tarpan was exterminated in about 1890. Tarpan-like horses still survive in zoos. Wood tarpan (last seen in Poland) died out earlier. Attempts to reconstruct the tarpan by breeding back have produced a stocky horse, clear to mouse-grey, nearly white in winter, and with short, erect mane, black stripe along back, and zebra-like stripes behind front legs.

5 Hunter

Bred for hunting and show jumping, and grouped into classes to suit different weights of rider. Vary in size and stamina according to type of country being hunted.

Goats

Most domesticated breeds are descended from wild bezoar goat, still surviving in mountains of south-west Asia. Horns in both sexes scimitar-shaped and flattened sideways. In domestic breeds these rise in a wider, more open spiral. Agility of goat is well-known and retained from its mountain ancestry. Earliest domestication was in Middle East about 10,000 years ago. Goats are kept mainly for milking. Female can produce up to eight pints daily. Usually kept for family use on small-holdings. Switzerland is the main European source of milking goats. Voracious feeders, they can do much damage to trees and hedges, so are usually kept tethered, but can be used to clear scrub. In some areas of world, especially around Mediterranean, goats have created desert conditions. Male called billy, female nanny, young a kid.

1 Alpine

A cross between British and Swiss stock. Slim build, coloured white, brown, grey or black. Ears erect. Billy more shaggy than nanny, with long hairs along back.

2 Toggenburg

Another cross between British and Swiss goats. Small size, colour brown with two white stripes down face and white around tail. Ears erect. Billy has a shaggy coat. Good milker. Smallest of Swiss breeds.

3 Saanan

Derived from Swiss valley of that name. White to creamy coat, nanny short-haired, billy more shaggy. Ears erect.

4 Anglo-Nubian

Originated from Nubia in north-east Africa. Has hanging ears, pronounced Roman nose, prominent forehead, long legs. Hair short, usually black and tan, may be mixed with white. Produces rich milk, but less so than Swiss breeds.

5 Bezoar

Also called ibex. Ancestor of domestic goats still surviving in mountains of south-west Asia, with further races in Spain, Alps, and some Greek islands. Large size, grey and grizzled, sometimes with dark markings; pale belly and lower legs. Large, curved horns with rings, smaller or missing in nanny.

Sheep

Domestic sheep are descended from mouflon, still found in mountains of south-west Asia, Corsica, Sardinia, and introduced into parts of Europe. Rather small size with short, non-fleecy coat. Horns in male (ram) massive, curved backwards and downwards, absent in female (ewe). Earliest domestication goes back some 9,000 years, to Neolithic farmers of Middle East. Wild Soay sheep of Outer Hebrides said to be direct descendants and resemble these early sheep. Selective breeding has produced woolly fleece to replace coarse, ancestral hair. Apart from New Zealand, Britain has largest number, about 40 breeds. Divided into long-wools, such as Romney Marsh and Border Leicester; short-wools, such as Suffolk and downland breeds; and hill sheep, such as Welsh mountain and blackface. Long-wools bred for making smooth woollen cloth, but meat is inferior. Short-wools have dark faces and legs, and fleece used in knitwear. Hill breeds provide coarser wool used in tweeds.

1 Romney Marsh

One of original breeds of long-wools in south-east England, on Romney Marsh, Kent, a land of flat fields enclosed with water ditches originally reclaimed from sea by Romans. Large, heavy-bodied on short legs, with wool on forehead forming 'top-knot'. Hornless with white face. Produces excellent lamb.

2 Border Leicester

Long-wool breed of Scottish border country. Long-bodied with pronounced chest, arched head and neck, white face, upright ears. Has been much used in crossing with hill breeds, such as Cheviot and Welsh (p.292).

3 Southdown

Well-known short-wool downland breed reared for meat production. Smallest of down breeds. Barrel-like body, fine white fleece which covers face and ears. Has helped to create other downland sheep, such as Suffolk, Dorset and Hampshire. Now a minority breed.

4 Suffolk

Derived from Southdown ram and Norfolk horn ewe, and developed to suit Anglian fenland. Long-bodied, short fleece, black face and legs. Horns form short buds. Has an early lambing season.

5 Dorset Horn

Horned breed derived from tan-faced Portland and Merino, giving an extra spiral to the large, down-curved horns, growing inwards and close to face in both sexes. Can lamb out of season. Face white and covered in wool. Grassland breed in southern England.

Sheep contd

1 Welsh Mountain

Small, hardy, agile mountain breed with white face and legs. Downcurved, forward-facing horns in ram only. Can subsist on mountain vegetation. Produces lean meat.

2 Scottish Blackface

Another mountain breed of heather moorland in Scottish Highlands. Originates from Pennines. Also occurs on Dartmoor. Heavily horned in both ram and ewe. Face and legs mixed black and white. Long, rather coarse fleece used to fill mattresses and make carpets.

3 Swaledale

Hill breed originating from northern Pennines, has spread to Scottish border. Britain's hardiest breed. Long, coarse outer coat with dense, finer inner coat, can withstand cold winds. Ram and ewe both heavily horned, similar to Dorset Horn. Face black with white nose, legs mottled. Wool used to make tweeds, carpets and thick sweaters.

4 Clun Forest

Grassland breed of west Midlands and Wales derived from hill and downland crosses. Face dark brown with short, dark, pricked ears and wool over head, legs dark. Long body, with small head held erect, giving alert expression.

5 Cheviot

Hill breed of Scottish borders, on grass moorland. Medium-sized, short-legged, white face and legs clear of wool, ears erect. Alert posture. Some rams are horned.

Sheep Breeding

Over the years British sheep-farming has consisted of combining old breeds of different types to improve the quality of hybrids. Hill sheep of hardy stock, such as Welsh and blackface, are raised in harsh mountain conditions, then transferred to low ground to mate with rams of more fertile breeds, such as Border Leicester. This produces a higher birthrate and milk yield, combining qualities of both parent stocks. They are then mated to a downland ram from Suffolk or Dorset to improve meat yield. The four main breeding groups are recognised as hill, crossing, down, and grassland sheep. Hill sheep, like their owners and sheepdogs (old English bobtail or collie) are a tough breed. They are brought down from hills to remove skin parasites in sheep dips after shearing in early summer.

1

2

3

4

5

Poultry

All breeds of chickens are descended from the red jungle fowl of India and south-east Asia. First domesticated in China, have since spread world-wide. Introduced into Britain for cock-fighting and for eating. Various breeds established over past 100 years include Leghorn and Wyandotte from America, and later the Rhode Island Red. Buff Orpington developed in Kent. These standard breeds are specialised for egg-laying or meat production and have formed the basis of considerable cross-breeding since Second World War. Modern factory farming in deep-litter houses and battery cages has extended the laying period, which normally starts in spring. Average hen can lay up to 200 eggs per year. Hybrid chicks are bred as broilers for the table, and raised by intensive methods in windowless buildings, under controlled lighting, humidity, temperature and feeding. Such techniques have greatly increased food supply but are open to criticism on animal welfare grounds. Modern chickens are classified according to economic value rather than breeds, as layers, table birds, general-purpose breeds, and fancy breeds. Free-range hens and eggs are now a side-line in poultry farming. Widespread hybridisation threatens the future of pure breeds.

1 Buff Orpington
Dual-purpose, orange-coloured.

2 Leghorn
White-coloured laying fowl producing white eggs.

3 Bantam
Small version of most standard breeds, with which it is crossed into many shapes and colours, about a quarter normal size. Bred more for ornament (and formerly for cock-fighting) than for eggs or meat. No commercial importance. An Old English bantam cock is shown here.

4 Rhode Island Red
Dual-purpose bird with reddish-brown plumage. A much-favoured breed which arrived from America in 1906.

5 Wyandotte
Dual-purpose, mottled black and white plumage.

Ducks

Most farm ducks in Britain are descended from wild mallard. Some are specialised for egg-laying, but most are bred as table birds, on mixed farms and in small units. Large-scale breeding mainly in East Anglia (Norfolk and Lincolnshire). Drake (male) is more colourful and has curled tail feathers. Ducks are hardy birds and independent, can forage on grass, worms, etc., but require extra food from owner, such as mash and cereals. They are messy feeders, and require a water trough or nearby pond or stream. Enclosed at night so that eggs are laid in morning, otherwise may stray and drop them haphazardly outdoors. Incubation of egg 28 days. Ducklings soon run about for food, can weigh up to six pounds at 12 weeks, but are usually killed for eating at eight weeks.

1 Aylesbury

A table bird, originally from Buckinghamshire, coloured off-white. Short orange legs, about the size of a mallard.

2 Indian Runner

Introduced from Malaya in 1836 as egg-layer. Very erect posture, no shoulders. Colour dark fawn or white, dark beak and legs.

3 Muscovy

Commonly kept in South America and Africa, occurs wild in central America where it nests in trees. Rather ungainly build. Wild bird is black with some white on wings. Domestic bird white, black, or mixture, occasionally somewhat lavender. Both sexes have bare red skin around eyes. Drake has small crest and fleshy knob at base of beak and down sides of cheeks. Duck half size of drake. Walks with see-saw movement of head. Does not quack, but makes a puffing sound. A table bird, also kept for ornament.

4 Khaki Campbell

Cross between Indian runner, mallard and Rouen. Drake (shown here) has blue-green head and neck, orange legs. Dual-purpose, but mostly for egg-laying (up to 300 per year, even more than a chicken).

5 Mallard

Familiar ancestral duck which becomes very tame in towns and villages, where it inhabits ponds, but retains wildness in countryside. Pairs during winter. After breeding in February-March, drake (shown here) moults to resemble duck's plumage, called the 'eclipse'. Duck well camouflaged for nesting on ground, occasionally in trees or on buildings, usually near water. At dusk and dawn makes regular flights in and out of town to roost and feed on reservoirs and estuaries, especially during winter. Flight rapid and direct, with fast wingbeats. Shot by wildfowlers. Occasional domestic birds resemble wild form (see also p.30).

Crops

In Neolithic times crude farming with primitive tools consisted of clearing patches of woodland to grow crops until the soil was exhausted, then moving on to another area. During the Middle Ages narrow strips separated by mounds or stakes (perhaps the origin of hedges) were worked on a communal basis. After harvesting, animals were allowed to move in to feed on stubble. Enclosed fields with surrounding hedges or stone walls appeared during Parliamentary Enclosures between 1760 and 1820.

1 Wheat

A main cereal crop in Britain, covering some 3 million acres, and used for making bread, cakes, and biscuits. Erect stem carrying upright seed-head, which tends to bend over on ripening. Grains protected by a stiff, spiked sheath, called chaff after threshing. Seed-head up to six inches (15cm), each grain oval-shaped with a cleft down one side. Grows on more fertile soils, mainly sown in autumn. Wild origin Middle East.

2 Timothy Grass

Soft-leaved perennial grass grown to provide both grazing and winter feed.

3 Meadow Fescue

Bred to give both grazing and cutting varieties, and like timothy grass one of the six grasses favoured by farmers for their nutritious qualities.

4 Barley

Most abundant cereal crop in Britain, mainly in south and east. Grain encased in close-fitting husk with elongated tip, the awn, which has tiny hooks. Two main forms, one with grain in two rows on each side of stem, other with six rows, and forming seed-head similar to wheat. Both derived from grasses in western Asia and north Africa. Made into barley bread in parts of Europe, also as malt for brewing beer. Given to pigs as mash. Straw used as animal litter.

5 Rye

Derived from wild grass in Asia Minor. Grown on small scale due to limited demand for products, such as rye-bread and crisp-bread. Tolerates poor soil. Occasionally sown as cattle fodder, and straw used in thatching.

6 Oats

Cultivated from wild ancestral grass, a probable native of Britain. Distinguished from other cereals by an open, hanging seed-head. Grains encased in tight-fitting husk with loosely attached chaff. Can grow on poorer soil, mainly in Scotland. Once a main food for horses, now grown more for human consumption, such as porridge and oat-cake.

7 Maize

The familiar American sweet corn. Grown in places for eating (corn on the cob) but mainly for silage. Single, stout stem with large leaves. Male flowers grow at top within broad blades, female lower down in angles of middle leaves. Originates in South America.

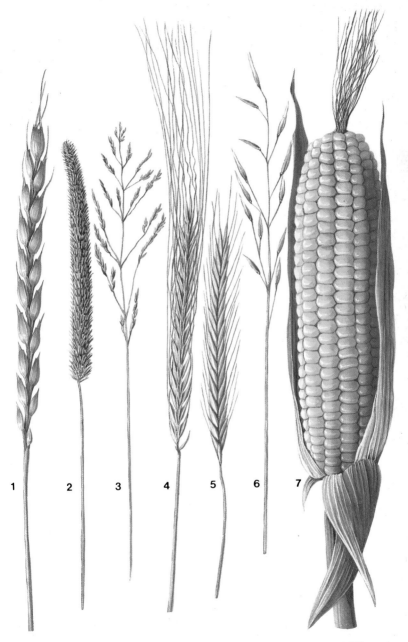

1   2   3   4   5   6   7

Crops contd

1 Medick

The main fodder crop sown with mixture of grass and clover is black medick or nonsuch. Low, prostrate, downy annual with clover-like leaves and long-stalked, rounded heads of small, yellow pea flowers. Fruit a curly, one-seeded, black pod. Irishmen wear it as shamrock on St Patrick's Day.

2 Rape

Leafy member of cabbage family grown as winter food for sheep and cattle. Many varieties with yellow, four-petalled flowers. Fodder rape resembles swede (p.302) above ground, but without swollen root. Is grown as substitute for mustard because of better flavour. (Two kinds of mustard, black and white, latter has pods covered in white hairs and is used in mustard-and-cress. Both have yellow flowers, can be confused with rape, but leaves more bristly and with large lobes at tip. Grown as condiment, also fodder, and helps to enrich soil when ploughed in as 'green manure'). Oil-seed rape (shown here), grown for seeds which produce oil used as lubricant and for cooking, is a new and increasing crop in Britain.

3 Lucerne

Common fodder plant. Hairless perennial with trefoil leaves, short bunches of violet pea flowers, many-seeded pods twisted into spiral. Also called alfalfa in America. Introduced during seventeenth century from Mediterranean. Deep-rooted, drought-resistant, grows mainly on light soils in south and east England. Escapes may occur along roadside verges.

4 Field Bean

Runner beans, broad beans and French beans are grown as human food. Broad beans with white flowers produce fleshy seeds. Runners with scarlet flowers and French with white ones are grown for edible pods. Field bean is a fodder crop for animals, including homing pigeons. One fragrant variety attracts bees. Ripening pod turns black.

5 Kale

Related to cabbage, widely grown as cattle and sheep fodder. Some varieties such as curly kale are used for human consumption. Large leaves on thick stem which contains nutritious pith, either made into silage or eaten by cattle and sheep in fields.

Root Crops

While cereals provide food from grains which grow above ground, root crops develop a swollen root below ground used for human consumption or as animal fodder. Latter usually stored on ground, piled up and covered with earth and straw.

1 Potato

Produces tubers which are not roots but swollen, undergound stems. The 'eyes' are buds which produce future shoots when small seed potatoes are planted in March-April. Crop harvested September-October. Introduced from South America in sixteenth century. Ireland suffered from great potato famine in 1840s due to fungus disease. Large crops were grown in Midlands during Industrial Revolution to feed workers. Still most important British root crop, grown in many varieties. Related to tomato.

2 Swede

Introduced from Sweden in eighteenth century. Related to turnip but is larger and more compact. Flesh yellow to orange. Grown in colder areas in north, fed as winter food to sheep and cattle, to lesser extent used as human food. May be dug up and left on ground for sheep to forage.

3 Sugar Beet

Derived from wild sea beet which grows around shore of Britain, and is also ancestor of beetroot and mangold. Develops a white, swollen, pointed root containing about 15 per cent sugar. Leaves lance-shaped. One acre provides up to two tons of sugar extract. Crop harvested by mechanical digger which slices off top to provide animal fodder. Root pulp also given to animals. Sugar first produced in Britain in 1912. Related fodder beet, more reddish colour, grown for animals.

4 Mangold

Large beet, turnip-like, reddish colour, tends to grow partly above ground. Leaves lance-shaped. Rather poor in food value, formerly a winter food for cattle, now replaced by more nourishing kale and grass. Also called mangel or mangelwurzel.

5 Turnip

Asiatic origin, introduced by Romans. Grown by sheep farmers for feeding livestock, also as human food, mainly in north. Top of plant also eaten as greens. Root round or oval, flesh white, leaves have broken, wavy border.

Rocks and Crystals

Rocks in the geological sense are beds of minerals which occur naturally in the earth's crust, and are formed in three different ways. Igneous (or 'fire') rocks are produced by volcanic eruptions. The lava cools and hardens into rocks with a crystalline nature, such as basalt and granite. Sedimentary (or 'laid down') rocks form mainly in water. Eroded particles are washed down by rivers, deposited in seas and lakes, and under pressure form into layers which become exposed with an uplift. Soft rocks such as clay or chalk have fine particles. Harder and coarser rocks, such as sandstone and limestone, have larger particles, and may stand out as tall cliffs or hills. Where the Earth's crust is exposed, as along a sea-cliff or the side of a quarry, different rock layers (strata) can be seen. Metamorphic (or 'changed in form') rocks result from the action of tremendous pressure, heat or water which changes igneous or sedimentary rock into a quite different type of rock. For example, shale may be changed into flat sheets of slate, while granite is changed into gneiss. Crystals occur in rocks as part of their structure, and usually attract attention by their sparkle. They can 'grow' into geometric shapes peculiar to each chemical.

1 Flint

A hard mineral composed of non-crystalline silica, a dull white when fresh, but weathers to dull grey. This common rock, found in beds between chalk, was used by early man in shaping his tools and weapons. It produces sparks when struck, and was used in flintlock guns. It is also used in road making.

2 Quartz

Composed of crystallised silica, the most abundant component of igneous rocks, occurs as sand grains. Hard and durable. Clear crystal is used as oscillators in radios. Some coloured forms treated as semi-precious, such as amethyst. Rock crystal once thought to be permanently frozen ice.

3 Granite

An igneous rock, mainly greyish or reddish, which has slowly cooled below ground (plutonic) to form large crystals of quartz, up to 30 per cent, with 60 per cent felspar and 10 per cent mica. China clay comes from felspar. Basalt, a black rock, solidifies rapidly at the surface, with finer crystals, and may cool into hexagonal columns, as at Giant's Causeway, Northern Ireland.

4 Calcite

Crystals of calcium carbonate, the raw material for quick-lime and cement, is usually white and effervesces with hydrochloric acid.

5 Schist

A metamorphic mineral derived from mica, quartz, or limestone, under severe pressure or temperature. Variable appearance, may show parallel veining.

6 Iron Pyrites

Also called fool's gold, from its colour. A crystalline form of iron sulphide, commonly found in coal and lead mines.

Common Fossils

Derived from the Latin *fossilis,* dug up, fossils are the remains or traces of prehistoric animals and plants preserved in the Earth's crust. They occur mainly in sedimentary rocks, since igneous and metamorphic rocks, which form under heat and pressure, usually destroy any such traces. The collecting and interpreting of fossils has provided convincing evidence of a story of evolutionary change from the dawn of life to the present day. Techniques for dating rocks have given ages to the fossils they contain. Hardened portions of animals and plants, such as bones, teeth, shells, and petrified wood are familiar fossils, as are imprints of leaves and bark, footprints, and worm casts. Even fossil eggs have been discovered. The interested layman can look for the smaller and commoner fossils where they are easily reached, as in rocks exposed along sea-cliffs, chalk, gravel and clay-pits, and in stone quarries. Some caves may also be productive. Take care if climbing, and seek permission from landowners.

1 Ammonites

A group of extinct marine molluscs related to modern squids and cuttlefish. They were provided with a coiled shell resembling a ram's horn, and named after the Egyptian ram god Ammon. They occur in chalk pits, usually as casts, and as petrified remains in Jurassic rocks, especially around Lyme Regis in Dorset and Whitby in Yorkshire.

2 Trilobites

Ancient marine crustaceans related to wood-lice, with hard, segmented outer skeletons divided into three lobes. May be found at Dudley, Worcestershire, and in old rocks in Wales and Scotland. Common during Cambrian period.

3 Mammoth Tooth

Molars and tusks, sometimes skulls and skeletons of mammoths turn up in gravel and clay pits along river valleys below the southern limit of the last ice-sheet.

4 Oyster Shell

Beds of oysters are usually uncovered during building operations or digging of tunnels, especially in London clay (Eocene period).

5 Fern Leaf

Imprints of ferns commonly occur in coal mines, in between the coal seams, and may be found on spoil heaps (Carboniferous period).

Weather

Weather in Britain, a constant subject of conversation due to its often unpredictable changes, is nevertheless free from extremes, which is due to our geographical position on the edge of the large land-mass of Eurasia. The maritime, temperate climate largely results from the vast expanse of Atlantic ocean to the west. The sea gains and loses heat more slowly than land, and so moderates our temperature. Much of Britain's wind and weather originates over the Atlantic, where cold and dry air from the Arctic and warmer, moisture-laden air from the sub-tropics meet to form an all too familiar depression or 'low'. This moves across the country with the prevailing south-westerly winds. Forced upwards by mountains it falls as rain, giving annual rainfall of as much as 200 inches in Wales and Scotland, far less in the drier, sunnier and more sheltered eastern parts.

A major influence is the Gulf Stream, a warm oceanic current flowing across from the Gulf of Mexico. Its effects are most noticeable in western Britain (palms even grow in northern Scotland), but the whole country enjoys a milder climate than regions at a similar latitude in Europe and North America.

In upland Britain temperature falls rapidly with height above sea-level, and the tree limit occurs at about 2,000 feet. Opposite sides of valleys show different kinds of plant life and uses. North-facing slopes are covered with rough grass and heather where sheep graze. South-facing slopes are used more for farming. Whereas the warmer south-west enjoys the benefit of the milder Atlantic air, the east of England can suffer bitter easterly winds from continental Europe.

Approaching clouds can give some idea of what kind of weather to expect. Clouds form where water vapour condenses into drops of water. This evaporates from the sea, rivers and lakes, and is transpired from plants. As a depression moves over Britain from the Atlantic the warmer air rises over cold air, and water vapour condenses into clouds. Droplets may then combine to produce rain. Clouds occur at various levels, and there are three main types — cumulus (heaped-up), cirrus (wispy), and stratus (layered).

1 Cirrus Clouds

The highest clouds, up to 50,000 feet. Long and wispy, sometimes called mares'-tails. They consist of ice crystals.

2 Cumulus Clouds

Have a woolly appearance, with blue sky between, indicating fair weather so long as they do not pile up. **Cumulo-nimbus clouds** (2a) are thunder clouds which have a ragged base and an anvil-shaped crown which may rise to 7,000 feet. At higher altitudes **alto-cumulus clouds** (2b) may form, between 7-20,000 feet, producing puffy patches in parallel lines, called a 'mackerel' sky.

3 Stratus Clouds

The lowest, sometimes almost at ground level, greyish flat sheets from which light rain may fall. As they thicken into **nimbo-stratus clouds** (3a) and blanket the sky, heavier rain may be expected.

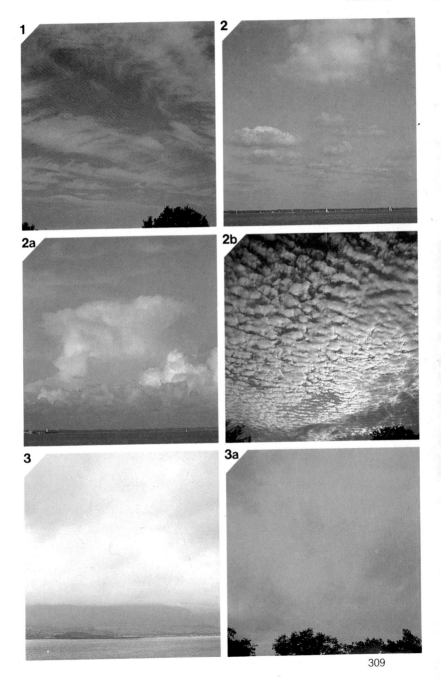

GLOSSARY OF TERMS

Annual A plant which flowers, sets seeds and dies in one year

Antennae The paired sensory organs on the head, used mainly of insects

Annelid Meaning ringed. True worms with segmented bodies visible as outer rings, e.g. earthworm

Anther The male organ of a flowering plant, which contains pollen

Arachnid Invertebrate group including spiders, scorpions and mites

Arboreal Tree-like or tree-dwelling

Arthropod Meaning jointed legs. Large group includes insects, myriapods, arachnids and crustaceans

Baleen Also called whalebone. Hanging plates in mouths of large whales, used for sieving sea-food

Basidium Reproductive cell in most larger fungi which produces spores

Biennial Herbaceous flowering plant which grows in one year and flowers in next

Bract A modified leaf, either at base of a flower stalk, or base of flower head, usually green

Bivalve A mollusc with two hinged shells, e.g. mussel

Calyx The outer covering of a flower, which is usually green and consists of sepals

Call note The inborn vocal cry of a bird or mammal which communicates a message, e.g. a food-call, danger call, mating call

Camouflage A visual method of concealment from an enemy or prey by some means of disguise, so as to resemble the background or to imitate an inedible object

Canine The dog-tooth of a carnivore

Capsule The container in lower plants (mosses, liverworts, ferns, horsetails and club-mosses) which liberates spores

Carpel The female organ in a flowering plant which contains the egg-cell

Catkin A crowded cluster of small flowers of one sex, some of which hang (e.g. hazel), others are vertical (e.g. willow)

Cerci Paired appendages, some long as in earwigs, at the tip of the abdomen of some insects

Chitin The hard and horny substance which covers many invertebrates, especially insects and crustaceans

Chlorophyll The green-coloured chemical in plants

Chromosomes Structures within the cell nucleus which carry and transmit the hereditary character

Chrysalis The pupal stage in butterflies and moths

Clitellum The glandular belt around an earthworm which secretes the egg-cocoon

Cotyledon The seed-leaf of an embryonic flowering plant, single in some (Monocotyledons), paired in others (Dicotyledons)

Commensal Meaning 'living from the same table', e.g. hermit crab and sea anemone. Also refers to animals associated with man, e.g. rat, sparrow

Common land Private land which by tradition can be used by the public and in some cases by the local commoners to exercise their ancient rights, e.g. pasturing cattle or ponies

Conifer A cone-bearing tree which grows needle-shaped leaves. In most cases these remain on the tree all year round

Coppice Trees lopped at ground level

Crustacean Class of arthropod animals, mostly marine, such as crabs, shrimps, barnacles. Includes freshwater crayfish and water-flea

Delayed implantation Condition in some deer and weasels in which the fertilised egg-cell remains unattached to the womb for a period, thus lengthening the gestation

Deciduous Shedding the leaves, usually in autumn, among broad-leaved trees

Dorsal Belonging to the back. The upper fin on the backs of fishes

Drey The nest of a squirrel

Echinoderm Meaning 'spiny skin'. Group of marine invertebrates including starfishes and sea-urchins

Eclipse A period in many ducks when the male moults, then assumes a temporary plumage resembling that of female

Elytra The horny wing cases in beetles

Erratic Boulders left behind by the retreating Ice Age

Feral Gone wild — usually a domestic animal in the wild state, e.g. town pigeon

Form A ground depression used as a resting place by a hare. The young occupy a milking form

Fronds Applied mainly to the leaves of ferns

Furcula The forked 'spring' of a springtail insect

Gasteropod Meaning 'Stomach-foot'. Group of molluscs with a single shell, and which move on a broad foot, e.g. snails

Gestation The period between conception and birth

Gregarious Living together in flocks or herds

Habitat The surroundings to which a plant or animal is adapted, e.g. woodland, pond, sea-shore

Habitat (artificial) A man-made situation exploited by plants or animals, e.g. birds on buildings, plants on waste-land

Halteres Balancing organs which replace the hind-wings of some flies

Haemoglobin The red oxygen-carrying pigment in red blood-cells

Hermaphrodite An animal or plant which carries both sex organs

Hibernation A deep winter sleep in which the body processes slow down and temperature falls

Honey guide Colour markings on flowers to guide insects towards the pollen or nectar

Hybrid A cross between two species which is usually infertile, e.g. mule from horse and donkey

Imago The adult stage of an insect

Incisors The front teeth in mammals, used for gnawing food, especially among rodents

Indigenous Native to its country

Labellum The lower petal of an orchid, usually marked and coloured to attract insects

Larva The young stage of an animal which differs from the adult, e.g. caterpillar, tadpole

Looper A caterpillar which moves its body in loops by drawing up its hindquarters and then extending the front part forwards

Lopping Cutting off branches from a tree

Mandible The lower jaw-bone in mammals; also refers to the biting mouthparts of insects and crustaceans

Mast The fruit of various trees and shrubs, such as nuts and acorns, eaten by birds and mammals, e.g. pigs

Metamorphosis A change in shape and form during the life of an animal, as in insects

Migration A regular movement from a breeding to a non-breeding area.

Mildew Minute parasitic fungus, e.g. mildew on rose

Molar A chewing tooth at rear of jaw

Mollusc Group of animals including snails, mussels and squids

Monogamous Keeping to a single mate

Mould Minute saprophytic fungus feeding on dead organic matter, e.g. on bread, clothing

Myriapod Group of invertebrates including millepedes and centipedes

Nematodes A large group of pale-coloured, unsegemented worm-like animals, aquatic or terrestrial (also called round-worms or thread-worms)

Nymph The larval stage in some insects which develops directly into an adult without a pupal stage, e.g. grass-hoppers, cockroaches

Omnivorous Feeding on both animals and plants

Operculum A covering or lid, such as the gill-cover of fishes, and the lid which closes the shell in some snails

Ovary The female organ

Oviparous Egg-laying

Ovipositor The egg-laying tube in some insects

Palmate Palm shaped

Palps Sensory structures around the mouths of insects, used in tasting

Parasite An animal or plant which lives and feeds on another organism, called the host

Parthenogenetic Reproducing by means of unfertilised eggs

Pecking order The order of dominance within a special group of animals

Pectoral (fin) The paired front fins in fishes

Pelvic (fin) The paired hind fins in fishes

Perennial Lasting year by year, as in some herbs and all trees

Pinion The last joint of a bird's wing. Also to cut a wing to prevent flight

Pinnate Having rows of leaflets along each side of the central axis

Plankton The drifting microscopic life in water

Pollard A tree cut at crown level

Polygamous Having more than one mate

Proboscis The elongated feeding tube in butterflies and moths

Pronotum The shield covering the head and thorax of some insects, e.g. grasshoppers

Prothallus The intermediate stage in a fern's life-history which carries the sex organs

Pupa The resting stage of an insect, in which the larva transforms into the adult, e.g. a chrysalis

Pupate Changing into a pupa.

Radula The tongue of snails and slugs

Reingestion Swallowing food a second time, as with rabbits eating their own dung

Rhyzome A horizontal, creeping, underground stem, as in irises

Rodent Mammals which nibble food with sharp incisor teeth, e.g. rats, squirrels

Roosting The communal sleeping among some birds and bats, e.g. on buildings, in trees and caves

Rufous A brownish red colouring

Ruminant Chewing the cud, as in deer and cattle

Rut Mating season of deer

Saprophyte A fungus which feeds on dead organic food, as opposed to a parasite

Scrape A shallow ground depression used as a nest site by some birds, also scratch marks made in soil by rabbits and squirrels

Sepal A member of the calyx in a flowering plant

Siphon The two openings in bivalve molluscs, e.g. mussel

Song The distinctive melody of a bird, usually learned and sometimes mimicked

Species The smallest classified unit of animal or plant which interbreeds with its own kind

Speculum The coloured feathers on the wings of ducks, also the white patch around the tail of deer

Spore The minute reproductive cells produced in vast numbers by lower plants, such as mosses and fungi

Sporophore The fruiting body of a fungus

Stamen The male organ of a flowering plant

Stigma The parts of a flowering plant's female organ which receive pollen

Striated Lined with parallel streaks or furrows

Stridulation The song of grass-hoppers, crickets and cicadas

Testa The outer coat of a seed

Thorax The chest region in insects

Tragus The small prominence at the entrance of the external ear, as in bats

Trefoil Three-lobed in shape

Trifoliate With three leaves or leaflets, as in clovers

Umbel A compound flower head whose branches resemble the spokes of an umbrella

Ungulate A hoofed mammal

Univalve A mollusc with a single shell, e.g. snail

Vestigial A reduced or functionless organ

Vertebrate A backboned animal

Viviparous Giving birth to young, as in birds and mammals

Volva The sheath at the base of the stem of some toadstools

Wattle A colourful, fleshy growth on the throat or head of some birds

Xerophyte A plant capable of resisting drought by some means, e.g. reduced leaf surface, rolled leaves, hairy surface

FURTHER READING LIST

Birds
Book of British Birds, Readers Digest
Field Guide to the Birds of Britain and Europe, R. Peterson, G. Mountfort, P. Hollom (Collins)

Mammals
Field Guide to the Mammals of Britain and Europe, F.H. van den Brink (Collins)
Handbook of British Mammals, ed. H.N. Southern (Blackwell Scientific)

Amphibians & Reptiles
Field Guide to the Reptiles and Amphibians of Britain and Europe, E. Arnold & J. Burton (Collins)
Reptiles and Amphibians of Europe, W. Hellmich (Blandford Press)

Insects
A Field Guide to the Insects of Britain and N. Europe, M. Chinery (Collins)
Insects Natural History, A. Imms (Collins)

Flowers
The Concise British Flora in Colour, W. Keeble Martin (Ebury Press)
The Pocket Guide to Wild Fowers, D. McClintock & R. Fitter (Collins)
A Handbook of British Flowering Plants, A. Melderis & E. Bangerter (Ward Lock)

Flowerless Plants
Collins Guide to Mushrooms and Toadstools, M. Lange & F. Hora (Collins)
Observer Book of Common Fungi, E. Wakefield (Warne)
Observer Book of Mosses and Liverworts, A Jewel (Warne)
Observer Book of Grasses, Sedges & Rushes, W. Stokoe (Warne)
Observer Book of Ferns, W. Stokoe (Warne)

Trees & Shrubs
Your Book of Trees, Miles Hadfield (Faber & Faber)
British Trees and Shrubs, R.D. Meikle (Eyre & Spottiswoode)

Pondlife
The Observer Book of Pondlife, J. Clegg (Warne)
Freshwater Life of the British Isles, J. Clegg (Warne)

Fishes
Guide to the Freshwater Fishes of Britain & Europe, A. Wheeler (Hamlyn)
The Pictorial Encyclopedia of Fishes, S. Frank (Hamlyn)

Seashore
Collins Pocket Guide to the Seashore, J. Barrett & C. Yonge (Collins)
The Observer Book of the Sea and Seashore, I. Evans (Warne)

Farm Animals
The Observer Book of Farm Animals, L. Alderson (Warne)

Soil
The World of the Soil, Sir E.J. Russell (Collins)

Rocks
The Observer Book of Geology, I. Evans (Warne)
Minerals and Rocks in Colour, F. Kircaldy (Blandford Press)

Weather
Weathercraft, L. Smith (Blandford Press)

Index